Streetwise German

Streetwise German

Speaking and Understanding Colloquial German

PAUL G. GRAVES, Ph.D.

University of Colorado

PASSPORT BOOKS

NTC/Contemporary Publishing Group

Library of Congress Cataloging-in-Publication Data

Graves, Paul G.
    Streetwise German : speaking and understanding colloquial
German / Paul G. Graves.
      p.   cm.
   ISBN 0-8442-2514-2
   1. German language—Conversation and phrase books—English.
2. German language—Slang.   3. German language—Spoken
German.   I. Title.
PF3121.G73   1998
438.3′421—dc21   98-10747
                                                CIP

To my wife, Eva Alkalay Graves

The assistance of Hugo Schmidt, Ph.D.,
University of Colorado, is gratefully acknowledged.

Cover photograph copyright © AA Photo Library, Hampshire, England

Published by Passport Books
A division of NTC/Contemporary Publishing Group, Inc.
4255 West Touhy Avenue, Lincolnwood (Chicago), Illinois 60712-1975 U.S.A.
Printed in the United States of America
International Standard Book Number: 0-8442-2514-2

8 9 10 11 12 13 VRS/VRS 0 5 4 3 2

Contents

Please note: Dialogues alternate between the colloquial speech of Northern Germany *(NG)* and that of Southern Germany and Austria *(SG)*.

Introduction

It goes without saying that studying colloquial German ("Streetwise German") from a book is no substitute for spending an extended period of time in Germany or Austria, hearing and absorbing the living language directly and personally. I hope that studying this text will lessen the shock that tourists experience when they realize that the language they learned in school is in many ways quite different from spoken German. This is not to say that their German studies were a waste of time. What it does say is that there is a substantial gap between High German (Hochdeutsch) and Streetwise German. This gap, obviously, is not exclusive to German. And there is no foolproof method by which it can be easily bridged. Your perseverance, your ear, and your feel for the language will be important factors. And this book will aid you in your efforts. By infusing a healthy portion of humor into a potentially dry subject, I hope for an occasional chuckle or smile on the part of the student.

Langenscheidt's *Großwörterbuch* classifies informal speech according to three categories: *colloq.* for colloquial, *sl.* for slang, and *vulg.* for vulgar. The word *Dreck,* e.g., is listed as *colloquial, Dreckskerl* as *slang,* and *Drecksau* as *vulgar.* In this book, the same classification has been applied.

I have been trying to keep my distance from the more pungent specimens of the "vulgar" kind—notably the so-called four-letter words. This I did, not on moral grounds, but to spare the student the embarrassment that might result from uncritical use of these terms. After spending a few weeks in a German language environment, the learner will sense more about how to use them with caution.

I would be hard put to advise any prospective students on just which colloquialisms or slang expressions to concentrate their efforts. More than anything else, the environment in which students choose to live or to spend their vacation determines which particular term or phrase will enrich their active vocabulary, and which will slide into their passive memory pool.

I am aware of the fact that these dialogues are chockful of colloquial, regional, and slangy phrases and words, common, funny, vulgar and weird. Do people really talk the way I make them talk? In other words, is the talk in this book "natural" enough? But what is "natural"? Try to tape the average conversation of two average persons, and you will find their dialogue "natural" all right—but also extremely boring, with no discernible design, structure, or punch line. Studying Streetwise German should be fun. And as to authenticity, I like to think that these dialogues qualify as authentic not unlike the ones found in a stage play in which the theater-goer recognizes his own human foibles. I cannot promise you that after finishing this book you will be streetwise in Germany. I can, however, assure you that there are a lot of native Germans, young and old, living in Germany today, who are not streetwise.

So take heart, and take the plunge!

Paul G. Graves

List of Abbreviations

adj.	adjective	*n. pl.*	neuter noun plural
adv.	adverb	*pp.*	past participle
coll.	colloquial	*prep.*	preposition
conj.	conjunction	*pron.*	pronoun
etw.	etwas	*R*	Review
f.	feminine noun	*S*	south German
f. pl.	feminine noun plural	*s.*	sich
jm.	jemandem (*dat.*)	*SG*	Southern Germany
jn.	jemanden (*acc.*)	*sg.*	singular
lit.	literally	*sl.*	slang
m.	masculine noun	*s.o.*	someone
m. pl.	masculine noun plural	*s.o.'s*	someone's
N	north German	*s.th.*	something
n.	neuter noun	*v.*	verb
NG	Northern Germany	*vulg.*	vulgar

Streetwise German

Dialog 1

Southern German

Im Restaurant

Otto, in a generous mood, invites his friend to a fancy restaurant.

JOSEF   Mensch, das is' saumäßig g'schmalzen. Ka Wunder—
weiße Tischtücher, wo ma' hinschaut und der Aufzug von
den Kellnern—

OTTO   Bist knapp bei Kasse, gell? Macht nix. Heut' bist mei' Gast.

JOSEF   Da schau her! Du zeigst di' heut' aber von deiner
großzügigen Seit'n. Mir hängt der Magen eh' schon in den
Kniekehlen. Ich könnt' reinhaun wie ein Scheunendrescher.

OTTO   Du alter Freßsack! Aber hier kannst dir was Richtig's
'neinziehn; kriegst auch alles, was d' willst.

JOSEF   Wirkli' alles?

OTTO   Ja, ja! Unlängst hab' ich Faultierfilet b'stellt—

JOSEF   Faultierfilet? Du verarscht mich. Und der Kellner?

In the Restaurant

JOSEF   Man, this is highway robbery. I'm not surprised—
tablecloths all over the place, and the monkey suits of the
waiters—

OTTO   Broke, ain't you? No sweat. This one's on me today.

JOSEF   Wow, thanks! You're sure generous today. I'm starved to
death. I could eat a horse.

OTTO   You old pig. But here you can really stuff your face. You can
get everything you want.

JOSEF   Really everything?

OTTO   Sure. The other day I ordered fillet of sloth.

JOSEF   Sloth? Don't give me that crap, man. And the waiter?

OTTO   Ja, der hat's g'schnallt. "Gewiß, mein Herr," hat er g'sagt. "Aber auf Faultier müssen's warten."

JOSEF   Und hat er's dann auch serviert?

OTTO   Dem Kellner sein G'sicht, zwei Stunden später, war ein Bild der Verzweiflung; "'Tschuldigen, der Herr," hat er g'sagt; "aber das letzte Stückl, das haben die Herrschaften drüben grad verspeist."

JOSEF   Herr Ober! Bitte schön, zwei Portionen gebratne Mammutkeule.

KELLNER   Jawohl! Kommt sofort!

(Josef and Otto continue talking. Waiter comes back shortly.)

KELLNER   Verzeihn die Herren . . .

JOSEF   Was is'? Nix mehr da?

KELLNER   Zuviel da. Das Dumme is' nur, das Fleisch hat an leichten Stich. *(lowering his voice)* Auf gut deutsch g'sagt, es is net ganz frisch.

Vocabulary

Aber hier kannst dir was Richtig's 'neinziehn. *(sl.)*	But here you can really stuff your face.
Aufzug *(m. coll.)*	getup
auf gut deutsch g'sagt *(coll.)*	frankly speaking
d' (du) *(pron.)*	you
Da schau her! *(sl.)*	Wow! Thanks!
das Dumme *(coll.)*	the trouble, the problem
Das Fleisch hat an (einen) leichten Stich. *(coll.)*	The meat is a little bit off.
Das is' saumäßig g'schmalzen. *(sl.)*	That's highway robbery.
Der hat's g'schnallt. *(sl.)*	(here) He swallowed it.
Du verarscht mich. *(sl.)*	Don't give me that crap.

OTTO   Yep. He swallowed it. "Certainly, sir," he says. "But for sloth you got to wait."

JOSEF   And did he finally really serve it?

OTTO   Two hours later, the waiter's face is a picture of despair. "Excuse me, sir," he says, "but the folks over there just now knocked off the last little piece."

JOSEF   Waiter!—Two portions of roasted mammoth loin, please.

WAITER   Right away.

(Josef and Otto continue talking. Waiter comes back shortly.)

WAITER   Sorry, gentlemen . . .

JOSEF   What's up? Out of it?

WAITER   Too much of it. The trouble is, the meat is a little bit off. *(lowering his voice)* Frankly speaking, it is not quite fresh.

Du zeigst di' heut' (dich heute) aber von deiner groß- zügigen Seit'n. *(coll.)*	You're sure generous today.
Freßsack *(m. sl.)*	old pig
Faultierfilet *(n.)*	fillet of sloth
gell? (nicht wahr?) *(sl.)*	ain't you? (isn't it so?)
grad (gerade) *(adv. coll.)*	just now
Herr Ober! *(coll.)*	Waiter!
Ich könnt' reinhaun wie ein Scheunendrescher. *(sl.)*	I could eat a horse.
ka (kein) *(adj. coll.)*	no
knapp bei Kasse sein *(coll.)*	to be broke
kriegen *(v. coll.)*	to get
ma' (man) *(pron.)*	one
Macht nix (nichts). *(coll.)*	No sweat.
mei' (mein) *(pron.)*	my

Mir hängt der Magen eh' **schon in den Kniekehlen.** (*sl.*)	I'm starved to death.
müssen's (müssen Sie) (*coll.*)	you must, you gotta
net (nicht) (*adv.*)	not
Nix mehr da? (*coll.*)	Nothing left?
Portionen (*f. pl.*)	servings
'Tschuldigen (Entschuldigen) (*v. coll.*)	to excuse
verspeist (*v. coll.*)	finished (eating), knocked off
Was is' (ist)? (*coll.*)	What's up?
wirkli' (wirklich) (*adv. coll.*)	really

A Smidgen of Streetwise Grammar
Fun with Idioms and Such

You will often notice:

☐   The omission of the vowels **e** or **u,** or of **ie** (of the pronoun **Sie**):

> auf deutsch **g'sagt** (gesagt)
> **gebrat'ne** (gebratene)
> Hat **er's** (er es) auch serviert?
> alles was **d'** (du) willst
> Auf Faultier **müssen's** (müssen Sie) warten.

☐   The omission of consonants:

> Was **is'** (ist) los?
> Heut' bist **mei'** (mein) Gast.
> Hast **scho'** (schon) genug?
> wo **ma'** (man) hinschaut

☐   The omission of an entire pronoun:

> Hier kannst (**du**) dir was Richtig's 'neinziehn.
> (**Du**) bist
> (**Es** or **'s**) macht nix.

☑ The omission of the terminal **e** (most common), as in **heut'** (heute):

>   Ich **fühl'** (fühle) etwas.
>   Da **könnt'** (könnte) ich mitgehn.
>   Unlängst **hab'** (habe) ich ihn g'sehn.

☐ When speaking Streetwise German, you generally try to avoid the genitive (possessive) form of the noun, the use of which is considered highfalutin.

>   Do not say:
>   **der Aufzug der Kellner**

>   Never say:
>   **der Kellner Aufzug**

>   Instead say:
>   **der Aufzug von den Kellnern**

>   You may also use this peculiar dative/possessive substitute in avoidance of the genitive:
>   **dem Kellner sein Aufzug**
>   **den Kellnern ihr Aufzug**
>   **der Frau ihr Mantel**
>   **den Frauen ihre Mäntel**
>   **Das ist dem Hans sein Bruder.**
>   **Was geht mich dem Fräulein ihr Bruder an?**

>   However, the genitive in **der Kellner war ein Bild der Verzweiflung** is acceptable, as it represents comic exaggeration.

☐ Essen und Fressen—reinhaun

>   Here are some more colorful terms:
>   **einkacheln, futtern, grasen, mampfen, reinspachteln, verdrücken, verputzen, verschnabulieren, vertilgen, wegmachen.**   to pig out
>   **Er hat sich den Wanst damit vollg'schlagen.**   He made a pig of himself.
>   **Er ist uns ins Essen g'fallen.**   He came at a bad time. (We were eating.)
>   **Das Essen fällt ihm aus'm G'sicht.**   He's vomiting.
>   **Er hat sich sein Essen redlich verdient.**   He worked hard.

Er hat sich ein Fressen draus gemacht.   He went to town doing it.

Sie ist zum Fressen süß.   She's so nice I could eat her alive.

Das war mir ein gefundenes Fressen.   That was just what I was waiting for.

Friß mi(ch) net gleich!   Don't bite my head off!

Ihn frißt der Neid.   He's green with envy.

Tea or Coffee?

WAITRESS	Tee oder Kaffee?	Tea or coffee?
GUEST	Kaffee ohne Sahne.	Coffee without cream.
WAITRESS	Sie müssen ihn ohne Milch trinken. Wir haben keine Sahne.	You'll have to drink it without milk. We have no cream.

Exercises

A. Complete the phrase by filling in the appropriate word from the list:

Faultierfilet, Freßsack, g'schnallt, knapp, Kniekehlen, Mammutkeule, 'neinziehn, Scheunendrescher, verarscht, Verzweiflung.

1. Unlängst hab' ich _____ bestellt.

2. Ja, der hat's _____.

3. Aber hier kannst dir was Richtig's _____.

4. Zwei Portionen gebrat'ne _____.

5. Du alter _Freßsack_!

6. Ich könnt' reinhaun wie ein _Schneu_____.

7. Dem Kellner sein G'sicht war ein Bild der _Verzweiflung_

8. Mir hängt der Magen schon in den _Kniekehlen_

9. Bist _knapp_ bei Kasse?

10. Du _verarscht_ mich.

B. True or False?

	T/F
1. Das Restaurant ist sehr billig.	_____
2. Faultierfilet wird sofort serviert.	_____
3. Josef ißt sehr viel.	_____
4. Das Fleisch ist nicht ganz frisch.	_____
5. Josef bestellt Schweinebraten.	_____
6. Otto ist knapp bei Kasse.	_____
7. Das letzte Stückl hat man grad' verspeist.	_____
8. Hier kriegt man alles, was man will.	_____
9. Josef ist überhaupt nicht hungrig.	_____
10. Otto ist heute sehr großzügig.	_____

C.   Match the German with the English:

1. __C__ knapp bei Kasse

2. __E__ Da schau her!

3. __I__ Jawohl! Kommt sofort!

4. __B__ 'Tschuldigen, der Herr.

5. __A__ Der hat's g'schnallt.

6. __H__ Du verarscht mich.

7. __D__ Du alter Freßsack!

8. __J__ Es hat an leichten Stich.

9. __F__ Ka Wunder!

10. __G__ Macht nix.

A. He swallowed it.

B. Excuse me, sir.

C. broke

D. You old pig!

E. Wow, thanks!

F. I'm not surprised.

G. No sweat!

H. Don't give me that crap.

I. Right away!

J. It isn't quite fresh.

D. Change the following phrases to make them sound less *hochdeutsch*.

Examples:

Ottos Faultierfilet
das Faultierfilet vom Otto

die Mäntel der Gäste
die Mäntel von den Gästen

Paulas Schuhe
die Schuhe von der Paula

1. Josefs Magen

   dem Josef sein Magen

2. Ottos Restaurant

   s Restaurant von Otto

3. Evas Kleid

   der Eva Ihr Kleid

4. die Portion des Gastes

   _____

5. der Preis der Lampe

   _____

6. die Bücher der Studenten

   _____

7. die Kinder der Olga

   _____

8. der Aufzug der Kellner

   _____

9. die Söhne der Soldaten

   _____

10. die Kleider der Studentinnen

    _____

E. Change the following phrases, using that peculiar dative/
    possessive substitute:

Example:
Ottos Faultierfilet
dem Otto sein Faultierfilet

1. das Haus des Herrn

_____

2. das Gesicht des Kellners

_____

3. die Hand des Onkels

_____

4. die Nase des Mädchens

_____

5. der Freund des Sohnes

_____

6. der Vater der Freundin

_____

7. die Töchter der Karla

_____

8. die Söhne des Kurt

_____

9. die Kleider der Gäste

_____

10. die Häuser der Verwandten

_____

Dialog 2

Northern German

Einerseits/Andererseits

This dialogue proves that there are two sides to everything.

HANS   Nun bin auch ich in den Hafen der Ehe eingelaufen.

GEORG   Und wie macht sich euer Eheglück?

HANS   Nicht so gut, weil das Leben mit meiner Alten kein
Honiglecken ist. Sie ist ein Biest mit Haaren auf den Zähnen.

GEORG   Warum haste dich darauf bloß eingelassen?

HANS   Weil ich fünfhundert Blaue dafür gekriegt hab'.

GEORG   Das ist doch super.

HANS   Nicht so super, weil ich jetzt aufgeschmissen bin: Ich hab'
nämlich mit dem Moos spekuliert und Pleite gemacht.

GEORG   Das ist beknackt.

On the One Hand/ On the Other Hand

HANS Well, now I got hitched, too.

GEORG And how is your married life?

HANS Not so wonderful, because life with my old lady is not exactly a ball. She's a bitch with a mean temper.

GEORG Then what did you do it for?

HANS 'Cuz I got a dowry of 50 000 marks.

GEORG That's cool.

HANS Not so cool, because I'm in a fix now: I speculated with the bread, and went broke.

GEORG That's rotten.

HANS   Nicht ganz so beknackt, weil ich trotz des ganzen Trabbels die Knete rechtzeitig nach Amerika abschieben konnte.

GEORG   Das ist echt geil.

HANS   Nicht so geil, weil die Bank dort Pleite gemacht hat und das Geld flöt'n war.

GEORG   Das ist blöd, Mensch.

HANS   Nicht so blöd, weil der Bankdirektor mein Freund war; also der hat sich verdrückt und ist mit den Kröten durchgebrannt.

GEORG   Das ist fetzig.

HANS   Nicht so fetzig, weil der Mann jetzt im Kittchen hockt.

GEORG   Das ist bescheuert.

HANS   Nicht so bescheuert, weil er den Zaster vorher vertuckelt hat.

GEORG   Das ist clever.

HANS   Nicht so clever, weil er verschwitzt hat, wo er ihn vertuckelt hat.

Vocabulary

abschieben *(v. coll.)*	to transfer
aufgeschmissen sein *(coll.)*	to be in a fix
beknackt *(adj. sl.)*	rotten
bescheuert *(adj. coll.)*	tough
Biest *(n. coll.)*	(here) bitch
(ein) Blauer *(m. coll.)*	a hundred-mark bill
clever *(adj. coll.)*	clever, smart
Das Leben mit meiner Alten ist kein Honiglecken.	Life with my old lady isn't exactly a ball.
Das ist blöd, (Mensch) *(coll.)*	That's messy, (man).
Das ist bescheuert *(sl.)*	That sucks.
durchbrennen *(v. coll.)*	to bolt, to run off
echt geil *(sl.)*	terrific, cool, a bitch
fetzig *(adj. sl.)*	super
flöt'n sein *(coll.)*	to be gone, evaporate

HANS   Not so rotten, because despite the jam I was in, I was able to transfer the bread to America just in time.

GEORG   That's terrific.

HANS   Not so terrific, because the bank there went bankrupt and the money was gone.

GEORG   Man, that's messy.

HANS   Not so messy, because the president of that bank was my buddy; he did a vanishing act, and split with the dinero.

GEORG   That's super.

HANS   Not so super, because the guy is sitting in the pen now.

GEORG   That's tough.

HANS   Not so tough, because he stashed the loot beforehand.

GEORG   That's smart.

HANS   Not so smart because he forgot where he stashed it.

Haare auf den Zähnen haben (*coll.*)	to have a mean temper
hocken (*v. coll.*)	to sit
in den Hafen der Ehe einlaufen (*coll.*)	to get hitched
Kittchen (*n. coll.*)	pen, jail
Knete (*f. sl.*)	money; dinero
Kröten (*pl. sl.*)	money
meine Alte (*coll.*)	my old lady
Moos (*n. coll.*)	bread, money
Pleite machen (*coll.*)	to go broke, to go into bankruptcy
super (*adj. coll.*)	cool
Trabbel (*m. sl.*)	difficulties; jam
(sich) verdrücken (*v. coll.*)	to do a vanishing act, to beat it
verschwitzen (*v. coll.*)	to forget
vertuckeln (*v. sl.*)	to stash away
Zaster (*m. sl.*)	money

A Smidgen of Streetwise Grammar

Fun with Idioms and Weird Words

☐ All about matrimony:

Eheknecht
Ehestandskrüppel } husband of a domineering woman
Ehefräulein   frigid wife
Ehehyäne   a female that alienates a husband from his wife
Eheschmiede   marriage license bureau
Ehetrott   marital routine
Ehegewitter   marital discord
Ehestandsgymnastik   sexual intercourse

☐ Twenty ways of talking Streetwise money:

**Asche, Kies, Knete, Klötze, Knöpfe, Kohle, Kröten,
Lappen, Leim, Mäuse, Moos, Moneten, Patte, Pinkepinke,
Pulver, Schotter, Steine, Streusand, Zaster, Zunder**

☐ What kind of Streetwise money?

dickes Geld   lots of money
großes Geld   big bucks
heißes Geld   counterfeit money
irres Geld   enormous amounts of money
schmutziges Geld   money from dubious sources
schnelles Geld   money made by speculation
schwarzes Geld   money made under the table

☐ More about money:

Geld bunkern   to stash money
Geld dreschen   to roll in dough
Geld zum Fressen haben   to be loaded
mit Geld gepolstert sein   to be well-heeled
Das Geld juckt ihm in der Tasche.   He cannot live within
his means.

Das läuft ins Geld.   That's upscale.
gutes Geld machen   to be up in the bucks
das Geld zum Fenster rausschmeißen   to throw money
  around, waste money
im Geld schwimmen   to have money to burn
nach Geld stinken   to be stinking rich

☐   All about the vanishing act:

Er ist abgepirscht, abgesockt.   He scrammed.
Er ist abgezogen, ausgerissen, ausgerückt.   He split.
**Er hat sich beurlaubt, hat sich davongemacht, hat sich
  dünne gemacht, verdünnisiert.**   He did a vanishing act.
**Er ist durchgegangen, hat sich empfohlen, hat sich
  fortgemacht.**   He took off.
**Er hat sich fortgestohlen, ist marschiert, hat sich
  gepackt.**   He faded out of sight.
**Er hat sich verkrümelt, hat sich verzogen, sich
  weggeschert.**   He went south.
**Er hat sich (auf) französisch, englisch, hintenrum
  verabschiedet.**   He took off.
Er hat sich aus dem Staub gemacht.   He hightailed it.
Er ist verduftet.   He beat it.

A Man with Imagination

BANKER	Sie haben sieben Jahre Bankerfahrung, ohne je einen Job gehabt zu haben?	You claim seven years of banking experience without ever having had a job?
APPLICANT	Haben Sie nicht die Stellung für einen Mann mit Phantasie ausgeschrieben?	Didn't you advertise the job for a man with imagination?

Exercises

A. Complete the phrase by filling in the appropriate word from the list:

Blaue, flöt'n, geil, Haare, Honiglecken, Knete, Moos, Pleite, verdrückt, vertuckelt.

1. Das Leben mit meiner Alten ist kein _Honiglecken_.

2. Ich habe mit dem _Moos_ spekuliert.

3. Der Bankdirektor hat sich _verdrückt_.

4. Er hat den Zaster _vertuckelt_.

5. Sie hat _Haare_ auf den Zähnen.

6. Das Geld war _flöt'n_.

7. Er hat _Pleite_ gemacht.

8. Er konnte die _Knete_ nach Amerika abschieben.

9. Er bekam fünfhundert _Blaue_ mit.

10. Das ist echt _geil_.

B. True or False?

T/F

1. Er ist mit den Kröten durchgebrannt. _T_

2. Jetzt hockt er im Kittchen. _T_

3. Er hat tausend Blaue mitbekommen. _T_

4. Er hatte Trabbel. _F_

5. Seine Alte ist sehr freundlich. _F_

6. Er hat mit dem Moos eine Wohnung gekauft. _F_

7. Er ist ledig geblieben. _F_

8. Seine Frau ist ein Biest. _T_

9. Er erinnert sich, wo er es vertuckelt hat. _F_

10. Hans war aufgeschmissen. _T_

C. Match the German with the English:

1. _D_ Er hat Pleite gemacht.

2. _F_ Sein Freund hat sich verdrückt.

3. _H_ Er ist in den Hafen der Ehe eingelaufen.

4. _C_ Das ist kein Honiglecken.

5. _J_ Er hat mit dem Moos spekuliert.

6. _I_ Das ist echt geil.

7. _A_ Das ist fetzig.

8. _B_ Das ist beknackt.

9. _E_ Das ist clever.

10. _G_ Das ist bescheuert.

A. That's super.
B. That's rotten.
C. It's not exactly a ball.
D. He went broke.
E. That's smart.
F. His friend did a vanishing act.
G. That sucks.
H. He got hitched.
I. That's really cool.
J. He speculated with the bread.

D. Underline the English term that comes closest in meaning to the German word on the left:

1. Moos   a. money   b. mouse   c. moth

2. Trabbel   a. drops   b. tears   c. jam

3. durchgehen   a. to burn   b. to split   c. to brake

4. beknackt   a. happy   b. noisy   c. rotten

5. Pleite   a. bankruptcy   b. play   c. pleasure

6. abschieben   a. to shove   b. to transfer   c. to shun

7. hocken   a. to sit   b. to hock   c. to heave

8. Kittchen   a. glue   b. jail   c. kitten

9. echt geil   a. real bad   b. dirty   c. cool

10. blöd   a. wonderful   b. ugly   c. messy

E. Underline the expressions that are *not* Streetwise German:

1. viel Geld verdienen

2. nach Geld stinken

3. Er hat sich dünne gemacht.

4. Er ist übersiedelt.

5. Sie hat sich verkrümelt.

6. Sie hat sich von uns verabschiedet.

7. mit Geld gepolstert sein

8. mit Geld versorgt sein

9. Geld bunkern

10. dickes Geld

worried about money

Dialog 3

Southern German

Mädchen unter sich

Mitzi, having lived in another city for a number of years, is visiting Fritzi, a former schoolmate.

MITZI *(coming in from the rain)* Heut' duscht's aber.

FRITZI Grüß dich! Du bist ja patschnaß. *(helping her out of the raincoat)* Jessas na! Du bist aufgegangen wie a Pfannkuchen; A Dampfnudel bist g'word'n, a richtige Blunzn.

MITZI Und du bist dünn wie ein Zwirnsfaden und flach wie ein Bügelbrett.

FRITZI Ja, ja, schon gut. Setz dich, bitte. Der Kaffee is' gleich fertig. Also was macht der Karl?

MITZI Der Mistkerl? Der Hallodri? Der kann mir den Buck'l runterrutschen, er und seine neueste Flamme.

FRITZI Eine neue Freundin?

Girl Talk

MITZI   *(coming in from the rain)* It's raining cats and dogs today.

FRITZI   Hi! Wow, you're dripping wet! *(helping her out of raincoat)* Holy cow! You swelled up like a balloon; you turned into a dumpling, a regular butterball.

MITZI   And you are skinny as a birdleg and flat as a pancake.

FRITZI   All right already. Sit down, please. Coffee will be ready in a minute. How's Karl?

MITZI   That slippery louse? That jerk? He can go to hell, he and his latest love.

FRITZI   A new girl?

MITZI   Red' kan Stuß. Ich mein' sein Stahlroß. Da muß ich jetz' in aner Tour mit ihm rumgondeln. Auf'm Sozius. Der Depp bringt mich noch um und sich auch.

FRITZI   Tu dir's net vermasseln mit ihm.

MITZI   *(smiling)* Bist deppert? Der will mich doch zum Altar schleppen.

FRITZI   Und? Kriegst kalte Füaß?

MITZI   *(solemnly)* Also für mich is' Heiraten auf immer und ewig. Da geht's um die Wurscht. Nimm die Laura und den Franz.

FRITZI   Saudummer Vergleich.

MITZI   Warum? Du meinst, weil sie eine Giftnudel und er ein Waschlappen is'?

FRITZI   Genau. Die Eh' war eh scho' im Eimer, eh' die Eh' noch a Eh' war; *(posing as the concerned friend)* aber sag': Wie stellt sich denn der Karl zu deinem Problem?

MITZI   Problem?

FRITZI   Ich mein' dein Freßproblem.

MITZI   Der kriegt, was er siacht.

FRITZI   No ja—aber so ein Bike is' doch nur für zwei gebaut . . . Wart', ich hab' die Lösung.

MITZI   Was?

FRITZI   Friß, soviel du willst, aber schau, daß du's net schluckst.

MITZI   Bei dir is das ka Kunststück. Wenn du Tomatensaft zutzelst, schaust du aus wie ein Thermometer.

FRITZI   Weißt was? Wenn ich so a Fettwanzn wär' wie du, möcht' ich mich aufhängen.

MITZI   Weißt was? Wenn's so weit is', benutz' ich dich als Strick.

MITZI   Get outta here! I mean his bike. Now I got to drive around with him all the time. On the back seat of his bike. That nerd's going to kill me one day, and himself too.

FRITZI   Don't mess it up for yourself.

MITZI   *(smiling)* Are you nuts? He wants to marry me.

FRITZI   So? Gettin' cold feet?

MITZI   *(solemnly)* Marriage for me is for keeps. It's do or die. Take Laura and Franz.

FRITZI   Dumb comparison.

MITZI   Why? You mean because she's a bitch and he's a wimp?

FRITZI   Exactly. And anyway, that marriage has been on the rocks for a long time, even before the marriage was a marriage; *(posing as the concerned friend)* but tell me: What does Karl think of your problem?

MITZI   What problem?

FRITZI   I mean your eating problem.

MITZI   What he sees is what he gets.

FRITZI   Okay—but a bike like that is built just for two. Wait! I got the solution.

MITZI   What?

FRITZI   Eat as much as you want, but watch out you don't swallow it.

MITZI   With you that's a piece o' cake. When you suck your tomato juice you look like a thermometer.

FRITZI   You know what? If I was a lard-ass like you, I would hang myself.

MITZI   You know what? At that point I'll use you for a rope.

Vocabulary

a (ein) *(coll.)*	a, an
auf immer und ewig	for keeps
Bist deppert? *(sl.)*	Are you nuts?
Blunzn *(f. sl.)*	butterball
Da geht's um die Wurscht! *(coll.)*	It's do or die!
Dampfnudel *(f. coll.)*	dumpling
Depp *(m. sl.)*	nerd
Der kann mir den Buck(e)l runterrutschen. *(sl.)*	He can go to hell.
Der kriegt, was er siacht (sieht) *(sl.)*	What he sees is what he gets.
Du bist aufgegangen wie ein Pfannkuchen. *(coll.)*	You swelled up like a balloon.
dünn wie ein Zwirnsfaden *(coll.)*	skinny as a birdleg
eh' (ehe) *(conj.)*	before
eh (sowieso) *(adv. coll.)*	anyway
Fettwanzn (Fettwanze) *(f. sl.)*	lard-ass
flach wie ein Bügelbrett *(coll.)*	flat as a pancake
Flamme *(f. coll.)*	flame; love
Freßproblem *(n. coll.)*	eating problem
Giftnudel *(f. sl.)*	bitch
Grüß dich! *(coll.)*	Hi!
Hallodri *(m. sl.)*	jerk
Heut' duscht's aber! *(coll.)*	It's raining cats and dogs today!
im Eimer *(sl.)*	on the rocks
in aner (einer) Tour *(coll.)*	all the time
ja, ja, scho' gut *(coll.)*	all right already
Jessas na! *(sl.)*	holy cow!
ka (kein) Kunststück *(coll.)*	a piece o' cake
Kriegst kalte Füaß? (= Füße) *(sl.)*	Getting cold feet?
Mistkerl *(m. sl.)*	*(lit.)* garbage guy; (here) slippery louse
net (nicht) *(coll.)*	not
patschnaß *(adj. coll.)*	dripping wet

Red' kan (keinen) Stuß! *(sl.)*	Don't talk nonsense! (here) Get outta here!
rumgondeln *(v. coll.)*	to drive around aimlessly
saudumm *(adj. sl.)*	(very) dumb
Stahlroß *(n. coll.)*	(motor)bike
Sozius *(m. coll.)*	backseat of a bike
vermasseln *(v. sl.)*	to mess up
Waschlappen *(m. coll.)*	wimp
Wenn's so weit is' *(coll.)*	at that point
zum Altar schleppen *(coll.)*	to drag to the altar; (here) to marry
zutzeln *(v. sl.)*	to suck

A Smidgen of Streetwise Grammar
Fun with Idioms and Such

☐ Some verbs with separable prefixes are shortened:

Er kann mir den Buckel **runterrutschen** (herunterrutschen).
Sag ihm, er soll **raufkommen** (heraufkommen).
Ich soll mit ihm **rumgondeln** (herumgondeln).
Das wird sich bald **rausstellen** (herausstellen). It will soon become apparent.
Er fällt **drauf rein** (darauf herein). He falls for it.

☐ Word order in Streetwise German is sometimes anti-grammatical. In the following sentences, all the rules are off:

Er möcht', daß ich mit ihm herumgondel in einer Tour.
(Er möcht', daß ich mit ihm in einer Tour herumgondel.)

Nix kann er machen ohne mich.
(Nix kann er ohne mich machen.)

Schaun Sie, ob alles in Ordnung is' für'n Winter.
(Schaun Sie, ob alles für'n Winter in Ordnung is'.)

☐   Definite articles precede a proper name:

> Was macht **der** Karl?
> (Was macht Karl?)

> Wohin fährt **die** Eva?
> (Wohin fährt Eva?)

☐   The uses of **Wurs(ch)t:**

> **Da geht's um die Wurscht.**   It's do or die.
> **Das ist mir Wurscht.**   I couldn't care less.
> **Sie macht Wurst aus ihm.**   She finishes him off.
> **Ich bin doch nicht ihr Wurschtl.**   I'm not her patsy.
> **Er wurstelt sich durch.**   He's muddling through.
> **Immer braucht er eine Extrawurst.**   He always asks for
>   special privileges.

☐   Die Eh' war eh scho' im Eimer.

> One could also say:
> **Die Eh' war in Scherben.**   in shambles
> **Die Eh' ist in Brüche gegangen.**   has collapsed.
> **Die Eh' ist hin**   (ruined).
> **Die Eh' ist hops gegangen.**   on the blink
> **Die Eh' ist futschikato.**   down the drain

☐   The adverb **eh':**

> Die Eh' war **eh'** scho' im Eimer.
> or:
> Die Eh' war sowieso scho' im Eimer.
> or:
> Die Eh' war ohnehin scho' im Eimer.

☐   The conjunction **eh':**

> **Eh'** sie noch eine Ehe war . . .
> or:
> Bevor sie noch eine Ehe war . . .

☐   Es regnet:

> **es pißt; es schifft.**
> (Caution: **pissen** and **schiffen** also mean to urinate).
>
> light rain:
> **es nieselt, es tröpfelt, es plätschert.**
>
> heavy rain:
> **es gießt, es schüttet, es strömt.**
> **Es regnet wie aus Eimern (Kübeln).**   cats and dogs

☐   Red' keinen Stuß:

> **Was du sagst, ist Blech** rubbish, **Gefasel** drivel, **Geschwafel**
> gabble, **a Schmarrn** nonsense, **Mumpitz** baloney, **Quatsch**
> bunk, **Mist** crap

☐   Additional terms denoting gain in weight or being fat:

> **Du hast Fett angesetzt.**   You turned chunky.
> **Du bist auseinandergegangen.**   You're a roly-poly.
> **Du hast dich herausgefuttert.**   You look like solid suet.
> **Du bist aus den Fugen gegangen.**   You're broad in the
>   beam.
> **Du bist gut wattiert. (gepolstert)**   You're well-padded.
> **Du bist kugelrund.**   You're round as a ball.
>
> A fat person might be called:
> **Dampfnudel** dumpling, **Dickbauch** tub of lard, **Dicksack**
> gutbucket, **Dickwanst** blubberguts, **Elefantenküken** baby
> elephant, **Fettwanst** fatso, **Mollenfriedhof** beerbelly, **Walroß**
> blimp

☐   Additional terms denoting loss of weight or being thin:

> **Du bist nur Haut und Knochen.**   You're skin and bones.
> **Du bist ein dürrer Hecht.**   You're scrawny as a stick.
> **Du siehst aus wie der Tod.**   You look like death warmed
>   over.
> Du bist: **eingeschrumpft** shriveled up, **eingelaufen**
>   shrunk, **eingetrocknet** dried up, **verkümmert** wizened,
>   **ein Splitter** splinter, **ein Streifen Haut** strip of skin,
>   **ein Hobelspan** wood shaving

Love and Kisses

SHE   *(tenderly)* Und sind meine Lippen die einzigen, die du je geküßt hast?

And are my lips the only ones that you ever kissed?

HE   Ja, mein Zuckergoscherl—und sie sind die süßesten von allen.

Yes, my sugarpuss; and they are the sweetest of all.

Exercises

A. Complete the phrase by filling in the appropriate word from the list:

Buckl, Eimer, Giftnudl, Pfannkuchen, rumgondeln, vermasseln, Waschlappen, Wurscht, zutzelt, Zwirnsfaden.

1. Der kann mir den _____ runterrutschen.

2. Tu dir's net _____.

3. Dünn wie ein _____.

4. Du bist aufgegangen wie a _____.

5. In aner Tour _____.

6. Da geht's um die _____.

7. Die Eh' war eh scho' im _____.

8. Fritzi _____ Tomatensaft.

9. Laura is' a _____.

10. Franz is' ein _____.

B. True or False?

T/F

1. Fritzi is' heut' ganz patschnaß.   _____

2. Mitzi is' sehr dick geworden.   _____

3. Karl hat ein Stahlroß.   _____

4. Fritzi ist flach wie ein Bügelbrett.   _____

5. Karl will die Mitzi nicht heiraten.   _____

6. Mitzi vergleicht die Laura mit dem Karl.   _____

7. Ein Bike ist nur für zwei gebaut.   _____

8. Fritzi serviert Kaffee.   _____

9. Mitzi ist Karls neuste Flamme.   _____

10. Mitzi hat ein Freßproblem.   _____

C. Match the German with the English:

1. _____ Da geht's um die Wurscht.   A. The marriage is on the rocks.

2. _____ Die Eh' is' im Eimer.   B. at that point

3. _____ auf immer und ewig   C. piece o' cake!

4. _____ in aner Tour   D. It's do or die.

5. _____ Red' kan Stuß!   E. Are you nuts?

6. _____ wenn's so weit is'   F. for keeps

7. _____ ka Kunststück   G. all the time

8. _____ Heut' duscht's aber!   H. Hi!

9. _____ Bist deppert?   I. Get outta here!

10. _____ Grüß dich!   J. It's raining cats and dogs.

D. Underline the synonyms:

1. Blunzn   a. Bügelbrett   b. Dampfnudl   c. Blondine

2. Buckl   a. Rücken   b. Schnalle   c. Ziege

3. saudumm   a. taub   b. schweinisch   c. idiotisch

4. Es duscht   a. Es schneit   b. Es regnet   c. Es hagelt

5. Depp   a. Fettwanze   b. Dummkopf   c. Depot

6. vermasseln   a. verderben   b. vermachen   c. verhaften

7. Stuß   a. Student   b. Stunde   c. Unsinn

8. Mistkerl   a. Straßenkehrer   b. Hallodri   c. Flamme

9. Stahlroß   a. Motorrad   b. Pferd   c. Dieb

10. rumgondeln   a. sich betrinken   b. segeln   c. herumfahren

E. Translate the following into Streetwise German:

1. _____

You swelled up like a balloon.

2. _____

She's a bitch, and he's a wimp.

3. _____

Don't mess it up for yourself!

4. _____

That slippery louse?

5. _____

It's do or die!

6. _____

What he sees is what he gets.

7. _____

He can go to hell!

8. _____

skinny as a birdleg

9. _____

Get outta here! (Don't talk nonsense!)

10. _____

You're dripping wet.

Dialog 4

Northern German

Leere Drohungen

Two men insulting each other—but it is all in good fun.

WILLY   Mensch, du bist 'n Zwilling, denn einer alleine kann ja
nich' so doof sein.

WALTER   Blubberheini, werd' nich' pampig, sonst zieh' ich dir eine.

WILLY   Sag' mal, haste nich' mehr alle? Nummerier' dir man schon
die Knochen, damit du sie nachher im Schnupptuch nach
Hause tragen kannst.

WALTER   Verzieh' dich, du Hirnie, oder du kriegst 'ne saftige
Abreibung.

WILLY   Du hast dich wohl selber lange nich' mehr quieken hören.
Soll ich dir erst mal die Fresse polieren, du Fliegengewicht?

WALTER   Dich vernasch' ich im Schnellschritt. Selbst Klein-Erna
würde dich mit 'nem kleinen Finger an' Nagel hängen.

WILLY   Und aus dir mach' ich Hackfleisch. Dir hau' ich doch nur
einmal auf'n Holzkopp, und deine Läuse fangen an zu
piepen, du Hampelmann und Lackaffe.

Empty Threats

WILLY   Man, you're a twin, because one alone couldn't be that stupid.

WALTER   Airhead, don't get snotty or I'll deck you.

WILLY   Hey, are you crazy? Number your bones, so you can lug 'em home in your hanky.

WALTER   Get lost, meathead, or I'll beat the living daylights out of you.

WILLY   Guess you haven't heard yourself squealin' for awhile, huh? Want me to smack you in the teeth, you wimp?

WALTER   I cream you in a sec. Even little Erna could hang you up on a nail with her pinky.

WILLY   I'll trash you. I'll bash your brains in until the lice start chirpin', you jellyfish, you candy ass.

WALTER   Kielholen müßte man dich. Warte nur! Dich vertrimm' ich, biste nach deiner Mama schreist und die Sternchen tanzen siehst.

WILLY   Dir ist wohl schon lange nich' mehr die Pupille übers Hemd gekleckert, wa?

WALTER   Du Kotzbrocken! Ich tret' dir vor'n Bauch, daß deinem Bandwurm das Trommelfell platzt. Dich stoß' ich aus'm Anzuch.

WILLY   Und ich mach' Frikadellen aus dir.

WALTER   Gesäß und Wäschestrick! Wo soll ich dir eine hinballern? Zwischen die Kiekerchen? Oder willste een Tritt in Hintern? Ein Hieb reicht. Der zweite wär' schon Leichenschändung.

WILLY   Noch ein Wort, du Sabbermaul, und in nullkommanix kannst du die Engel singen hören.

Vocabulary

auf'n Holzkopp hau(e)n *(sl.)*
to bash one's brains in

Aus dir mach' ich Hackfleisch *(sl.)*
(lit) I'll make mincemeat of you. (here) I'll trash you.

biste (bist du) *(coll.)*
you are

Blubberheini *(m. sl.)*
airhead

Dich stoß' ich aus'm Anzuch (Anzug). *(sl.)*
I'll squeeze you out of your suit.

Dich vernasch' ich im Schnellschritt. *(sl.)*
I'll cream you in a sec.

doof *(adj. sl.)*
stupid

Du kriegst 'ne saftige Abreibung. *(sl.)*
(here) I'll beat the living daylights out of you.

Fliegengewicht *(n. coll.)*
flyweight, wimp

die Fresse polieren *(sl.)*
to smack s.o. in the teeth

Frikadelle *(f. coll.)*
(here) Big Mac, hamburger

Gesäß und Wäschestrick! *(vulg.)*
Christ!

WALTER   I ought to beat the shit out of you. You just wait! I'll blast
          you till you cry for your mommy and see little stars dancin'.

WILLY   How long has it been since your eyeball slithered down
          your shirt, tell me?

WALTER   You piece of vomit! I'll slam you in the guts until your
          tapeworm busts its eardrums open. I squeeze you out of
          your suit.

WILLY   And I'll mash you into ground beef.

WALTER   Christ! Where do I belt you one first? Between the little
          blinkers? How 'bout a kick in the ass? One whack is
          enough. The next would waste a corpse.

WILLY   One more word, dweeb, and, before you know what hit
          you, you'll hear the angels singing.

Hampelmann *(m.)*   (here) jellyfish
Haste (Hast du) nich' mehr   (here) Are you crazy? Did you
alle? *(sl.)*   freak out? (see grammar
                                         section)
hinballern *(v. sl.)*   to belt
Hintern *(m. sl.)*   behind; ass
Hirnie *(m. sl.)*   meathead
Ich tret' dir vor'n Bauch. *(sl.)* I'll slam you in the guts.
in nullkommanix *(coll.)*   before you know
Kiekerchen *(pl. sl.)*   little eyes; blinkers
Kielholen müßte man dich!   (here) I ought to beat the shit out
(sl.)   of you! (see grammar section)
kleckern *(v. sl.)*   to slither
Klein-Erna   little Erna (see grammar section)
Kotzbrocken *(m. sl.)*   piece of vomit
Lackaffe *(m. sl.)*   candy ass
Nummerier' dir man schon   number your bones
die Knochen *(sl.)*
pampig *(adj. sl.)*   snotty
piepen *(v. coll.)*   to chirp

quieken *(v. sl.)*	to scream, to squeal
Sabbermaul *(n. sl.)*	dweeb
Schnupptuch (Schnupftuch) *(n. coll.)*	hankie
Sonst zieh' ich dir eine. *(sl.)*	I'll deck you, hit you.
(die) Sternchen tanzen sehen *(coll.)*	to see little stars dance
vertrimmen *(v. sl.)*	to blast
Verzieh' dich! *(sl.)*	Get lost!
wa? (was?) *(coll.)*	what, tell me
willste (willst du) *(coll.)*	do you want

A Smidgen of Streetwise Grammar
Fun with Idioms and Weird Words

☐ Haste nich' mehr alle?

This is the short version of **Haste nich' mehr alle Tassen im Schrank?** or **Bist du nich' richtig im Dachstübchen?** Are you out of your mind? crazy? insane? Did you freak out?

☐ Klein-Erna:

In Northern Germany there are many jokes and anecdotes about a girl named **Klein-Erna,** Little Erna.

☐ Kielholen müßte man dich.

Recalcitrant sailors used to be towed from one side of the ship to the other ("keelhauled")—a painful punishment.

☐ Gesäß und Wäschestrick!

Other interjections of heightened annoyance: **Himmel, Arsch und Wolkenbruch! Himmel, Sack und Pfeife! Himmel, Arsch und Zwirn! Arsch und Donnerwetter!**

☐   Here are a dozen ways of slapping someone's face:

> **Ich knall' dir eine.**
> **Ich schmier' dir eine.**
> **Ich funk' dir eine.**
> **Ich geb' dir eine.**
> **Ich kleb' dir eine.**
> **Ich lang' dir eine.**
> **Ich latsch' dir eine.**
> **Ich schnalz' dir eine.**
> **Ich verabreich' dir eine.**
> **Ich zwitscher' dir eine.**
> **Ich hau' dir eine runter.**
> **Ich näh' dir gleich 'nen Knopf an die Backe.**

☐   Gipsschädel, Holzkopf, Hornochs, Mondkalb

Here are some more pejoratives; most of them are self-explanatory:

Depp dope, **Dussel** dummy, **Blödmann** idiot, **Trutsch** nerd, **Fatzke** dude, **Flachkopf, Hammel, Heuochs, Kalb, Kamel, Kuh, Heini** birdbrain, **Rindvieh, Schaf, Schafskopf, Schwachkopf, Strohkopf, Trampeltier** camel, **Wasserkopf**

☐   die Fresse polieren

More about **Fresse:**
die Fresse bis an die Ohren aufreißen   to grandstand
jm. die Fresse polieren   to hit s.o. in the face
eine große Fresse haben   to brag
die Fresse hängen lassen   to look sad
jm. die Fresse hinhalten   to stand up for s.o.
jm. die Fresse massieren   to slap s.o.
jm. in die Fresse spucken   to tell s.o. off
jm. die Fresse stopfen   to shut up s.o.

Question and Answer

| PROFESSOR | (to student during oral exam) Ist Ihnen die Frage zu schwierig? | Do you find the question too difficult? |
| STUDENT | Die Frage ist kein Problem, Herr Professor. Ich zerbrech' mir den Kopf über die Antwort. | The question is no problem, sir. It's the answer that gives me a headache. |

Exercises

A. Complete the phrase by filling in the appropriate word from the list:

Abreibung, Anzuch, Hackfleisch, hinballern, kielholen, Hintern, nummerier', piepen, polieren, Schnellschritt.

1. Du kriegst 'ne saftige _____.

2. Und aus dir mach' ich _____.

3. Deine Läuse fangen an zu _____.

4. _____ müßte man dich.

5. _____ dir man schon die Knochen.

6. Soll ich dir erst mal die Fresse _____?

7. Dich stoß ich aus'm _____.

8. Oder willste een Tritt in _____?

9. Wo soll ich dir eine _____?

10. Dich vernasch' ich im _____.

B. True or False?

T/F

1. Mit "Kiekerchen" meint Walter die Augen. _____

2. Wenn man glücklich ist, hört man die Engel singen. _____

3. "Frikadellen" sind gekochte Nudeln. _____

4. Wenn Willy "Fresse" sagt, meint er den Mund. _____

5. Walter nennt Willy "Blubberheini". _____

6. Willy möchte aus Walter Hackfleisch machen. _____

7. Man braucht das Schnupptuch für die Nase. _____

8. Willy nennt Walter klug. _____

9. Walter nennt Willy einen Kotzbrocken. _____

10. "Sabbermaul" ist ein Kompliment. _____

C. Match the German with the English:

1. _____ Ich zieh' dir eine.

2. _____ in nullkommanix

3. _____ Dir hau' ich auf'n Holzkopp.

4. _____ Haste nich' mehr alle?

5. _____ Ich tret' dir vor'n Bauch.

6. _____ Werd' nich' pampig!

7. _____ Willste een Tritt in Hintern?

8. _____ Aus dir mach' ich Hackfleisch.

9. _____ Verzieh' dich!

10. _____ Dich vernasch' ich im Schnellschritt.

A. I'll trash you.
B. Don't get snotty.
C. I'll cream you in a sec.
D. I'll deck you.
E. How 'bout a kick in the ass?
F. I'll bash your brains in.
G. Get lost!
H. Are you crazy?
I. I'll slam you in the guts.
J. before you know what hit you

D. Translate the following into Streetwise German:

1. _____

   Get lost, meathead!

2. _____

   I'll cream you in a sec.

3. _____

   I'll squeeze you out of your suit.

4. _____

   I ought to beat the shit out of you.

5. _____

   Where do I belt you one first?

6. _____

   The next (blow) would waste a corpse.

7. _____

   Airhead, don't get snotty!

8. _____

   I'll blast you till you cry for your mommy.

9. _____

   You can lug 'em home in your hanky.

10. _____

   I'll beat the living daylights out of you.

E. Underline the English term that comes closest in meaning to the
    German word on the left.

1. Blubberheini   a. whale   b. airhead   c. wiseguy

2. Kiekerchen   a. blinkers   b. kicks   c. cakes

3. Hintern   a. death   b. ass   c. Mars

4. Frikadellen   a. sardines   b. hamburgers   c. fricassee

5. Fliegengewicht   a. flier   b. fleetfoot   c. wimp

6. hinballern   a. to belt   b. to boil   c. to ballot

7. Schnupptuch   a. snapshot   b. hankie   c. snoot

8. vertrimmen   a. to trim   b. to blast   c. to trifle

9. pampig   a. snotty   b. spoiled   c. grassy

10. doof   a. doodle   b. stupid   c. tough

Dialog 5

Southern German

Liebe übers Grab hinaus

A married couple. Helmut wants to be left alone, and Karla is the anxious type.

KARLA   Süßer, falls ich vor dir abkratz', möchst mir was versprechen?

HELMUT   Was denn?

KARLA   Versprich mir, daß mein Grab immer schön grün sein wird.

HELMUT   Ach du meine Güte! Geht's dir net gut? Was schwafelst denn vom Sterben? Du kommst mir pumperlg'sund vor. Schaust aus wie's blühende Leben. Darf ich jetzt lesen?

KARLA   Hast recht, Hasi. Momentan fühl' ich mich auch pudelwohl, aber ich möcht' eben auf Nummer sicher geh'n, daß d' mir mein Grab nicht verkommen laßt, wenn ich amol net mehr bin. Was passiert wenn dich a andre aufreißt? Dann hast die am Hals, und mi' vergißt schnurstracks.

Love Beyond the Grave

KARLA   Honeybunch, in case I croak before you, would you promise me something?

HELMUT   What is it?

KARLA   Promise me, my grave will always be nice and green.

HELMUT   Holy Moses! Are you sick? What's that yak about dying? To me you look fit as a fiddle, alive and kicking.—May I read now?

KARLA   You're right, sweetie. At the moment I feel like a million bucks. But I'd like to be absolutely certain that you won't neglect my grave when I'm not around anymore. What is going to happen if another woman picks you up? Then you got her on your back, and you'll forget me immediately.

HELMUT   Was redst denn saublöd so daher, Karla? Du überlebst
mich noch, da kannst Gift drauf nehmen. — Darf ich jetzt
lesen?

KARLA   Bubi, sei net bös, aber ich kann mir net helfen. Ich bin so
heikel in der Beziehung. Schatzi, bist du sicher, daß mein
Grab immer grün sein wird?

HELMUT   Ich versprech' dir's.

KARLA   Mausi, da fällt mir a großer Stein vom Herzen. Aber ich
möcht', daß du's mir ein bißl feierlicher versprichst.
Schnucki, bist du hundertprozentig vollkommen sicher,
mein Grab wird immer . . .

HELMUT   Karla, dein verdammtes Grab wird grün sein, und wenn
ich's selber grün anstreichen muß.

Vocabulary

abkratzen *(v. sl.)*   to croak
Ach du meine Güte! *(coll.)*   Holy Moses!
amol (einmal) *(coll.)*   sometime
auf Nummer sicher geh'n   to be absolutely certain
  (coll.)
aufreißen *(v. sl.)*   to pick up
Bubi *(m. coll.)*   little boy (endearing term);
                                                        (here) angel

Da fällt mir a (ein) großer   That takes a big load off my
  Stein vom Herzen. *(coll.)*   mind.
Da kannst du Gift drauf   You can bet your sweet life.
  nehmen. *(coll.)*
Dann hast du die am Hals.   Then you have her on your back.
  (Dann mußt du für sie
  sorgen.) *(coll.)*
ein bißl (bißchen) feierlicher   to promise with more feeling,
  versprechen   passion
Geht's dir net (nicht) gut?   Are you sick?
  (coll.)
Hasi *(n. coll.)*   bunny, little hare (endearing
                                                        term); (here) sweetie

heikel *(adj. coll.)*   finicky

HELMUT   Don't talk nonsense, Karla. You're going to outlive me, you can bet your sweet life. — May I read now?

KARLA   Angel, don't be mad, but I can't help it. I'm so finicky in that respect. Precious, are you sure my grave will always be green?

HELMUT   I'm sure.

KARLA   Love, that takes a big load off my mind. But I'd like you to say it with more feeling. Sweetheart, are you one hundred percent absolutely sure that my grave will always . . .

HELMUT   Karla, your goddamn grave will be green even if I have to paint it green myself.

---

hundertprozentig vollkommen (*coll.*)	100% absolutely sure
Ich kann mir net (nicht) helfen. (*coll.*)	I can't help it.
Mausi (*n. coll.*)	little mouse (endearing term); (here) love
pudelwohl (ich fühl mich pudelwohl) (*coll.*)	(I feel) like a million bucks; on top of the world
pumperlg(e)sund (*adj. coll.*)	fit as a fiddle
saublöd daherreden (*sl.*)	to talk nonsense
Schatzi (*n. coll.*)	little treasure (endearing term); (here) precious
Schnucki (*n. coll.*)	(here) honeybunch
schnurstracks (*adv.*)	immediately, straight away
schön grün (*coll.*)	nice and green
schwafeln (*v. sl.*)	to yak
Süßer (*m. coll.*)	sweetheart, honeybunch
verdammtes Grab (*vulg.*)	goddamn grave
verkommen lassen (*v.*)	to neglect
Wenn ich amol net mehr bin. (*coll.*)	When I'm not around anymore
wie's blühende Leben (*coll.*)	alive and kicking

Note: The above-listed terms of endearment (**Bubi, Hasi, Mausi, Schatzi, Süßer** and **Schnucki**) are, of course, interchangeable.

A Smidgen of Streetwise Grammar
Fun with Idioms and Such

☐   Note the abbreviated form **möchst:**

Möchst du mir was versprechen?
(Möchtest du mir etwas versprechen?)

☐   The uses of **schön:**

a. to invigorate the adjective following it:
schön grün   nice and green
Sei **schön** brav und geh schlafen.   Go to bed like a good
boy.

b. To reinforce the verb following or preceding it:
Da hat er sich aber **schön** in den Dreck reing'setzt.
He sure got himself into a mess there.

c. meaning the opposite of what it says:
Damit ist er **schön** angekommen.   He came to the wrong
address.

☐   The manifold uses of **was:**

a. **was** vs. **wo:**
Für was (Wofür) hältst du mich?
Mit was (Womit) schreibst du?
Von was (Wovon) spricht er?
Vor was (Wovor) hast du Angst?

b. **was** with **sein** and **haben:**
Er ist was.   He is an important man.
Er hält sich für weiß Gott was.   He thinks a lot of
himself.
Er hat was.   He is in a bad mood; or, something is wrong
with him.

c. **was** taking the place of **warum** or **wieviel:**
Was (Warum) regen Sie sich so auf?
Was (Wieviel) bin ich Ihnen schuldig?

d. **was** as the shortened form of **etwas:**
Ich will dir **was** (etwas) sagen.
Es hat **was** (etwas) für sich.   There's something to be said for it.

☐   Sie fühlt sich pudelwohl.

You can also say:
Sie ist wieder auf dem Damm.   She is in good shape again.
Sie ist wieder auf der Höhe.   She is on her feet again.
Sie ist wieder gut beisammen.   She has it together again.
Sie ist die Gesundheit selbst.   She is in the pink.
Er (sie) ist:
  kerngesund   sound as a bell
  quicklebendig   full of pep
  frisch und munter   hale and hearty

Talking with a Neighbor

FRAU SCHMIDT	Wie geht's denn Ihrem Mann?	How is your husband?
FRAU SCHULZ	Ja der führt ein Hundeleben.	He leads a dog's life.
FRAU SCHMIDT	Was meinen's denn?	What d'you mean?
FRAU SCHULZ	Er knurrt den ganzen Tag und schnarcht die ganze Nacht.	He growls all day, and snores all night.

Exercises

A. Complete the phrase by filling in the appropriate word from the list:

abkratz', aufreißt, gut, Güte, helfen, Leben, pudelwohl, pumperlg'sund, saublöd, schwafelst.

1. Momentan fühl' ich mich _____.

2. falls ich vor dir _____

3. Was _____ denn vom Sterben?

4. Du kommst mir _____ vor.

5. Was redst denn so _____ daher?

6. Wenn dich a andre _____.

7. Ach, du meine _____!

8. Geht's dir net _____?

9. Ich kann mir net _____.

10. wie's blühende _____

B. True or False?

	T/F
1. Helmut möchte gern lesen.	_____
2. Karla ist heikel in dieser Beziehung.	_____
3. Sie denkt nie ans Sterben.	_____
4. Karla sieht sehr krank aus.	_____
5. Helmut wird ihr Grab selber grün anstreichen.	_____
6. Karla möchte auf Nummer sicher gehen.	_____
7. Sie wird Gift nehmen.	_____
8. Helmut kauft einen Grabstein.	_____

9. Karla wird ihn am Hals haben.   _____

10. Da fällt ihr ein Stein vom Herzen.   _____

C. Match the German with the English:

1. _____	Ich bin so heikel in der Beziehung.	A. Are you sick?
2. _____	Geht's dir net gut?	B. Then you got her on your back.
3. _____	Mich vergißt du schnurstracks.	C. What's that yak about dying?
4. _____	Ich fühl' mich pudelwohl.	D. That takes a big load off my mind.
5. _____	Was schwafelst denn vom Sterben?	E. I'm so finicky in that respect.
6. _____	Du kannst Gift drauf nehmen.	F. Holy Moses!
7. _____	Dann hast du sie am Hals.	G. I feel like a million bucks.
8. _____	Da fällt mir ein großer Stein vom Herzen.	H. I'd like to be absolutely certain.
9. _____	Ich möcht' auf Nummer sicher gehn.	I. You can bet your sweet life.
10. _____	Ach du meine Güte!	J. You'll forget me immediately.

D. Try to replace words like *wofür, worauf, warum, wieviel, etwas,* by using *was* in the following sentences:

1. Wofür ist das gut?

   _____

2. Wozu braucht man das?

   _____

3. Woran denkst du?

_____

4. Worauf basiert das?

_____

5. Sie hat etwas gefunden.

_____

6. Hast du etwas gehört?

_____

7. Wieviel haben Sie dafür bezahlt?

_____

8. Warum machst du so einen Lärm?

_____

E.   Translate the following into Streetwise German:

1. I'm so finicky in this respect.

_____

2. That takes a big load off my mind.

_____

3. You can bet your sweet life.

_____

4. You got her on your back.

_____

5. I feel like a million bucks.

_____

6. Are you sick?

_____

7. What's that yak about dying?

_____

8. You look fit as a fiddle.

_____

9. In case I croak . . .

_____

10. You'll forget me immediately.

_____

Answers
Dialogs 1 through 5

Dialog 1

A.
1. Faultierfilet
2. g'schnallt
3. 'neinziehn
4. Mammutkeule
5. Freßsack
6. Scheunendrescher
7. Verzweiflung
8. Kniekehlen
9. knapp
10. verarscht

B.
1. F   3. T   5. F   7. T   9. F
2. F   4. T   6. F   8. T   10. T

C.
1. C   3. I   5. A   7. D   9. F
2. E   4. B   6. H   8. J   10. G

D.
1. der Magen vom Josef
2. das Restaurant vom Otto
3. das Kleid von (der) Eva
4. die Portion vom Gast
5. der Preis von der Lampe
6. die Bücher von den Studenten
7. die Kinder von (der) Olga
8. der Aufzug von den Kellnern
9. die Söhne von den Soldaten
10. die Kleider von den Studentinnen

E.
1. dem Herrn sein Haus
2. dem Kellner sein Gesicht
3. dem Onkel seine Hand
4. dem Mädchen seine Nase
5. dem Sohn sein Freund
6. der Freundin ihr Vater
7. der Karla ihre Tochter
8. dem Kurt seine Söhne
9. den Gästen ihre Kleider
10. den Verwandten ihre Häuser

Dialog 2

A. 1. Honiglecken   5. Haare   8. Knete
    2. Moos   6. flöt'n   9. Blaue
    3. verdrückt   7. Pleite   10. geil
    4. vertuckelt

B. 1. T   3. F   5. F   7. F   9. F
    2. T   4. T   6. F   8. T   10. T

C. 1. D   3. H   5. J   7. A   9. E
    2. F   4. C   6. I   8. B   10. G

D. 1. a   3. b   5. a   7. a   9. c
    2. c   4. c   6. b   8. b   10. c

E. 1, 4, 6, 8

Dialog 3

A. 1. Buckl   5. rumgondeln   8. zutzelt
    2. vermasseln   6. Wurscht   9. Giftnudl
    3. Zwirnsfaden   7. Eimer   10. Waschlappen
    4. Pfannkuchen

B. 1. F   3. T   5. F   7. T   9. F
    2. T   4. T   6. F   8. T   10. T

C. 1. D   3. F   5. I   7. C   9. E
    2. A   4. G   6. B   8. J   10. H

D. 1. b   3. c   5. b   7. c   9. a
    2. a   4. b   6. a   8. b   10. c

E.   1. Du bist aufgegangen wie a Pfannkuchen.
     2. Sie is' eine Giftnudl, und er is' ein Waschlappen.
     3. Tu dir's net vermasseln mit ihm.
     4. Der Mistkerl?
     5. Da geht's um die Wurscht.
     6. Der kriegt, was er siacht.
     7. Der kann mir den Buckl runterrutschen.
     8. dünn wie ein Zwirnsfaden
     9. Red kan Stuß!
    10. Du bist ja patschnaß.

Dialog 4

A. 1. Abreibung   5. Nummerier'   8. Hintern
    2. Hackfleisch   6. polieren   9. hinballern
    3. piepen   7. Anzuch   10. Schnellschritt
    4. kielholen

B. 1. T   3. F   5. T   7. F   9. T
    2. F   4. T   6. T   8. F   10. F

C. 1. D   3. F   5. I   7. E   9. G
    2. J   4. H   6. B   8. A   10. C

D.   1. Verzieh' dich, du Hirnie!
     2. Dich vernasch' ich im Schnellschritt.
     3. Dich stoß' ich aus'm Anzuch.
     4. Kielholen müßte man dich.
     5. Wo soll ich dir eine hinballern?
     6. Der zweite wär' Leichenschändung.
     7. Blubberheini, werd' nich' pampig!
     8. Dich vertrimm' ich, biste nach deiner Mama schreist.
     9. Du kannst sie im Schnupptuch nach Hause tragen.
    10. Du kriegst 'ne saftige Abreibung.

E. 1. b   3. b   5. c   7. b   9. a
    2. a   4. b   6. a   8. b   10. b

Dialog 5

A. 1. pudelwohl   5. saublöd   8. gut
    2. abkratz'   6. aufreißt   9. helfen
    3. schwafelst   7. Güte   10. Leben
    4. pumperlg'sund

B. 1. T   3. F   5. T   7. F   9. F
    2. T   4. F   6. T   8. F   10. T

C. 1. E   3. J   5. C   7. B   9. H
    2. A   4. G   6. I   8. D   10. F

D. 1. Für was ist das gut?
    2. Zu was braucht man das?
    3. An was denkst du?
    4. Auf was basiert das?
    5. Sie hat was gefunden.
    6. Hast du was gehört?
    7. Was haben Sie dafür bezahlt?
    8. Was machst du so einen Lärm?

E. 1. Ich bin so heikel in der Beziehung.
    2. Da fällt mir ein großer Stein vom Herzen.
    3. Da kannst du Gift drauf nehmen.
    4. Dann hast du die am Hals.
    5. Ich fühl' mich pudelwohl.
    6. Geht's dir net gut?
    7. Was schwafelst denn vom Sterben?
    8. Du schaust aus wie's blühende Leben.
    9. Falls ich vor dir abkratz' . . .
    10. Du vergißt mich schnurstracks.

Review
Dialogs 1 through 5

Exercises

A. Replace the word(s) in parentheses with the Streetwise German synonyms from the right:

1. Ich könnt' (essen) _____ wie ein Scheunendrescher.

2. Der hat's (geschluckt) _____.

3. Er hat mit dem (Geld) _____ spekuliert.

4. Er hat's (vergessen) _____.

5. Red' kan (Unsinn) _____.

6. Er kann mir den (Rücken) _____ runterrutschen.

7. Einer allein kann nicht so (dumm)

    _____ sein.

8. Wo soll ich dir eine (hinschlagen)

    _____.

9. Ich fühl' mich (wunderbar) _____.

10. Was (redst) _____ denn vom Sterben?

A. Moos
B. doof
C. Buckl
D. hinballern
E. reinhaun
F. schwafelst
G. verschwitzt
H. g'schnallt
I. Stuß
J. pudelwohl

B. Underline the word in parentheses that makes sense when completing the sentence:

1. Hier kannst dir was richtiges ('tschuldigen, 'neinziehn, verarschen).

2. Das is' saumäßig (cool, pudelwohl, g'schmalzen).

3. Das Leben mit ihr war kein (Honiglecken, Kittchen, Zaster).

4. Er hat das Geld vorher (verdrückt, verschwitzt, vertuckelt).

5. Du bist flach wie ein (Bügelbrett, Zwirnsfaden, Buckl).

6. Die Eh' war eh scho' im (Hallodri, Waschlappen, Eimer).

7. Du kriegst 'ne saftige (Fresse, Abreibung, Pupille).

8. Nummerier' dir man schon die (Knochen, Läuse, Sternchen).

9. Karla fürchtet, daß sie vor ihm (abkratzt, schwafelt, lebt).

10. Dann hat er sie am (Grab, Hals, Stein).

C. Complete the following words:

1.	F					

| 2. | E | |

| 3. | T | | | |

| 4. | T | | | | | | |

| 5. | W | | | | | | | | | |

| 6. | A | | | |

| 7. | N | |

| 8. | Z | | | | |

| 9. | E | | | |

1. super
2. anyway
3. wonderful
4. difficulties
5. wimp
6. getup
7. nothing
8. dough
9. real

D. Circle the words in the grid:

A	C	D	G	L	M	H	I	N
O	R	S	A	N	A	C	G	H
L	M	O	B	L	U	N	Z	N
P	R	E	L	G	S	U	U	Z
D	N	O	H	L	I	A	T	A
C	P	L	E	I	T	E	Z	D
D	O	P	I	R	E	L	E	N
C	L	G	K	H	X	N	L	D
D	O	D	E	P	P	G	N	L
E	H	B	L	O	R	C	E	U
M	I	S	T	K	E	R	L	A
D	R	N	C	U	G	H	I	L
B	N	O	D	I	H	N	M	O
Z	I	R	G	R	L	A	O	D
B	E	N	G	O	C	G	L	A

Expressions for:

(vertical):	meathead, finicky, sweetie, to suck
(horizontal):	butterball, bankruptcy, nerd, anyway, slippery louse

Answers to Review

Dialogs 1 through 5

A. 1. E   3. A   5. I   7. B   9. J
   2. H   4. G   6. C   8. D   10. F

B. 1. 'neinziehn   5. Bügelbrett   8. Knochen
   2. g'schmalzen   6. Eimer   9. abkratzt
   3. Honiglecken   7. Abreibung   10. Hals
   4. vertuckelt

C. 1. fetzig   4. Trabbel   7. nix
   2. eh   5. Waschlappen   8. Zaster
   3. toll   6. Aufzug   9. echt

D. (vertical):   Hirnie, heikel, Mausi, zutzeln
   (horizontal):   Blunzn, Pleite, Depp, eh, Mistkerl

Dialog 6

Northern German

Eine sympathische Dame

Two friends having an adult conversation. Wouldn't you hate to be their target?

KLARA Sie trägt zu viel von nicht genug.

LAURA Sie trägt Fetzen, die zu spät anfangen und zu früh aufhören.

KLARA Aber das Frauenzimmer hat nie was zum Anziehn mit drei Schränken voll von Klamüsern, von kessen und flotten Klamotten.

LAURA Das Pech ist, sie glaubt, sie ist eine Sirene—doch sie klingt bloß wie eene.

KLARA Sie hat 'nen Tratschfimmel und 'ne spitze Zunge. Sie flunkert und schwefelt und tratscht und klatscht, wo sie geht und steht.

LAURA Die hat man mit 'ner Plattenspielernadel geimpft—

KLARA —und davon hat sie dann prompt die Mauldiarrhoe gekriegt.

A Nice Lady

KLARA   She wears too much of not enough.

LAURA   She wears rags that start late and end early.

KLARA   But the broad never has anything to wear with three closets full of duds, of stylish threads and fancy togs.

LAURA   The bummer is, she thinks she is a siren—but she only sounds like one.

KLARA   She is afflicted with the gabbing disease. God, she has a sharp tongue! She fibs and twaddles, gabs and yaps at every turn.

LAURA   Vaccinated with a phonograph needle—

KLARA   —she promptly developed diarrhea of the mouth.

LAURA   Und dabei ist sie so verschwiegen wie 'ne Litfaßsäule.

KLARA   Wenn die mal in die Nüsse geht, muß man ihr die Schnute extra totschlagen.

LAURA   Aber der Alfred, ihr Mann, nennt sie seine "flotte Biene" und er ist bestimmt nicht ihr Jasager. Wenn sie "nein" sagt, sagt er "nein", da kannste Gift drauf nehmen.

KLARA   Und doch ist sie arm dran. Hat schon seit Jahren keinen Geburtstag mehr gehabt.

LAURA   Es geht das Gerücht, eine hat sie mal gefragt, ganz unerwartet: "Wie alt bist du denn eigentlich?" Da hat sie sich endlicht verplappert und hat ausgepackt: "Nun, ich war vierzig;" aber sie sagte nicht, wann.

KLARA   Alfred ist total in sie verschossen und nennt sie "mein Tuttchen, mein steiler Zahn, mein Wonneproppen, mein Schmackeduzchen." Sie hat alles, womit sich ein Mann gewöhnlich dicktut: starke Knochen, Muskeln und einen Schnurrbart.

LAURA   Sie heißt Alice, und weißt du, warum? Als die Eltern sie zuerst sahen, schrien sie: "Das is' alles!"

Vocabulary

arm dran sein *(coll.)*	to be a poor shnook, a wretched soul
(mit etw.) auspacken *(v. coll.)*	to spill the beans
Da kannst du Gift drauf nehmen. *(coll.)*	You can bet (your life) on that.
(sich) dicktun *(v. sl.)*	to be self-satisfied
Es geht das Gerücht . . . *(coll.)*	Rumor has it . . .
Fetzen *(pl. coll.)*	rags (clothes)
flotte Biene *(f. sl.)*	pretty girl; (here) classy chassis
flunkern *(v. coll.)*	to fib
Frauenzimmer *(n. coll.)*	broad
in die Nüsse gehen *(sl.)*	to kick the bucket
Klamüser *(pl. sl.)*	duds

LAURA   Yeah, she's as discreet as a billboard.

KLARA   When she finally kicks the bucket, you'll have to kill her trap separately.

LAURA   But her husband Alfred calls her his "classy chassis," and he is definitely not her yes-man. When she says no, he says no. You can bet on that.

KLARA   And yet, she's a poor shnook. Hasn't had a birthday for years.

LAURA   Rumor has it, some woman once asked her, unexpectedly, "How old are you actually?" It was then that she spilled the beans: "Well, I was forty"—but she didn't say when.

KLARA   Alfred is nuts about her, calling her his dreamboat, his super girl, his centerfold, his pussycat. She's got everything a man usually likes to show off: massive bones, muscles, and a moustache.

LAURA   Her name is Alice, and you know why? When her parents first saw her, they shouted: "Das is' alles!" [no more!]

---

kesse und flotte Klamotten *(pl. coll.)*	fancy togs
klatschen *(v.)*	to yap, gab
Mauldiarrhöe *(f. sl.)*	diarrhea of the mouth
'ne (eine) spitze Zunge haben *(coll.)*	to have a malicious, sharp tongue
Pech *(n. coll.)*	bad luck; a bummer
Schmackeduzchen *(n. sl.)*	pussycat
Schnute *(f. sl.)*	mouth, trap
schwefeln *(v. sl.)*	to twaddle, gab
steiler Zahn *(m. sl.)*	supergirl
tratschen *(v. coll.)*	to gab, gossip
Tratschfimmel *(m. sl.)*	gabbing disease, 'rapping' rash
Tuttchen *(n. coll.)*	dreamboat
(sich) verplappern *(v. coll.)*	to forget oneself and spill the beans

(in jn.) verschossen sein *(coll.)*   to be nuts about s.o.
verschwiegen wie 'ne (eine)   as discreet as a billboard
  Litfaßsäule *(coll.)*
wo sie geht und steht *(coll.)*   at every turn
Wonneproppen *(m. coll.)*   roly-poly baby; (here) centerfold

A Smidgen of Streetwise Grammar

Fun with Idioms and Weird Words

☐ Frau

>   **eine Frau in den besten Mannesjahren**   a woman between
>   40 and 50
>   **eine Frau im goldenen Mittelalter**   a woman just over 40
>   **eine heiße Frau**   a sexy woman
>   **eine zweigleisige** (double-tracked) **Frau**   a woman with a
>   lover besides her husband

☐ Pech

>   **Pech an den Fingern haben**   to hate to pay; to be a thief
>   **jn. ins Pech reiten**   to be a rip-off artist
>   **wie Schwefel und Pech zusammenhalten**   to stick together;
>   to be faithful to each other
>   **Pech gehabt!**   Too bad! Bad luck!
>   **pechrabenschwarz**   jet-black
>   **Pechmarie**   unlucky girl
>   **Pechsträhne**   consecutive mishaps
>
>   (Note: **Pech** literally means "pitch.")

☐ Tratsch und Klatsch

>   **Sie nimmt kein Blatt vor den Mund.**   She doesn't mince
>   words.
>   **Sie verbrennt sich den Mund.**   She gets into hot water.
>   **Sie kann 's Maul nicht halten.**   She can't keep her trap shut.

Sie ist nicht auf den Mund gefallen.   She knows all the
answers.

Sie zerreißt sich darüber das Maul.   She likes to chew the
fat.

☐   Klatchbase

Klatschweib gossip monger, **Plaudertasche** chatterbox,
Faselhans gasser, **Quasselstrippe** blabbermouth

☐   'ne flotte Biene

flinke Biene   highpowered girl
kesse Biene   pert girl
scharfe Biene   sexy girl

☐   Da kannst du Gift drauf nehmen.

Er spuckt Gift und Galle.   He blows his top.
Sie hat ihn mit Gift bespritzt.   She bad-mouthed him.
Das ist Gift für ihn.   That screws him up.
Sie ist ein blondes Gift.   She's a stunning blonde.

Their Favorite Pastime

ELKE	Was du da über Alice vorbringst, ist nicht wert, wiederholt zu werden. Die ganze Geschichte—	What you tell about Alice isn't worth repeating. The whole story—
HEIKE	—ist noch zu jung. Gib ihr Zeit.	—is still too young. Give it time.
LIA	Ich weiß nur Gutes über sie zu sagen.	I know nothing but good about her.
PIA	Dann tratschen wir von jemand andern.	Then let's gab about someone else.

Exercises

A. Complete the phrase by filling in the appropriate word from the list:

Biene, dicktut, Fetzen, Klamüsern, Litfaßsäule, Mauldiarrhöe, Schnute, Tratschfimmel, verplappert, verschossen.

1. Sie hat 'nen _____.

2. Und davon hat sie die _____ gekriegt.

3. Dabei ist sie so verschwiegen wie eine _____.

4. Man muß ihr die _____ extra totschlagen.

5. Alfred nennt sie eine flotte _____.

6. Da hat sie sich endlich _____.

7. Sie hat alles, womit sich ein Mann _____.

8. Alfred ist total in sie _____.

9. Sie hat drei Schränke voll von _____.

10. Sie trägt _____, die zu spät anfangen.

B. True or False?

	T/F
1. Alice spricht sehr wenig.	_____
2. Alfred ist nicht ihr Jasager.	_____
3. Sie glaubt, sie ist eine Sirene.	_____
4. Alice trägt nur lange Kleider.	_____
5. Alfred nennt sie "mein Tuttchen."	_____
6. Sie hat eine spitze Zunge.	_____

7. Sie ist bloß dreißig Jahre alt. _____

8. Sie trägt zu viel von nicht genug. _____

9. "Sie ißt gern Nüsse", heißt es im Dialog. _____

10. Man hat sie mit einer Plattenspielernadel geimpft. _____

C. Match the German with the English:

1. _____ Sie hat ausgepackt.

2. _____ Es geht das Gerücht . . .

3. _____ Sie ist arm dran.

4. _____ Das Frauenzimmer hat nichts zum Anziehen.

5. _____ Sie flunkert und schwefelt.

6. _____ Da kannste Gift drauf nehmen.

7. _____ Er nennt sie "mein Wonneproppen."

8. _____ Alfred ist in sie verschossen.

9. _____ Wenn sie in die Nüsse geht . . .

A. The broad has nothing to wear.
B. She fibs and twaddles.
C. You can bet on that.
D. She's a poor shnook.
E. When she kicks the bucket . . .
F. She spilled the beans.
G. Rumor has it . . .
H. He calls her "my centerfold."
I. Alfred is nuts about her.

D. Underline the English term that comes closest in meaning to the German word on the left:

1. sich dicktun   a. to thicken   b. to brag   c. to smile

2. Schnute   a. trap   b. rope   c. ship

3. schwefeln   a. to tail   b. to twaddle   c. to sulfurate

4. Fetzen   a. rags   b. hats   c. fat

5. Tuttchen   a. dove   b. tussle   c. dreamboat

6. tratschen   a. to gab   b. to trash   c. to travel

7. Frauenzimmer   a. ladies' room b. broad   c. chamber

8. Klamüser   a. duds   b. clams   c. Klan

9. Litfaßsäule   a. litterbag   b. billboard   c. liquor bottle

10. Pech   a. bummer   b. peck   c. peak

E. Translate the following into Streetwise German:

1. She is afflicted with the gabbing disease.

_____

2. She's as discreet as a billboard.

_____

3. She's a poor shnook.

_____

4. The broad never has anything to wear.

_____

5. She gabs and yaps at every turn.

_____

6. Alfred is nuts about her.

_____

7. He calls her his pussycat.

_____

8. She has everything a man brags about.

_____

9. When she finally kicks the bucket . . .

_____

10. She spilled the beans.

_____

Dialog 7

Achtung, bissiger Hund!

All about man's best friend.

KARL Also mei' Spezi, der Max, der hat an Wachhund, der is'
prima. Wenn der Max an Kerl ums Haus rumschnüffeln
siecht, no dann weckt er den Hund einfach auf und der fangt
in nullkommanix zum Belln an.

HANS Wasd' net sagst! Da hat er aber ein Mordsschwein! Mein
Freund, der Toni, also der muß sich leider ohne an Hund
g'fretten, der is' bettelarm. Also wenn der Schiß kriegt, dann
fangt er halt selber zum Belln an.

KARL Ha, ha! Wer's glaubt, wird selig! Haltst mich zum Narrn?

HANS Waßt, die Leut' sagn, der Hund is' dem Menschen sein bester
Freund. Und weißt auch, warum?

KARL Ich hab' keinen blassen Schimmer.

Beware of the Dog

KARL My friend Max, now he has a watchdog that is great. When Max sees some bum snooping around the house, he wakes the dog, and the dog starts barking on the double.

HANS No kiddin'! Max sure got all the breaks! My friend Toni, now he got to do without a dog 'cause he's poor as a church mouse. When he gets spooked, he starts barking himself.

KARL Ha, ha! My eye! Who you're ribbin'?

HANS Y' know, people say, a dog is man's best friend. You know why?

KARL Search me.

HANS　Nummer eins, ein Hund geht dir net auf'n Wecker. Nummer zwei, er haut' dich net um Geld an; und Nummer drei, er hat keine Schwiegereltern.

KARL　Und er ratscht net wie auf'zog'n. Und billiger is' er auch als ein Weibsbild, b'sonders wenn sie a Bißgurn is', wie das ja öfters passiert. Weil die Lizenz kost' so gut wie nix, und an Pelz hat er eh schon, den mußt ihm net erst anschaff'n.

HANS　Logo! Und er is' auch der einzige Freund, den man sich kaufen kann.

KARL　Find' ich ja auch! Glaubst, können Hund' reden?

HANS　Hörst, du bist aber strohdumm. Ich garantier' dir, daß wenn a Hund dir sagt, er kann reden, dann erzählt er dir an Kas.

KARL　Vielleicht net reden, aber mei' Freund der Gottfried, also der hat an Hund, der spielt Poker—das geb' ich dir schriftlich.

HANS　Hörst, du bist aber ein Depp. Du hast an Schuß, das glaubst doch net wirklich.

KARL　No und ob! Aber mein Freund is' ein bißl enttäuscht über'n Hund. Weil jed's Mal, daß der Gottfried ein gutes Blatt kriegt, wedelt das Hundsviech mit'm Schwanz.

Vocabulary

(jm.) auf'n (auf den) Wecker gehn (sl.)	to make s.o. jumpy, to disturb
bettelarm (adj.)	poor as a church mouse
Bißgurn (f. sl.)	nagging woman; bitch
Dann erzählt er dir an (einen) Kas (Käse). (coll.)	He feeds you a line.
Das geb' ich dir schriftlich. (coll.)	That I can give you in writing.
Du hast an (einen) Schuß. (sl.)	You're touched in the head.
ein gutes Blatt (coll.)	a good hand (in a card game)
Find' ich ja auch! (coll.)	You got it!
(sich) g'fretten (sl.)	to do without

HANS   Number one, he don't make you jumpy. Number two, he won't bug you for money. And number three, he has no in-laws.

KARL   And he don't gab round the clock. And he's cheaper than a wife, especially if she's a bitch, as often happens. Besides, the license costs next to nothing, and he already has a fur coat; now that's a deal.

HANS   Makes sense. And he also is the only friend that you can buy.

KARL   You got it! Do you think dogs can talk?

HANS   You sure are stupid. I guarantee if a dog tells you he can talk, he's just feeding you a line.

KARL   OK, so maybe he can't talk; but my friend Gottfried has a dog that plays poker—*that* I can give you in writing.

HANS   You sure are a dope. You're touched in the head.

KARL   You wanna bet! But my friend is disappointed with the dog. Each time Gottfried gets a good hand, the damn dog wags his tail.

Haltst (Hälst) mich zum Narr(e)n? *(coll.)*	Who you're ribbin'? Who are you kidding?
haut dich net um Geld an *(sl.)*	doesn't bug you for money
Ich hab' keinen blassen Schimmer. *(coll.)*	I have no idea; search me.
Kerl *(m. coll.)*	(here) bum
kost' (kostet) so gut wie nix *(coll.)*	costs next to nothing
Logo! *(adj. sl.)*	Logical! Makes sense!
ein Mordsschwein haben *(sl.)*	to get all the breaks
net (nicht)	not
no (na, nun) *(coll.)*	well, then
No und ob!	You wanna bet! You can say that again!
in nullkommanix *(sl.)*	right away, on the double

prima *(adj. coll.)*	great, terrific
ratschen *(v. coll.)*	to gab
rumschnüffeln *(v. coll.)*	to snoop around
strohdumm *(adj. sl.)*	stupid
Schiß kriegen *(vulg.)*	to get spooked
siecht (sieht) *(v. coll.)*	sees
Spezi *(m. sl.)*	friend
Wasd' net sagst! (Was du nicht sagst!) *(coll.)*	You don't say!
waßt (weißt) *(v.)*	Do you know
Weibsbild *(n. coll.)*	(here) wife
Wer's glaubt, wird selig! *(coll.)*	My eye!
wie aufzog'n (aufgezogen) ratschen *coll.)*	to gab constantly ('round the clock)

A Smidgen of Streetwise Grammar

Fun with Idioms and Weird Words

☐ Logo!

Other expressions expressing consent or agreement:
selbstredend   natch
und ob   I should say
Das muß man dir lassen. You sold me.
Geht in Ordnung.   Okay.
Bin dafür zu haben.   You got it.
Also das machen wir.   It's a deal.
Es wär' mir ein Fest.   I drink to that.
Es wär' mir eine Wonne und ein Grunzen.   You said a mouthful.

☐ Du bist aber ein Depp!

Other pejoratives:
Du bist saublöd.   You are stupid.
Hornochse   pinhead

Kamel camel
Mostschädel numbskull
Quadratschädel knucklehead
Rindvieh meathead
Schafskopf dumbo
Strohkopf cabbagehead

One could also say of him:
Er hat das Schießpulver nicht erfunden.   He's no big deal.
dumm geboren und nichts dazugelernt   born a fool,
   always a fool
Er hat ein Brett vorm Kopf.   He's missing a few marbles.
Er hat die Dummheit mit'm Löffel gefressen.   He doesn't
   know the time of day.
Er ist dümmer, als die Polizei erlaubt.   He's the world's
   prize pinhead.
Er ist so dumm, daß es weh' tun muß.   It must hurt to be
   that stupid.

☐   Ein Hund is' billiger als ein Weibsbild.

Weib, Weibsbild has a derogatory connotation nowadays,
except in such phrases as:
Wir sind jetzt Mann und Weib.
Er hat Weib und Kinder.   He has a wife and a family.

But the expressions that follow are anything but
complimentary:
Weibergewäsch, Weibergeschwätz   women's gossip
Weiberheld   ladykiller
Weiberherrschaft   petticoat rule
Weiberlaune   woman's whim

☐   Der Hund is' prima.

Er ist auf den Hund gekommen.   He's flat broke.
Da liegt der Hund begraben.   That's the ticket.
Das ist eine Hundearbeit.   That's a grind, an awful job.
Mir ist hundeelend.   I'm sick as a dog.
Das ist ein Hundefraß.   That's garbage.
Ich bin hundemüde.   I'm beat.

Going to the Dogs

DOGCATCHER	Wann's net bis Dienstag a Lizenz für'n Hund ham, sitzen's in der Scheißgass'n.	If you don't have a license for the dog by Tuesday, you'll be in deep shit.
DOG OWNER	Machen's die Ohrwatscheln auf: Vorigen Monat is' mei' Haus ab'brannt. Vorige Woch'n is' mei' Frau mit mei'm besten Freund durchgebrannt. Vorgestern hab'ns' ma' mein' Sohn wegen Einbruch arretiert. Gestern hat ma' mir mei' Auto g'stohl'n. In der Scheißgass'n, sag'n's? Ja, wo glauben's denn, sitz' i' jetzt?	Listen, man, and listen good: Last month my house burned down. Last week my wife took off with my best friend. Day before yesterday they arrested my son on a burglary charge. Yesterday someone stole my car. I'll be in deep shit, you say? Where d'you think I'm now?

Exercises

A. Complete the phrase by filling in the appropriate word from the list:

Depp, g'fretten, Mordsschwein, Narr'n, nix, ratscht, Schimmer, selig, Spezi, strohdumm.

1. Er _____ wie auf'zog'n.

2. Der muß sich ohne Hund _____.

3. Du bist aber ein _____.

4. Wer's glaubt, wird _____.

5. Das kost' so gut wie _____.

6. Ich hab' keinen blassen _____.

7. Du bist aber _____.

8. Haltst mich zum _____?

9. Da hat er aber ein _____.

10. Mei' _____, der Max . . .

B. True or False?

	T/F
1. Karl ist sehr intelligent.	_____
2. Sein Freund ist enttäuscht über'n Hund.	_____
3. Max hat ein Mordsschwein.	_____
4. Der Hund ist dem Menschen sein bester Freund.	_____
5. Wenn der Tony an Schiß kriegt, fangt er zum Lachen an.	_____
6. Ein Hund is' billiger als ein Weibsbild.	_____
7. Der Hund ratscht wie auf'zog'n.	_____
8. Die Lizenz kostet sehr wenig.	_____
9. Ein Hund geht dir auf'n Wecker.	_____
10. Toni hat viel Geld.	_____

C. Match the German with the English:

1. _____ Wer's glaubt, wird selig.
2. _____ Der haut dich net ums Geld an.
3. _____ Haltst mich zum Narr'n?
4. _____ Du hast an Schuß.
5. _____ Wasd' net sagst!
6. _____ Tony kriegt Schiß.
7. _____ Du bist aber strohdumm.
8. _____ Ich hab' kan blassen Schimmer.
9. _____ Find' ich ja auch!
10. _____ Der is' bettelarm.

A. Search me.
B. You got it!
C. He won't bug you for money.
D. You sure are stupid.
E. My eye!
F. Who you're ribbin'?
G. He's poor as a church mouse.
H. You're touched in the head.
I. No kiddin'!
J. Tony gets spooked.

D. Translate the following into Streetwise German:

1. He starts barking on the double.

_____

2. He sure got all the breaks.

_____

3. A dog does not make you jumpy.

_____

4. He don't blather round the clock.

_____

5. You sure are a dope.

_____

6. My eye!

_____

7. He got to do without a dog.

_____

8. You can say that again!

_____

9. He feeds you a line.

_____

10. Makes sense!

_____

E. Underline the synonyms:

1. Spezi   a. Speck   b. Platz   c. Freund

2. Mordsschwein a. Glück   b. Geselchtes   c. Totschläger

3. Schiß   a. Kugel   b. Angst   c. Schach

4. ratschen   a. reden   b. anzeigen   c. rumschnüffeln

5. anhaun   a. angeben   b. anbetteln   c. anmachen

6. Depp   a. Depot   b. Deposit   c. Dummkopf

7. prima   a. großartig   b. sauber   c. früh

8. Bißgurn   a. Gurke   b. Hausdrache   c. Beißkorb

Dialog 8

Northern German/Southern German

Sprachschwierigkeiten

Man from Hamburg visits Vienna.

SEDLMAYR   Also da drüben sehn Sie die Oper.

CLAUSEN   Ach ja—die olle Oper. Na ja, die ist knorke.

SEDLMAYR   Knorke? Ja, was heißt denn das?

CLAUSEN   Knorke ist zweimal so scharf wie dufte. Kapito?

SEDLMAYR   Kruzitürken! Was reden's denn so deppert daher!

CLAUSEN   Was ist los, Männeken? Haste Spätzündung?

SEDLMAYR   Regen's Ihnen ab!

CLAUSEN   Pustekuchen! *(to himself)* Doof bleibt doof, da helfen keine Pillen.

SEDLMAYR   Und Sie können mich auch! *(to himself)* Die halbete Zeit waß i net, was der zamredt.

Problems in
Communication

SEDLMAYR   Over there you can see the opera.

CLAUSEN   Ah—the old opera. That's wild.

SEDLMAYR   Wild?—What d'you mean?

CLAUSEN   Wild is twice as cool as nifty. Capísh?

SEDLMAYR   Damn you! Don't give me that bunk!

CLAUSEN   What's wrong, little man? Not all there?

SEDLMAYR   Knock it off!

CLAUSEN   Rubbish! *(to himself)* Doesn't know which way is up and nothing can help.

SEDLMAYR   You know what *you* can do. *(to himself)* Half the time I don't know what the hell the bastard is saying.

CLAUSEN   Ach—da drüben laufen Streifen.

SEDLMAYR   Streifen?

CLAUSEN   Filme. Kinofilme, Dussel. Daß du von der plietschen Seite bist, kann man auch nich' gerade behaupten.

SEDLMAYR   Gehn's tun's Ihnen net aufpudeln. *(to himself)* Der Piefke macht mi' ganz narrisch. *(to Clausen)* Also das is' die Hofburg. An der hat man 500 Jahre gebaut.

CLAUSEN   So 'n Kokolores! Mein Baumeister macht das in zwo kurzen Jährchen.

SEDLMAYR   *(to himself)* Der hat an Wurm in der Marilln. *(to Clausen)* Und das hier is' das Burgtheater. Also für das ham's zehn Jahr' braucht. Unter'm Kaiser Franz Josef.

CLAUSEN   Ich denk', mich laust 'n Affe. So was stampfen wir in sechs Wochen aus'm Boden. Das ist ja zum Beömmeln.

SEDLMAYR   Und hier is' das Rathaus. Neugotisch.

CLAUSEN   Da soll mich der Klabautermann holen! Jetzt bleibt mir aber die Spucke weg! Fünf Jahre für das, oder?

SEDLMAYR   Also ob Sie's glauben oder net, wie ich heut' früh in die Stadt einig'fahr'n bin, da war's noch gar net da.

Vocabulary

Da drüben laufen Streifen. *(coll.)*
There's a cinema over there.

Da soll mich der Klabautermann holen. *(coll.)*
(interjection denoting astonishment; here) Now you got me with my pants down.

Das ist ja zum Beömmeln. *(sl.)*
That really cracks me up.

Der hat an Wurm in der Marilln. *(sl.)*
He's zonked out.

Der Piefke macht mi' (mich) ganz narrisch. *(sl.)*
That loudmouth (from up north) drives me nuts.

CLAUSEN   Ah—there's a flick over there.

SEDLMAYR   Flick?

CLAUSEN   Movie theater, dummy. Nobody could say you're very
           quick on the draw.

SEDLMAYR   Now don't get snotty with me. *(to himself)* That
           loudmouth drives me nuts. *(to Clausen)* Now this is the
           imperial palace. Took 500 years to build.

CLAUSEN   What a grind! My builder would put that up in two years
           flat.

SEDLMAYR   *(to himself)* Zonked out. *(to Clausen)* And this here is the
           Burgtheater. Ten years labor for that. Under the emperor
           Francis Joseph.

CLAUSEN   Well, I'll be damned! This kind of thing we do in six
           weeks. That really cracks me up!

SEDLMAYR   And this is City Hall. Neo-Gothic.

CLAUSEN   Now you got me with my pants down! It boggles the
           mind! Five years for that, eh?

SEDLMAYR   Believe it or not, but when I drove downtown this
           morning, it wasn't there yet.

**Die halbete Zeit waß (weiß) i
(ich) net, was der zamredt
(zusammenredet).** *(sl.)*

Half the time I don't know what
he's saying.

**Doof bleibt doof, da helfen
keine Pillen.** *(sl.)*

Doesn't know which way is up
and nothing can help.

Dussel *(m. sl.)*

dummy

**Gehn's tun's Ihnen net (nicht)
aufpudeln.** *(sl.)*

Now don't get snotty with me.

ham's (haben Sie) *(coll.)*

Do you have

Haste (hast du) Spätzündung?
(sl.)

Not all there? Slow on the
uptake?

**in die Stadt einifahrn
(hineinfahren)** *(sl.)*

to drive downtown

Jetzt bleibt mir aber die Spucke weg! *(sl.)*	It boggles the mind!
Kapito? *(sl.)*	Capísh? (understand?)
knorke *(adj. sl.)*	wild, cool, heavy, prima
Knorke ist zweimal so scharf wie dufte. *(sl.)*	Wild is twice as cool as nifty.
Kruzitürken! *(sl.)*	Damn you!
Männeken *(n. sl.)*	little man
Mich laust der Affe! *(sl.)*	Well, I'll be damned!
oder? *(coll.)*	(here) eh?
olle (alte) *(adj. coll.)*	old
Pustekuchen! *(sl.)*	Rubbish! Bull!
Regen's Ihnen ab! *(coll.)*	Knock it off!
so 'n (ein) Kokolores! *(m. sl.)*	misplaced efforts; (here) what a grind!
So was stampfen wir in sechs Wochen aus'm (aus dem) Boden. *(sl.)*	This kind of thing we do in six weeks.
Und Sie können mich auch! *(vulg.)*	You know what *you* can do!
von der plietschen Seite sein *(sl.)*	to be quick on the draw
Was reden's denn so deppert daher! *(sl.)*	Don't give me that bunk!
zwo (zwei)	two

A Smidgen of Streetwise Grammar

Idioms for the Fearless Traveler. Don't Leave Home without Them.

☐   Doof is' doof

    auf doof gehen   to play dumb
    jn. doof und dusselig reden   to fast-talk s.o.
    doof auf beiden Backen sein   to be a dimwit
    jn. für doof verkaufen   to play s.o. for a sucker
    Das schmeckt gar nich' so doof.   It's not half bad.

☐ Spucke, spucken

> **Er sieht aus wie Spucke und Asche.**   He looks like death
> warmed over.
> **Die Spucke wird lang.**   It gets to be a bore.
> **nich die Spucke wert**   not worth a damn
> **sich in die Hände spucken**   to buckle down to work
> **sich nicht auf den Kopf spucken lassen**   to take no bull
> **Leute, wohin man spuckt**   crawling with people
> **Es ist zum Spucken!**   It makes you puke!

☐ Pustekuchen! Kokolores!

More Streetwise German terms denoting disagreement or
rejection:

Vienna	Hamburg	New York
An Schmarrn!	**Möwendreck!**	Thumbs down!
Ich kann mich beherrschen.	**Bei mir ist Pause.**	Count me out.
Is' mir scheiß- egal!	**Interessiert mich nich' die Bohne.**	You should live so long.
Daß i net lach'!	**Ja, Pfeifendeckel!**	Thanks, but no thanks!
Ka Spur!	**Quatsch!**	No way!

☐ Mir bleibt die Spucke weg!

More Streetwise German terms of amazement:

Vienna	Hamburg	New York
Wenn das wahr is', fress' i an Besen!	**Ach du liebe Schande!**	I'll be darned!
Da schau her!	**Da stockt mir die Milch.**	I'm bowled over.
Das is' allerhand!	**Da wackelt der Balkon!**	I'm all shook up.
Da steht mir der Verstand still.	**Donner und Hagel!**	I'm flabbergasted!
Ich bin paff!	**Ich bin baff!**	I'm blown away!
Jessasna!	**Nee, nanu!**	I'm floored!
Das is' a Wahnsinn!	**Nu' schlägt's dreizehn!**	It beats me!
		Now I've heard everything!

☐   Klabautermann

>   Ship's goblin, according to popular belief, performing a variety
>   of services for the crew as long as the ship is safe.

A Viennese on a Visit in Hamburg

MAN FROM VIENNA	Ein Momenterl bitte, der Herr. Möchten Sie mir gefälligst den Weg zur Reeperbahn zeigen?	One little moment, the gentleman, please. Could you kindly direct me to the reeperbahn?
MAN FROM HAMBURG	Zwei Straßen geradeaus, dann links. Straße kreuzen, nächste Straße rechts. Platz kreuzen, nächste Straße scharf links. Dann halb rechts und Sie sind dort.	Two blocks straight ahead, then left. Cross the street, next street right. Cross the square, next street sharp left. Then half right, and you're there.
MAN FROM VIENNA	Vielen Dank für die Auskunft, mein Herr. Und wenn Sie nächstens nach Wien kommen sollten—	Thanks a lot for the information, sir. And if you should come to Vienna next time—
MAN FROM HAMBURG	Kokolores, Mensch! Wiederholen Sie die Weisungen!	Nonsense, man. Repeat the instructions!

Exercises

A. Complete the phrase by filling in the appropriate word from the list:

aufpudeln, beömmeln, deppert, knorke, laust, Marilln, Piefke, Pillen, Spucke, Streifen.

    1. Was reden's denn so _____ daher?

    2. Da helfen keine _____.

    3. Der _____ macht mi' ganz narrisch.

    4. Das ist ja zum _____.

    5. Gehn's tun's Ihnen net _____.

    6. Jetzt bleibt mir aber die _____ weg.

    7. Da drüben laufen _____.

    8. Ich denk', mich _____'n Affe.

    9. Der hat an Wurm in der _____.

  10. Na ja, die ist _____.

B. True or False?

                                               T/F

    1. Sedlmayr versteht Clausen sehr gut.   _____

    2. An der Hofburg hat man 100 Jahre lang gebaut.   _____

    3. Clausen glaubt, Sedlmayr ist dumm.   _____

    4. "Streifen" bedeutet Filme.   _____

    5. Clausen bewundert die Oper.   _____

    6. In Hamburg baut man langsamer als in Wien.   _____

    7. Knorke ist zweimal so scharf wie dufte.   _____

    8. Sedlmayr nennt den Hamburger "Piefke".   _____

9. Clausen nennt Sedlmayr "Pustekuchen". _____

10. Kokolores ist ein Getränk. _____

C. Match the German with the English:

1. _____ Jetzt bleibt mir aber die Spucke weg.

2. _____ Regen's Ihnen ab!

3. _____ Das ist ja zum Beömmeln!

4. _____ Da drüben laufen Streifen.

5. _____ Was ist los, Männeken?

6. _____ Gehn's, tun's Ihnen net aufpudeln.

7. _____ So'n Kokolores!

8. _____ Der Piefke macht mi' ganz narrisch.

9. _____ Und Sie können mich auch!

10. _____ Haste Spätzündung?

A. That loudmouth drives me nuts.

B. What a grind!

C. You know what *you* can do!

D. Not all there?

E. It boggles the mind.

F. Knock it off!

G. There's a cinema over there.

H. What's wrong, little man?

I. Now don't get snotty with me.

J. That really cracks me up.

D. Translate the following into Streetwise German:

1. Don't give me that bunk!

_____

2. Now don't get snotty with me!

_____

3. Knock it off!

_____

4. You know what *you* can do!

_____

5. That really cracks me up.

_____

6. Now you got me with my pants down!

_____

7. What a grind!

_____

8. Zonked out.

_____

9. Damn you!

_____

E. The following are north German expressions. Try to write down
    their Viennese equivalents:

    1. Bei mir Pause. _____

    2. Ja, Pfeifendeckel! _____

    3. Nu' schlägt's dreizehn! _____

    4. Nee nanu! _____

    5. Quatsch! _____

    6. Möwendreck! _____

    7. Donner und Hagel! _____

    8. Da wackelt der Balkon! _____

    9. Nich' die Bohne! _____

    10. Da stockt mir die Milch! _____

Northern German

Betrachtungen über das Eheleben

A valuable exchange on the part of two experts.

ADELE   Dein Mann Tony ist 'n Schlauberger. Der denkt zweimal,
bevor er nix sagt.

BERTA   Mehr Ehemänner würden Hals über Kopf Leine ziehen,
wenn sie wissen würden, wie man 'nen Koffer packt.

ADELE   Immer wenn ich mir 'n Typen abschleppe, der ein guter
Fang sein könnte, hat ihn schon eine geködert. Ich kann ein
Lied davon singen.

BERTA   Ja, die, die in Frage kommen, kann man an einer Hand
abzählen. Du kennst doch meine Freundin Liese. Also die
legt für ihren Mann die Hand ins Feuer, und weißt du
warum?

ADELE   Nee, ich hab' null Ahnung.

BERTA   Nun, weil sie selber mit ihm überall hintrottelt.

Reflections on Married Life

ADELE   Your husband Toni is a smart ass. He thinks twice before he says zilch.

BERTA   More married men would take a hike real quick if they only knew how to pack a suitcase.

ADELE   Whenever I pick myself a guy who might make a fine catch, it turns out that someone has caught him. I can tell you a thing or two about that.

BERTA   Yes, eligible men are more scarce than hens' teeth. I'm sure you know my friend Liese. Now she will always stick up for her husband, and do you know why?

ADELE   Search me.

BERTA   Because she always goes everywhere he goes.

ADELE   Die hat eben Grütze im Kopf. Das ist ein tolles Weib.

BERTA   Ja, die ist cool. Die Männer wissen alle, wo und wann sie
         sich in den Eheschlamassel gestürzt haben; aber für's
         "Warum" sind sie nicht plietsch genug.

ADELE   Was für'n Ehemann soll ich mir anlachen?

BERTA   Sei man nich so dusselich. Ehemänner, die kannste nich'
         brauchen. Sieh zu, daß du dich an 'nen Junggesellen
         ranmachst.

ADELE   Ein Mann ist in Butter, solang er die Hosen voll hat. Dann ist
         er brav und auch weniger bockig als sonst. Sag, Berta,
         warum habt ihr mich und meinen Ex nie zusammen zu
         euch eingeladen? Habt ihr den Kerl wirklich nicht verdauen
         können?

BERTA   Au Backe! Tatsache ist, dein Ex sieht piekfein aus; in
         Wirklichkeit ist er ein stinkfaules Aas, 'n billiger Ganove,
         Lauaffe und Weichei, an dem Hopfen und Malz verloren ist.
         Ich freu' mich, daß du ihm schließlich den Laufpaß gegeben
         hast.

ADELE   Weißte was? Wenn du mein Mann wärst, würde ich dir Gift
         in den Kaffee schütten.

BERTA   Weißte was? Wenn du meine Frau wärst, würde ich ihn
         trinken.

Vocabulary

Aber für's (für das) "Warum" sind sie nicht plietsch genug. (*sl.*)	But they aren't smart enough to know why.
an einer Hand abzählen (*coll.*)	to be rare as hens' teeth, can count them on one hand
An dem ist Hopfen und Malz verloren. (*coll.*)	He's a lost cause.
(sich jn.) anlachen (*sl.*)	to get one for oneself, smile at, flirt with

ADELE   She's got horse sense. She's quite a gal.

BERTA   Yes, she's cool. Every man remembers where and when he took the plunge into marital misery. But he's not smart enough to know why.

ADELE   What kind of a husband should I pick for myself?

BERTA   For Chrissake, don't be dopey. You don't need any married men. Better look around for a bachelor.

ADELE   I believe a man is OK as long as he's got a guilty conscience. Then he watches his step and is less ornery than usual. Tell me, Berta, why didn't you ever invite me and my ex to your house? Did the guy really seem that obnoxious to you?

BERTA   Oh boy! Your ex looks like a straight arrow, but in reality he's a lazy no-good bum, a cheap crook, an impossible character, in short, a lost cause. I'm glad you finally blew him off.

ADELE   You know what? If you were my husband, I would put poison in your coffee.

BERTA   You know what? If you were my wife, I would drink it.

Au Backe! (*coll.*)	Oh boy!
abschleppen (*v. sl.*)	to pick
bockig (*adj. coll.*)	ornery
brav sein (*coll.*)	to be well-behaved
geil, cool (*adj.*) (*pronounced as in English*)	cool
Dein Ex sieht piekfein aus. (*sl.*)	Your former husband looks like a straight arrow.
die Hosen voll haben (*sl.*)	to have a guilty conscience
Die legt für ihren Mann die Hand ins Feuer. (*coll.*)	She sticks up for her husband.
dusselich (*adj. coll.*)	dopey

Eheschlamassel *(m. or n. coll.)*	marital misery
ein guter Fang *(m. coll.)*	a good catch
Ex *(m. sl.)*	(here) ex-husband
Ganove *(m. sl.)*	crook
geködert (ködern) *(v. coll.)*	to catch
Grütze im Kopf (haben) *(coll.)*	(to have) horse sense
Habt ihr den Kerl wirklich nicht verdauen können? *(coll.)*	Did he seem that obnoxious to you?
Hals über Kopf *(coll.)*	headlong; real quick
Ich kann ein Lied davon singen. *(coll.)*	I can tell you a thing or two about that.
Immer wenn ich 'n (einen) Typen abschleppe. *(sl.)*	Whenever I pick myself a guy.
in Butter sein *(sl.)*	to be OK
in Frage kommen *(coll.)*	(here) to be eligible
Lauaffe *(m.)* **und Weichei** *(n. sl.)*	pushover and sissy
(jm. den) Laufpaß geben *(coll.)*	to blow s.o. off
Leine ziehen *(sl.)*	to take a hike
man (or **mal**) *(adv.)*	only
Nee (Nein), ich hab' null Ahnung. *(sl.)*	Search me.
nix (nichts) *(sl.)*	nothing
(sich) ranmachen *(v. coll.)*	to look around (for), sidle up to s.o.
sauber *(adj. coll.)*	clean; (here) welcome, good, fine
Schlauberger *(m. coll.)*	smartass
(ein) stinkfaules Aas *(sl.)*	a lazy no-good bum
(ein) tolles Weib *(coll.)*	quite a gal
überall mit jemand hintrotteln *(coll.)*	to be at someone's side every step of the way
Weißte? (weißt du) *(coll.)*	Do you know?

A Smidgen of Streetwise Grammar
Idioms, Funny and Weird

☐   hintrotteln:

Playing on the similarity of two distinct German words, **der Trott** and **der Trottel. Trott** derives from the slow, somewhat ponderous gait of horses which, in human terms, denotes a person's same old daily routine, as in **Er geht immer im gleichen Trott. Trottel** means idiot, moron, nincompoop. When combined (as in **hintrotteln**), these two words mean mindlessly (or like a fool) walking the same old route, doing the same old thing.

☐   Der Mann ist in Butter. The man is OK.

More buttery idioms:
Sie hat ein Herz wie Butter.   She's got a soft spot.
Er läßt sich nicht die Butter vom Brot nehmen.   You can't put anything over on him.
etwas um ein Butterbrot bekommen   to get s.th. dirt cheap
etwas für ein Butterbrot tun   to do s.th. for peanuts
Alles in Butter.   Everything's hunky-dory.

☐   Er hat Grütze im Kopf.

This can be expressed in different ways:
Er kennt sich aus.   He knows his way around.
Er läßt sich kein X für ein U vormachen.   You can't fool him.
Der ist nicht auf den Kopf gefallen.   He's no dope.
Der läßt sich nicht überfahren.   You can't push him around.
Der läßt sich nicht an der Nase herumführen.   He's no sucker.

☐   Die Hosen voll haben

freche Hosen
enge Hosen
scharfe Hosen
auf die Haut gespritzte Hosen
} tight pants

Er hat leere Hosen.   He's a loser.

Ich hab' ihm die Hosen ausgezogen.   I took the shirt off his back.

Er hat sich die Hosen durchgewetzt.   He wore out his pants.

Dem kann man im Gehen die Hosen flicken.   He is very slow.

Bei ihm geht die Hose allein.   He wears very baggy pants.

Mach dir nicht in die Hosen!   Don't get scared!

Besser als in die Hosen gemacht!   Better than nothing!

☐   ein tolles Weib

Please note that **toll** may have different meanings:

Bist du toll?   Are you out of your skull?

Dieser Lärm macht mich ganz toll.   This noise is enough to drive me nuts.

Er studiert wie toll.   He hits the books like mad.

Das war eine tolle Woche.   That was a wild week.

In dem Kleid siehst du toll aus.   You look great in this dress.

Das ist ja eine tolle Wirtschaft!   That sure is an awful mess!

Gestern hat es ganz toll geregnet.   Yesterday it rained like hell.

For Better or for Worse

ANJA	Zwanzig Jahre lang waren mein Mann und ich unbeschreiblich glücklich.	For twenty years my husband and I were indescribably happy.
DÖRTE	Und was ist dann passiert?	And then what happened?
ANJA	Wir haben uns kennengelernt.	We met.

Exercises

A. Complete the phrase by filling in the appropriate word from the list:

bockig, Eheschlamassel, Ganove, Grütze, Laufpaß, Leine, Malz, null, piekfein, tolles.

1. Dein Ex sieht _____ aus.

2. An ihm ist Hopfen und _____ verloren.

3. Nee, ich hab' _____ Ahnung.

4. Du hast ihm den _____ gegeben.

5. Sie haben sich in den _____ gestürzt.

6. Er hat eben _____ im Kopf.

7. Er ist 'n billiger _____.

8. Das ist ein _____ Weib.

9. Sie würden Hals über Kopf _____ ziehen.

10. Dann ist er weniger _____ als sonst.

B. True or False?

	T/F
1. Liese hat Grütze im Kopf.	_____
2. Sie geht immer allein aus.	_____
3. Toni ist ein Schlauberger.	_____
4. Lieses Mann hat die Hosen voll.	_____
5. Für's "Warum" sind sie nicht plietsch genug.	_____
6. Männer wissen, wie man Koffer packt, sagt sie.	_____
7. Berta kann den Kerl nicht leiden.	_____
8. Liese legt für ihren Mann die Hand ins Feuer.	_____

9. Adele kann ein Lied davon singen. _____

10. Sie möchte nie heiraten. _____

C. Match the German with the English:

1. _____ Sei man nich' so dusselich.

2. _____ Er ist 'n billiger Ganove.

3. _____ Der Mann ist in Butter.

4. _____ Er ist ein guter Fang.

5. _____ Ich hab' null Ahnung.

6. _____ Er sieht piekfein aus.

7. _____ Dann ist er weniger bockig.

8. _____ Die hat Grütze im Kopf.

9. _____ Er hat die Hosen voll.

10. _____ Sie hat ihm den Laufpaß gegeben.

A. Then he's less ornery.
B. She blew him off.
C. She's got horse sense.
D. Don't be dopey.
E. He's got a guilty conscience.
F. The man is OK.
G. He is a fine catch.
H. He looks like a straight arrow.
I. Search me.
J. He's a cheap crook.

D. Fill in the blank with the letter, indicating your best choice in reference to a dialogue you read.

1. Dein Mann Tony ist ein _____.
   a. Depp   b. Schlauberger   c. Genie

2. Der hat eben _____ im Kopf.
   a. Grütze   b. Unsinn   c. nichts

3. Was für'n Ehemann soll ich mir _____?
   a. lachen   b. anlachen   c. verlachen

4. Für's "Warum" sind sie nicht _____ genug.
   a. dumm   b. plietsch   c. schnell

5. Ein Mann ist in _____, solange er die Hosen voll hat.
   a. Speck   b. Fett   c. Butter

6. Dann hat ihn schon eine _____.
   a. geködert   b. angeschaut   c. besprochen

7. Der denkt _____, bevor er nix sagt.
   a. nach   b. zweimal   c. daran

8. Sieh, daß du dich an ihn _____.
   a. ranmachst   b. erinnerst   c. wendest

9. Ich freu' mich, daß du ihm den _____ gegeben hast.
   a. Teppich   b. Brief   c. Laufpaß

10. Dein Ex sieht _____ aus.
    a. miserabel   b. piekfein   c. krank

E. Translate the following into Streetwise German:

1. He is a lazy no-good bum.

   _____

2. He is a lost cause.

   _____

3. More men would take a hike.

   _____

4. Don't be dopey.

   _____

5. They are more scarce than hens' teeth.

   _____

6. She will always stick up for him.

   _____

7. Did that guy really seem that obnoxious to you?

   _____

8. He looks like a straight arrow.

   _____

9. Then he is less ornery.

   _____

Dialog 10

Southern German

Wofür hat man Freunde?

What is a Borzoi? Buyer beware.

ALOIS   Jetz' sitz' ich aber wirklich in der Tint'n.

ANTON   Was is' dir über die Leber g'laufen? Kann ich dir behilflich sein?

ALOIS   Nett von dir, aber ich hab' ein Mordsproblem. Ich steh' wie der Ochs' vorm Berg. Du kennst doch meine Alte. Also die is' außer Rand und Band.

ANTON   Ehetrouble? Hast was ausg'fressen? Ah—ich weiß. Du hast nebenrausg'haut.

ALOIS   Red' kan Stiefel zam. Meiner Frau ihr Borzoi is' weg.

ANTON   Weg, sagst? Du meinst, verschütt' gegangen?

ALOIS   Futsch! Futschikato!

ANTON   Vielleicht hat ihn wer mitgehn lassen. Vielleicht habts Ihr die Tür offeng'lassen.

What are Friends for?

ALOIS   Now I'm really in the soup.

ANTON   What's come over you? Can I help you?

ALOIS   Thanks loads, but I've got a heavy problem. Fact is I'm stumped. You know my old lady. She's all shook up.

ANTON   Marital mishaps? Your conscience bothering you? Ah—I know. You were fooling around.

ALOIS   Bull. Her Borzoi is gone.

ANTON   Gone, you say? You mean, lost?

ALOIS   Disappeared.

ANTON   Maybe someone stole it. Maybe you left the door open.

ALOIS   Kann sein. Aber ich bin der Sündenbock, und ich kann doch wirklich nix dafür diesmal. Das kost' mich an Batzen Geld.

ANTON   Alois, du hast mehr Schwein als Verstand.

ALOIS   Is' dirs Gehirn in den Hintern gerutscht?

ANTON   Genau so ein Borzoi is' mir gestern unterkommen.

ALOIS   No geh! Du hast einen Borzoi?

ANTON   Und er is' dein, alter Strizzi; dein für 1 000 Mark.

ALOIS   Was redst denn da? 1 000 Mark?

ANTON   Was ich selber dafür hab' blechen müssen.

ALOIS   1 000 Mark is' ein Haufen Geld . . .

ANTON   Und du hast an Haufen Ärger; also 900 Mark, weil du's bist.

ALOIS   Mehr als 800 könnt' ich net zusammenkratzen.

ANTON   Du machst mich fix und fertig, alter Freund.

ALOIS   Also wann kann ich ihn sehn? Morgen?

ANTON   Morgen. *(Exit Alois)* Jetz' muß ich nur noch rauskriegen, was der Geier so ein Borzoi eigentlich is'.

Vocabulary

alter Strizzi *(m. coll.)*	old chum
an (ein) Batzen Geld *(sl.)*	big bucks
außer Rand und Band sein *(coll.)*	to be all shook up
blechen *(v. coll.)*	to dish out, to pay
Du machst mich fix und fertig. *(coll.)*	(here) You kill me.
Ehetrouble *(m. coll.)*	marital mishaps
ein Haufen Geld *(coll.)*	a heap of money
Futsch! (Futschikato!) *(adj. coll.)*	Gone! Disappeared! Down the tube!
Hast was ausg'fressen? *(sl.)*	Is your conscience bothering you?

ALOIS   Maybe. But I'm the patsy, and this time I'm really innocent. That'll cost me big bucks.

ANTON   Alois, you're a lucky dog.

ALOIS   Have you got your head up your ass?

ANTON   Yesterday I came across a borzoi just like that.

ALOIS   Honest? You got a borzoi?

ANTON   And it's yours, old chum; yours for 1 000 marks.

ALOIS   What are you saying? 1 000 marks?

ANTON   Just what I had to dish out myself.

ALOIS   1 000 marks is a heap of money . . .

ANTON   And you got a heap of trouble; well, 900 marks, just for you.

ALOIS   800 is all I could cough up.

ANTON   You kill me, old buddy.

ALOIS   Well—when can I see it? Tomorrow?

ANTON   Tomorrow. (*Exit Alois*) Now I got to figure out what the heck a borzoi really is.

---

in der Tint'n (Tinte) sitzen (*coll.*)	to be in the soup
Is' dirs (Ist dir das) Gehirn in den Hintern gerutscht? (*sl.*)	Have you got your head up your ass?
mehr Schwein als Verstand haben (*coll.*)	to be a lucky dog
meine Alte (*coll.*)	my old lady
(etwas) mitgehn (mitgehen) lassen (*coll.*)	to steal s.th.
Mordsproblem (*n. sl.*)	a heavy problem, a terrible problem
nix (nichts) dafür können (*coll.*)	to be really innocent
nebenraus hauen (*v. sl.*)	to fool around
No geh! (*coll.*)	Honest.

rauskriegen *(v. coll.)*	to figure out
Red kan' (keinen) Stiefel zam (zusammen)! *(coll.)*	Bull!
Sündenbock *(m. coll.)*	patsy, scapegoat
unterkommen *(v. coll.)*	to come across
verschütt' gehen *(v. sl.)*	to get lost
Vielleicht habts Ihr die Tür offeng'lassen.	See grammar section.
Was der Geier! *(coll.)*	What the heck!
Was is' dir über die Leber g'laufen (gelaufen)? *(coll.)*	What's come over you?
weil du's (du es) bist *(coll.)*	because it's you; specially for you
wie der Ochs vorm Berg stehen *(coll.)*	to be in a quandary, to be stumped
zusammenkratzen *(v. coll.)*	to cough up

A Smidgen of Streetwise Grammar

Fun with Idioms

☐ The use of **-n:** instead of the dative singular **-e,** you may add **-n** to the stem of some feminine nouns. (These endings used to be quite respectable way back.)

in der **Tint'n** (Tinte):
Jetz' sitz' ich in der Tint'n.

in der **Tasch'n** (Tasche):
Sie hat Geld in der Tasch'n.

Also quite common are these phrases:
auf der Gass'n or **auf der Straß'n**

☐ The uses of **wer, wem,** *and* **wen** (substituted for **jemand**):

Is' dir **wer** auf die Hühneraugen gestiegen?
(Is' dir jemand auf die Hühneraugen gestiegen?)

Hast du das **wem** gegeben?
(Hast du das jemandem gegeben?)

Hat er dort **wen** getroffen?
(Hat er dort jemanden getroffen?)

☐ The use of **wie** (Avoid using **als** in the comparative of Streetwise German. The use of **wie,** the grammatically correct form for the positive, is much preferred.):

ärger **wie** das (ärger als das)
Gretl is' kleiner **wie** ihre Schwester. (Gretl is' kleiner als ihre Schwester.)

☐ Borzoi

As per Webster's New Collegiate Dictionary: any of a breed of large long-haired dogs of greyhound type developed in Russia, esp. for pursuing wolves.

☐ Was is' dir über die Leber gelaufen?

Er befeuchtet sich die Leber.   He hits the bottle.
Er hat eine trockene Leber.   He's in a bad mood.
Bei mir knistert schon die Leber.   I'm dry as dust.
Es liegt ihm auf der Leber.   It rubs him the wrong way.
Er sauft sich die Leber aus'm Leib.   He goes on a bender.

☐ Is' dir's Gehirn in den Hintern gerutscht?

Er hat einen eisernen Hintern.   He's a hard ass.
Er sitzt sich den Hintern breit.   He has a desk job.
Damit ist er auf den Hintern gefallen.   There he made a boo-boo.
Da möcht' man sich in den Hintern beißen.   There I screwed up.

☐ Vielleicht **habts** Ihr die Tür offeng'lassen?

The correct grammatical form would be **habt.** Here the ancient *dual* crops up, the obsolete pronoun **ös** (meaning you two), but reduced to **-s,** and attached to the verb in the second person plural. It is commonly used in southern Germany and Austria.

Other examples:

Was **machts** denn da?   What are you doing there?

Wo **warts** denn?   Where were you?

Sonst **wißts** nix?   Is that all you know?

Tit for Tat

KRUPP	Und wie ham Sie sich Ihr Vermögen erworben?	And how did you make your fortune?
HUGENBERG	Ich bin der Teilhaber von einem reichen Mann g'worden. Er hat 's Geld g'habt und ich die Erfahrung.	I became the partner of a rich man. He had the money, and I had the experience.
KRUPP	Und wie hat Ihnen das genützt?	And how did that help you?
HUGENBERG	Jetz' hat er die Erfahrung und ich hab' 's Geld.	Now he has the experience, and I have the money.

Exercises

A. Complete the phrase by filling in the appropriate word from the list:

Batzen, blechen, Hintern, Leber, Ochs, Stiefel, Strizzi, Tint'n, verschütt', weg.

1. Ich steh' wie der _____ vor'm Berg.

2. Das kost' mich an _____ Geld.

3. Meiner Frau ihr Borzoi is' _____.

4. Was ich selber dafür hab' _____ müssen.

5. Was is' dir über die _____ g'lauf'n?

6. Du meinst, _____ gegangen?

7. Is' dir's Gehirn in den _____ gerutscht?

8. Jetz' sitz' ich in der _____.

9. Und er is' dein, alter _____.

10. Red' kan _____ zam.

B. True or False?

	T/F
1. Alois hat ein Mordsproblem.	_____
2. Das kostet ihn sehr wenig.	_____
3. Zwanzig Mark is' ein Haufen Geld.	_____
4. Diesmal kann er wirklich nix dafür.	_____
5. Der Borzoi is' weg.	_____
6. Anton hat einen anderen Borzoi, sagt er.	_____
7. Aber er will ihm nicht helfen.	_____
8. Anton ist außer Rand und Band.	_____
9. Und er glaubt, Alois hat nebenrausg'haut.	_____
10. Alois is' der Sündenbock.	_____

C. Match the German with the English:

1. _____ Ich kann doch wirklich nichts dafür diesmal.

2. _____ Ich sitz' in der Tint'n.

3. _____ Du hast mehr Schwein als Verstand.

4. _____ Was ist dir über die Leber gelaufen?

5. _____ Ich steh' wie der Ochs' vor'm Berg.

6. _____ Hast was ausg'fress'n?

7. _____ Is' dir's Gehirn in den Hintern gerutscht?

8. _____ Die is' außer Rand und Band.

9. _____ Mehr könnt' ich net zusammenkratzen.

10. _____ Du hast nebenrausg'haut.

A. She's all shook up.
B. Your conscience bothering you?
C. That's all I could cough up.
D. I'm really innocent this time.
E. You were fooling around.
F. You're a lucky dog.
G. Now I'm in the soup.
H. What's come over you?
I. Fact is, I'm stumped.
J. Have you got your head up your ass?

D. Translate the following into Streetwise German:

1. What's come over you?

_____

2. Maybe someone stole it.

_____

3. He has a heavy problem.

_____

4. Is your conscience bothering you?

_____

5. What the heck . . .

_____

6. marital mishaps

_____

7. a heap of money

_____

8. my old lady

_____

9. You kill me!

_____

10. Honest!

_____

E. Underline the expressions that are *not* Streetwise German.

1. Er hat Geld in der Tasche.

2. Das Kind spielt auf der Gass'n.

3. Hat sie dort jemand gesehn?

4. Hast du wen gesehn?

5. Habt's Ihr euch gut unterhalten?

6. Hat ihn wer gegrüßt?

7. Der Junge spielt auf der Wies'n.

8. Wo wart Ihr denn?

Answers
Dialogs 6 through 10

Dialog 6

A.
1. Tratschfimmel
2. Mauldiarrhöe
3. Litfaßsäule
4. Schnute
5. Biene
6. verplappert
7. dicktut
8. verschossen
9. Klamüsern
10. Fetzen

B.
1. F
2. T
3. T
4. F
5. T
6. T
7. F
8. T
9. F
10. T

C.
1. F
2. G
3. D
4. A
5. B
6. C
7. H
8. I
9. E

D.
1. b
2. a
3. b
4. a
5. c
6. a
7. b
8. a
9. b
10. a

E.
1. Sie hat 'nen Tratschfimmel.
2. Sie ist verschwiegen wie 'ne Litfaßsäule.
3. Sie ist arm dran.
4. Das Frauenzimmer hat nie was zum Anziehen.
5. Sie klatscht, wo sie geht und steht.
6. Alfred ist total in sie verschossen.
7. Alfred nennt sie sein Schmackeduzchen.
8. Sie hat alles, womit sich ein Mann dicktut.
9. Wenn die mal in die Nüsse geht . . .
10. Sie hat ausgepackt.

Dialog 7

A. 1. ratscht   5. nix   8. Narr'n
   2. g'frett'n   6. Schimmer   9. Mordsschwein
   3. Depp   7. strohdumm   10. Spezi
   4. selig

B. 1. F   3. T   5. F   7. F   9. F
   2. T   4. T   6. T   8. T   10. F

C. 1. E   3. F   5. I   7. D   9. B
   2. C   4. H   6. J   8. A   10. G

D. 1. Der fangt in nullkommanix zum Bell'n an.
   2. Da hat er aber ein Mordsschwein.
   3. Ein Hund geht dir net auf'n Wecker.
   4. Er ratscht net wie auf'zog'n.
   5. Hörst, du bist aber ein Depp.
   6. Wer's glaubt, wird selig.
   7. Der muß sich ohne an Hund g'frett'n.
   8. Na und ob!
   9. Er erzählt dir an Kas.
   10. Logo!

E. 1. c   3. b   5. b   7. a
   2. a   4. a   6. c   8. b

Dialog 8

A. 1. deppert   5. aufpudeln   8. laust
   2. Pillen   6. Spucke   9. Marilln
   3. Piefke   7. Streifen   10. knorke
   4. beömmeln

B. 1. F   3. T   5. T   7. T   9. F
   2. F   4. T   6. F   8. T   10. F

C.

1. E	3. J	5. H	7. B	9. C
2. F	4. G	6. I	8. A	10. D

D.
1. Was reden's denn so deppert daher?
2. Gehn's tun's Ihnen net aufpudeln.
3. Regen's Ihnen ab!
4. Und Sie können mich auch!
5. Das ist ja zum Beömmeln.
6. Da soll mich der Klabautermann holen!
7. So'n Kokolores!
8. Der hat an Wurm in der Marilln.
9. Kruzitürken!

E.
1. Ich kann mich beherrschen.
2. Daß i' net lach'!
3. Das is' ja Wahnsinn!
4. Jessasna!
5. Ka Spur!
6. An Schmarr'n!
7. Da steht mir der Verstand still.
8. Das is' allerhand!
9. Is' mir scheißegal!
10. Da schau her!

Dialog 9

A.

1. piekfein	5. Eheschlamassel	8. tolles
2. Malz	6. Grütze	9. Leine
3. null	7. Ganove	10. bockig
4. Laufpaß		

B.

1. T	3. T	5. T	7. T	9. T
2. F	4. F	6. F	8. T	10. F

C.

1. D	3. F	5. I	7. A	9. E
2. J	4. G	6. H	8. C	10. B

D. 1. b   3. b   5. c   7. b   9. c
    2. a   4. b   6. a   8. a   10. b

E. 1. Er ist ein stinkfaules Aas.
    2. An ihm ist Hopfen und Malz verloren.
    3. Mehr Ehemänner würden Leine ziehen.
    4. Sei man nich' so dusselich.
    5. Die kann man an einer Hand abzählen.
    6. Die legt immer für ihren Mann die Hand ins Feuer.
    7. Habt Ihr den Kerl wirklich nicht verdauen können?
    8. Dein Ex sieht piekfein aus.
    9. Dann ist er weniger bockig.

Dialog 10

A. 1. Ochs   5. Leber   8. Tint'n
    2. Batzen   6. verschütt'   9. Strizzi
    3. weg   7. Hintern   10. Stiefel
    4. blechen

B. 1. T   3. F   5. T   7. F   9. T
    2. F   4. T   6. T   8. F   10. T

C. 1. D   3. F   5. I   7. J   9. C
    2. G   4. H   6. B   8. A   10. E

D. 1. Was is' dir über die Leber g'laufen?
    2. Vielleicht hat ihn wer mitgehn lassen.
    3. Er hat ein Mordsproblem.
    4. Hast was ausg'fress'n?
    5. Was der Geier . . .
    6. Ehetrouble
    7. ein Haufen Geld
    8. meine Alte
    9. Du machst mich fix und fertig!
    10. No geh!

E. 1. 3. 8.

Review
Dialogs 6 through 10

Exercises

A. Replace the words in parentheses with the Streetwise German synonyms from the right:

1. Was reden's denn so (dumm) _____ daher?

2. Da drüben laufen (Filme) _____.

3. Ich hab' (keine) _____ Ahnung.

4. Die hat eben (Verstand) _____ im Kopf.

5. Red' kan (Unsinn) _____ zam.

6. Er ist (verloren) _____ gegangen.

7. Sie ist eine flotte (Dame) _____.

8. Er ist in sie (verliebt) _____.

9. Sie ratscht wie (aufgedreht) _____.

10. Der Max is' mei' (Freund) _____.

A. null
B. verschütt'
C. Biene
D. deppert
E. Streifen
F. verschossen
G. Spezi
H. Grütze
I. Stiefel
J. auf'zog'n

B. Underline the word in parentheses that makes sense within the context of the dialogue you read, and which completes the sentence:

1. Regen's Ihnen (zu, ab, bei).

2. Ich denk', mich laust 'n (Bär, Fuchs, Affe).

3. Dieser Mann ist in (Butter, Margarine, Speiseöl).

4. Schließlich gab sie ihm den (Schlauberger, Ehemann, Laufpaß).

5. Hast was (ausg'fress'n, mitg'fress'n, abg'fress'n)?

6. Jetz' sitz' ich aber wirklich in der (Wanne, Supp'n, Tint'n).

7. Sie tratscht, wo sie geht und (näht, steht, dreht).

8. Alfred ist total in sie (verschossen, vergossen, verflossen).

9. Karl hat keinen blassen (Hund, Glimmer, Schimmer).

10. Ein Hund geht dir net auf'n (Wecker, Stecker, Bäcker).

C. Fill in the blank with the letter indicating your best choice in reference to a dialogue that you read before:

1. Der _____ macht mi' ganz narrisch.

    a. Baumeister   b. Piefke   c. Pudel

2. Und Sie können mich _____.

    a. nicht   b. sehen   c. auch

3. Habt Ihr den Kerl wirklich nicht _____ können?

    a. verdauen   b. vergessen   c. verlassen

4. Dann ist er brav und weniger _____.

    a. freigebig   b. stolz   c. bockig

5. Ich kann doch wirklich nix _____.

    a. dabei   b. dafür   c. daran

6. Du hast mehr _____ als Verstand.

    a. Schwein   b. Pferd   c. Maus

7. Sie hat drei Schränke voll von _____.

    a. Sprotten   b. Motten   c. Klamotten

8. Man muß ihr die _____ totschlagen.

    a. Schnute   b. Schnecke   c. Schnulze

9. Haltst mich zum _____?

    a. Depp'n   b. Narr'n   c. Spezi

10. Wer's glaubt, wird _____.

    a. selig   b. fromm   c. gesund

D. Unscramble the words below, and write them into the appropriate squares below the numbers on top:

1. NZEFET
2. TOFLT
3. LSUDSE
4. EOAGNV

5. GKOBIC
6. NHEBLCE
7. NZAKABRTE
8. HRANRSCI

E. Complete the following words:

1.	M							
2.	O			
3.	R											
4.	D		
5.	S					
6.	P								
7.	R								
8.	O		
9.	B		
10.	L		
11.	E												
12.	M					

Wanted: the Streetwise German equivalents of the following expressions:

1. little man
2. old (NG, f.)
3. to snoop around
4. stupid
5. chum
6. rubbish!
7. to find out
8. waiter
9. little boy
10. makes sense
11. marital mishap
12. ass

Answers to Review

Dialogs 6 through 10

A. 1. D   3. A   5. I   7. C   9. J
     2. E   4. H   6. B   8. F   10. G

B. 1. ab   5. ausg'fress'n   8. verschossen
     2. Affe   6. Tint'n   9. Schimmer
     3. Butter   7. steht   10. Wecker
     4. Laufpaß

C. 1. b   3. a   5. b   7. c   9. b
     2. c   4. c   6. a   8. a   10. a

D. 1. Fetzen   4. Ganove   7. abkratzen
     2. flott   5. bockig   8. narrisch
     3. Dussel   6. blechen

E. 1. Männeken   5. Strizzi   9. Bubi
     2. olle   6. Pustekuchen   10. Logo
     3. rumschnüffeln   7. rauskriegen   11. Eheschlamassel
     4. doof   8. Ober   12. Hintern

Dialog 11

Northern German

Ein sympathischer Herr

Paula and Eva talk about the most obnoxious man they know.

PAULA   Wer braucht Feinde, wenn man diesen Saukerl zum Freund hat?

EVA   Ja, das is' 'n ausgekochter Fatzke. Und immer da, wenn er dich braucht. Es ist zum Auswachsen.

PAULA   Ich glaube, es ist höchste Eisenbahn, daß man ihm 'nen Dämpfer aufsetzt—

EVA   —und gehörig aufs Dach steigt. Aber mich wird er nie mehr reinlegen. Bei mir ist der abgemeldet. Und mit seinen finanziellen Projekten kann er baden geh'n.

PAULA   Ja, der wollte sich da ins gemachte Bett legen. Aber dem Kerl kann man ja nicht vertrauen. Was immer er von sich gibt, ist erstunken und erlogen.

EVA   Du kannst ihm nicht glauben, auch wenn er schwört, daß er lügt. Aber bei mir muß er da früher aufsteh'n.

A Nice Gentleman

PAULA Who needs enemies if you got that sleazeball for a friend?

EVA Yes, he's a tricky hotshot, always there when he needs you. It drives me up the wall.

PAULA I think it's high time somebody told him off.

EVA Yes, someone should bawl him out real good. But he won't sucker *me* anymore. He's sidelined in *my* book. And he can shove his financial projects.

PAULA Yeah, he was looking for a cozy niche. But you can't trust that guy. Whatever he spouts is a lot of bull.

EVA You can never believe him, even when he swears that he lies. But he won't play games with me.

PAULA Ich schmeiß' ihn achtkantig hinaus, wenn er sich herzukommen traut.

EVA Aber eines Tages geht das Aas zu weit—

PAULA —und wir alle hoffen, er bleibt dort.

EVA Der könnte seine eignen Eltern killen und dann um Gnade fleh'n, weil er 'n Waisenkind geworden ist.

PAULA Und 'n Geizkragen ist er auch. Unlängst, hör' ich, hat er versucht, seiner Frau einzureden, daß sie in einem Pelzmantel zu dick aussieht. Und dabei ist sie dünn wie 'ne Bohnenstange.

EVA Und dabei hat er Geld wie Dreck.

PAULA Leider ist er mit allen Wassern gewaschen und hat es faustdick hinter den Ohren.

EVA Außerdem hat er 'n dickes Fell, du kannst ihm nichts anhaben und ich muß meine Wut in mich hineinfressen.

PAULA Gib ihm Saures, Eva!

Vocabulary

Aas *(n. sl.)*	bastard
(jm.) aufs Dach steigen *(coll.)*	to bawl out s.o.
ausgekocht *(adj. coll.)*	tricky
baden geh'n (gehen) *(sl.)*	to shove it
Bei mir ist der abgemeldet. *(sl.)*	He's sidelined in my book.
Bei mir muß er da früher aufsteh'n. *(coll.)*	He won't play games with me.
(ein) dickes Fell haben *(coll.)*	to have a thick skin
dünn wie 'ne (eine) Bohnenstange *(coll.)*	thin as a beanpole
erstunken und erlogen *(sl.)*	a lot of bull
Es ist höchste Eisenbahn. *(coll.)*	It's high time.
Es ist zum Auswachsen. *(coll.)*	It drives me up the wall.

PAULA   Should he have the nerve to show up, I'd throw him out on his ass.

EVA   But one day the bastard will go too far—

PAULA   —and everybody hopes he'll stay there.

EVA   He's the kind of man who could kill his own parents, and then beg for mercy on the grounds of being an orphan.

PAULA   And he's a miser, too. The other day, I'm told, he tried to convince his wife that she looks too fat in a fur coat. But she's thin as a beanpole.

EVA   And we know he got money to burn.

PAULA   Trouble is he knows the score, and is a sly dog.

EVA   He also has a thick skin. You can't get at him, and it burns me up.

PAULA   Let 'im have it, Eva!

---

es faustdick hinter den Ohren haben *(coll.)*	to be a sly dog
Fatzke *(m. sl.)*	hotshot
gehörig *(adj.)*	proper; (here) real good
Geizkragen *(m. coll.)*	miser
Geld wie Dreck haben *(sl.)*	to have money to burn
Gib ihm Saures! *(sl.)*	Let him have it!
Ich muß meine Wut in mich hineinfressen. *(sl.)*	I got to swallow my anger; it burns me up.
Ich schmeiß' ihn achtkantig hinaus. *(sl.)*	I throw him out on his ass.
Kerl *(m. coll.)*	guy
killen *(v. sl.)*	to kill
mit allen Wassern gewaschen sein *(coll.)*	to know the score
(jm.) 'nen (einen) Dämpfer aufsetzen *(coll.)*	to tell s.o. off
(jn.) reinlegen *(v. coll.)*	to cheat s.o.; to sucker s.o.

Saukerl *(m. vulg.)*   sleazeball
sich ins gemachte Bett legen   to find a cozy niche
  (coll.)

A Smidgen of Streetwise Grammar
Wild and Woolly Words

☐ hinausschmeißen—more about **schmeißen:**

> **Das hat ihn geschmissen.**   That was his undoing.
> **eine Runde Bier schmeißen**   to pay for a round of beer
> **eine Sache schmeißen**   to do a good job
> **das Studium hinschmeißen**   to quit studying
> **sich auf etwas schmeißen**   to concentrate on s.th.
> **den Laden schmeißen**   to run the store, to accomplish s.th.
> **Sie hat sich ihm förmlich an den Hals geschmissen.**
>   She literally threw herself at him.

☐ erstunken und erlogen—all about liars and lying:

> **Er lügt das Blaue vom Himmel herunter.**   He lies through
>   his teeth.
> **Er lügt wie gedruckt.**   He lies his head off.
> **Er lügt, daß sich die Balken biegen.**   He tells a pack of lies.
> **sich etwas aus den Fingern saugen**   to cook up s.th.
> **etwas aus der Luft greifen**   to tell a cock-and-bull story
> **jn. hinters Licht führen**   to pull the wool over s.o.'s eyes
> **jm. einen Bären aufbinden**   to take s.o. for a ride
> Er ist ein:
> **Aufschneider** show-off, **Bauerfänger** con man, **Lügenmaul**
> shameless liar, **Schaumschläger** fourflusher, **Scharlatan**
> fraud, **Windbeutel** windbag.

☐ Dreck

> **Das geht ihn einen Dreck an.**   That's none of his damn
>   business.
> **Dreck am Stecken haben**   to have a criminal record

Dreck im Hirn haben   to be stupid
im Dreck sitzen   to be all screwed up
jn. mit Dreck bewerfen   to sling mud at s.o.
jn. wie den letzten Dreck behandeln   to treat s.o. like dirt
sich einen Dreck draus machen   to give a damn
sich um jeden Dreck kümmern   to poke one's nose into
everything

☐   das Aas (*lit.:* animal corpse)

As a term of abuse:
blödes Aas   stupid fellow
falsches Aas   phony guy
faules Aas   loafer (lazy guy)
feiges Aas   coward
freches Aas   fresh fellow

In a more positive vein:
gerissenes Aas   man who knows his way around
goldiges Aas   lovable girl
reiches Aas   wealthy man
schlaues Aas   shrewd fellow

☐   reinlegen

Here is a small selection of synonyms:
**anschmieren, bemogeln, belemmern, beschummeln,
beschupsen, einseifen, einwickeln, hochnehmen,
lackieren, lackmeiern, leimen, neppen**

How popular can you get?

LOTTE   Es gibt Menschen, die ihm gern ihre Dienste widmen würden: Totengräber, zum Beispiel.

There are people who would be delighted to offer him their services: gravediggers, for instance.

GERHARD   Er ist so ekelhaft, nicht mal sein eigner Schatten mag ihm Gesellschaft leisten.

He is so obnoxious, not even his own shadow likes to keep him company.

| ILSE | Jemand sollte ihn an einen kurzsichtigen Messerschleuderer im Zirkus vermieten. | Somebody should rent him out to a near-sighted knife-thrower in the circus. |

Exercises

A. Complete the phrase by filling in the appropriate word from the list:

abgemeldet, achtkantig, Dämpfer, Dreck, Eisenbahn, erlogen, Fatzke, Bett, reinlegen, Saures.

1. Der ist 'n ausgekochter _____.

2. Er wird mich nie mehr _____.

3. Ich schmeiß' ihn _____ hinaus.

4. Er hat Geld wie _____.

5. Was er sagt, ist erstunken und _____.

6. Ich muß ihm einen _____ aufsetzen.

7. Gib ihm _____, Eva!

8. Der wollte sich ins gemachte _____ legen.

9. Bei mir ist der _____.

10. Ja, es ist höchste _____.

B. True or False?

	T/F
1. Eines Tages geht das Aas zu weit.	____
2. Paula ist ein Waisenkind geworden.	____
3. Eva steht immer früh auf.	____
4. Er ist aber sehr arm.	____

5. Paula nennt ihn einen Saukerl.   _____

6. Eva möchte ihm aufs Dach steigen.   _____

7. Dem Kerl kann man nicht vertrauen.   _____

8. Er muß seine Wut in sich hineinfressen.   _____

9. Was er sagt, ist die reine Wahrheit.   _____

10. Aber er hat ein dickes Fell.   _____

C. Match the German with the English:

1. _____ Der ist ein ausgekochter Fatzke.

2. _____ Bei mir ist der abgemeldet.

3. _____ Ich schmeiß' ihn achtkantig hinaus.

4. _____ Mit seinen Projekten kann er baden geh'n.

5. _____ Er hat's faustdick hinter den Ohren.

6. _____ Bei mir muß er da früher aufsteh'n.

7. _____ Jemand sollte ihm gehörig aufs Dach steigen.

8. _____ Sie ist dünn wie 'ne Bohnenstange.

9. _____ Es ist höchste Eisenbahn.

10. _____ Es ist zum Auswachsen!

A. She's thin as a beanpole.

B. He can shove his projects.

C. It's high time.

D. He's sidelined in *my* book.

E. It drives me up the wall!

F. I'll throw him out on his ass.

G. He's a tricky hotshot.

H. He's a sly dog.

I. He won't play games with me.

J. Someone should bawl him out real good.

D. Underline the English expression that comes closest in meaning to the German word:

1. Fatzke

   a. fatso   b. hotshot   c. rag

2. höchste Eisenbahn

   a. high time   b. express train   c. excellent

3. Geizkragen

   a. high collar   b. goose   c. miser

4. Aas

   a. ace   b. bastard   c. donkey

5. abgemeldet

   a. sidelined   b. announced   c. recalled

6. ausgekocht

   a. cooked out   b. caught   c. tricky

7. Saukerl

   a. drunkard   b. sleazeball   c. sniper

8. kann baden gehn

   a. can shove it   b. can take a bath   c. can clean it up

9. Geld wie Dreck

   a. dirty money   b. money to burn   c. money like dirt

10. reinlegen

   a. to clean up   b. to lie down   c. to sucker

E. Translate the following into Streetwise German:

1. He's a tricky hotshot.

2. She'll throw him out on his ass.

3. Someone should bawl him out real good.

_____

4. He got money to burn.

_____

5. He's sidelined in *my* book.

_____

6. He drives me up the wall.

_____

7. He won't play games with me.

_____

8. It burns me up.

_____

9. It's high time.

_____

10. a lot of bull

_____

Dialog 12

Southern German

In Mosers Gemischt-warenhandlung

Imagine a medium-sized, family-run grocery store in a small township where the American-style supermarket model has not yet penetrated.

MOSER Nix mehr auf Pump, gnä' Frau. Jetz stecken's scho' zu tief in der Kreid'n. Sie woll'n doch net, daß ich die Bud'n zurieg'l?

KUNDE Jessasmariaundjosef, Herr Moser. Tun's Ihnen net versündigen. Was schuld' ich Ihnen denn?

MOSER Mehr als es sein sollt', Frau Zehetbauer.

KUNDE Also dann bezahl' ich Ihnen halt was es sein sollt' und mir sind quitt.

MOSER Sie sind so g'spaßig, gnä' Frau, mit Ihnen gibt's immer a Hetz und a Gaudi. Aber die Situation is' kein Jux nicht mehr. Vielleicht könnten's mir die Schulden abstottern, in gleinen Zahlungen, ich mein', tröpferlweis'.

In Moser's
Grocery Store

MOSER   Nothing more on credit, ma'am. You're too deep in the red as is. D'you want me to close up the joint?

CUSTOMER   Jesus, Herr Moser, don't ever say that. How much do I owe you?

MOSER   More than it should be, Frau Zehetbauer.

CUSTOMER   Tell you what, I'll pay you what it should be, and we are even.

MOSER   You are a scream, ma'am, always chipper, a real gas. But this situation is no longer a laughing matter. Maybe you could pay me back in small installments, I mean, little by little.

KUNDE   Ja, ja, schon gut. Schöne Trauben haben's da. Glauben's, hat man die bestaubt? Mit einem Gift?

MOSER   Naa, Frau Zehetbauer. Das Gift kriegen's separat in der Drogerie. Aber wenn Sie und der Herr Gemahl was wirklich Gut's woll'n, dann schaun's Ihnen doch die Karpfen an, also wie springlebendig die sind.

KUNDE   Ja, aber sind die auch frisch? Ah—hier haben's die Eier. Aber Herr Moser, 2 Mark 50 für 10 Eier. 25 Pfennig für ein Ei?

MOSER   Dafür daß ein Hendl den ganzen lieben Tag auf dem einen Ei hocken tut, is' das doch spottbillig. Aber Sie ham recht, Frau Zehetbauer, die Fressalien sind gepfeffert heutzutag'.

KUNDE   Und sind die Eier auch frisch?

MOSER   Das werden wir sogleich ausschecken. Du liabe Zeit! Die ham sich ja alle bereits gründlich ausgekühlt.

KUNDE   Aber 2 Mark 50 für 10 Eier, Herr Moser? Also das reißt doch ein Loch in die Kasse, und dabei sind sie noch so glein.

MOSER   Da kann ma' halt nix mach'n, gnä' Frau. Der Bauer, der sie mir liefert, nimmt sie halt immer zu früh aus'm Nest heraus.

Vocabulary

abstottern (v. sl.)	to pay off in installments
auf Pump (sl.)	on credit
ausschecken (v. sl.)	to find out
(die) Bud'n zuriegeln (sl.)	to close up the joint, the shop
dabei (adv.)	(here) on top of it
dafür daß	(here) considering the fact that
Da kann ma' (man) halt nix mach'n (nichts machen). (coll.)	Sorry, there's nothing we can do about it.
Das reißt ein Loch in die Kasse. (coll.)	That's real steep.

CUSTOMER   Yes, yes, all right. You have some nice grapes here. Were they sprayed? With poison?

MOSER   No, Frau Zehetbauer. The poison, you get separate in the drug store. But if you want to treat yourself and your hubby to a real delicacy, look at those carp, how perky they are.

CUSTOMER   Yes, but are they fresh? Ah—here are your eggs. But Herr Moser, 2 mark 50 for 10 eggs. 25 pfennigs for one egg?

MOSER   Try to think of that little hen sitting on one egg all day long; now that's dirt cheap. But you're right. Eats are outta sight nowadays.

CUSTOMER   And are the eggs fresh?

MOSER   That we'll check out on the double. Look at that! They are all cooled off already.

CUSTOMER   But 2 mark 50 for 10 eggs, Herr Moser, that's real steep, and on top of it, they are so small.

MOSER   Sorry, there's nothing we can do about it, ma'am. The farmer who makes the delivery takes them out of the nest too early.

---

den ganzen lieben Tag *(coll.)*	all day long
Du liabe (liebe) Zeit!	Look at that!
Fressalien *(pl. coll.)*	food; eats; chow
Gemischtwarenhandlung *(f.)*	family-run grocery store
gepfeffert *(adj. coll.)*	(here) expensive; outta sight
glein (klein) *(adj. coll.)*	little
gnä' Frau (gnädige Frau) *(coll.)*	ma'am
Hendl (Henne) *(n. coll.)*	little hen
hocken *(v. coll.)*	to sit
immer a Hetz (eine Hetze) und a (eine) Gaudi *(sl.)*	always chipper, a real gas
in der Kreid'n *(sl.)*	in the red
Jessasmariaundjosef! *(sl.)*	Jesus!
Jux *(m. coll.)*	joke, a laugh

mir (wir) *(sl.)*	we
naa (nein) *(sl.)*	no
quitt sein *(coll.)*	to be even
Sie ham (haben) recht. *(coll.)*	You're right.
Sie sind so g'spaßig (gespaßig). *(sl.)*	You're a scream.
spottbillig *(adj. coll.)*	dirt cheap
springlebendig *(adj. coll.)*	perky
tröpferlweis' (tröpferlweise) *(adj. sl.)*	little by little
Versündigen Sie sich nicht! *(coll.)*	(here) Don't ever say that!
was wirklich Gut's *(coll.)*	a real delicacy

A Smidgen of Streetwise Grammar
Fun with Idioms

☐ hops gehn (to go bankrupt)

> More of the same:
> **den Pleitegeier auf dem Dach sitzen haben**   to have the wolves at the door
> **sich die Schulden abschminken**   to get rid of debts
> **umschmeißen**   to go belly up
> **pleite machen**   to go under

☐ Das is' kein Jux nicht mehr.

> The double negative, intensifying the negative aspect of a given situation, is quite frequent in Streetwise German.

☐ billig . . .

> **kost' so gut wie nix**   costs next to nothing
> **kost' eine Bagatelle**   it's cut rate
> **wird einem nachg'schmissen**   it's a real steal
> **für an Apfel und an Ei**   for a song
> **spottbillig**   very cheap, a bargain

☐   . . . und teuer

> **kost' eine Stange Geld**   costs a pile of money
> **so teuer, daß einem die Augen übergehn**   paying through
>   the nose
> **unverschämte Preise**   highway robbery
> **sauteuer**   very expensive

☐   Das Hendl hockt auf dem Ei.

> Humans *hock* also:
> **Er ist ein Stubenhocker.**   He's a homebody.
> **Sie hockt über ihren Büchern.**   She's poring over her books.
> **Er hockt auf seinem Geld.**   He sits on his money.

☐   Das reißt ein Loch in die Kasse.

> **Er reißt das Gespräch an sich.**   He grabs, monopolizes the
>   conversation.
> **Ich reiß' mich nicht um sie.**   I can do without her.
> **Die Ware findet reißenden Absatz.**   The merchandise sells
>   like hot cakes.
> **Mir reißt die Geduld.**   I'm losing my patience.

Matching Wits

KUNDE	Was kost' denn ein halbes Kilo von dem Schinken?	How much is half a kilogram of that ham?
MOSER	70 Schilling.	70 schillings.
KUNDE	Aber in dem andern G'schäft kost' der nur 60 Schilling.	But in the other store it costs only 60 schillings.
MOSER	Ja, warum kaufen's ihn dann net dort?	So why don't you buy it there?
KUNDE	Die ham kan mehr.	They don't have any left.
MOSER	Also wenn ich kan mehr hab', verkauf' ich ihn um 50 Schilling.	Well, when I don't have any left, I'll sell it for 50 schillings.

Exercises

A. Complete the phrase by filling in the appropriate word from the list:

abstottern, Fressalien, Gaudi, g'spaßig, halt, Jux, Kasse, Kreid'n, Pump, spottbillig.

    1. Sie sind so _____ .

    2. zu tief in der _____

    3. Die Situation is' kein _____ nicht mehr.

    4. Da kann ma' _____ nix machen.

    5. Nix mehr auf _____ .

    6. Die _____ sind gepfeffert heutzutag'.

    7. immer a Hetz' und a _____

    8. Das reißt doch ein Loch in die _____ .

    9. Vielleicht könnten's mir die Schulden _____ .

    10. Dafür is' das doch _____ .

B. True or False?

	T/F
1. Sie möchte ihre Schulden tröpferlweis' bezahlen.	_____
2. Die Karpfen sind alle tot.	_____
3. Die Eier sind ganz frisch.	_____
4. Die Situation ist kein Jux.	_____
5. Herr Moser hat keine Trauben.	_____
6. Das Gift kriegt man in der Drogerie.	_____
7. Frau Zehetbauer findet, daß die Eier zu groß sind.	_____
8. Die Fressalien sind gepfeffert.	_____

9. Ein Ei kostet 75 Pfennig. _____

10. Frau Zehetbauer möchte, daß Moser das Geschäft _____
    zusperrt.

C. Match the German with the English:

1. _____ Zahlen's mir tröpferlweis'.

2. _____ Du liebe Zeit!

3. _____ Sie sind so g'spaßig.

4. _____ Das werd'n wir
    ausschecken.

5. _____ Nix mehr auf Pump.

6. _____ zu tief in der Kreid'n

7. _____ Tun's Ihnen net
    versündigen!

8. _____ Die Fressalien sind
    gepfeffert.

9. _____ kein Jux nicht mehr

10. _____ a Hetz und a Gaudi

A. Nothing more on
   credit.
B. Pay me little by
   little.
C. always chipper, a
   real gas
D. Look at that!
E. Don't ever say that!
F. no longer a
   laughing matter
G. You're a scream.
H. That we'll smell out.
I. too deep in the red
J. Eats are outta sight.

D. Underline the synonyms:

1. Fressalien

   a. Lebensmittel   b. Erfrischungen   c. Sorgen

2. ausschecken

   a. bezahlen   b. inspizieren   c. beruhigen

3. hocken

   a. versetzen   b. schneiden   c. sitzen

4. Jux

   a. Spaß   b. Jazz   c. Würfel

5. Bud'n

   a. Bier   b. Laden   c. Knospe

6. abstottern

   a. abzahlen   b. abstauben   c. abstecken

7. zuriegeln

   a. zusammenkratzen   b. zutzeln   c. zusperren

8. auf Pump

   a. mit Pomp   b. auf Kredit   c. auf Schuhen

E. Translate into English:

1. Mit Ihnen gibt's immer a Hetz' und a Gaudi.

   _____

2. Sie woll'n doch net, daß ich die Bud'n zuriegl?

   _____

3. Sie sind so g'spaßig!

   _____

4. Tun's Ihnen net versündigen!

   _____

5. Der frische Karpfen wär' wirklich was Gut's.

   _____

6. Die Situation ist kein Jux nicht mehr.

   _____

7. Jetz' stecken's scho' zu tief in der Kreid'n.

   _____

8. Nix mehr auf Pump, gnä' Frau!

_____

9. Und mir sind quitt.

_____

10. Ich mein', tröpferlweis'.

_____

Dialog 13

Northern German

Sterben ist der schönste Tod

Please skip this chapter if you are afraid of the Grim Reaper.

JÜRGEN	Und Wolfgang?
KONRAD	Der Quengelfritze? Der pfeift aus'm letzten Loch.
JÜRGEN	Kann sich nich' mehr hochrappeln?
KONRAD	I wo! Der Kerl riecht nach Tannenholz.
JÜRGEN	Und sein Bruder, der lange Lulatsch?
KONRAD	Abgeschnappt.
JÜRGEN	Draufgegangen?
KONRAD	Aber sicher! Der hat den Löffel abgegeben.
JÜRGEN	Und deine Puppe? Noch immer so knackig?
KONRAD	Nee, sieht aus wie Geist Leo.

Heading for
the Last Roundup

JÜRGEN	And Wolfgang?
KONRAD	That grouch? He's on his last leg.
JÜRGEN	And can't pick himself up?
KONRAD	No way! The guy's a goner.
JÜRGEN	And his brother, that lamppost?
KONRAD	Keeled over.
JÜRGEN	Bit the dust?
KONRAD	You bet. Grounded for good.
JÜRGEN	And your old lady? Still so cute?
KONRAD	No, looks like death warmed over.

JÜRGEN   War doch 'n schönes Weibsstück.

KONRAD   Tja! Die ist geliefert. Die hört den Kuckuck nich' mehr schrei'n.

JÜRGEN   Und der Herr Schulze?

KONRAD   Du meinst das arme Luder mit dem Dünnschißproblem?

JÜRGEN   Ich mein' den ollen Knülch mit der dicken Knolle.

KONRAD   Der ist über den Jordan gegangen.

JÜRGEN   Hat auch ins Gras beißen müssen?

KONRAD   Der sieht jetzt die Radieschen von unten wachsen.

JÜRGEN   Apropos Radieschen, ich hab'n Kohldampf bis unter die Arme.

KONRAD   Komm laß uns was zwischen die Beißerchen schieben. Haste Bock auf'n Köm?

JÜRGEN   Das wäre lecker.

Vocabulary

Aber sicher! (*coll.*)	You bet!
abschnappen (*v. sl.*)	to keel over, die
Apropos . . . (*coll.*)	Speaking of . . .
aus'm (aus dem) letzten Loch pfeifen (*coll.*)	to be on one's last leg
Das arme Luder. (*sl.*)	This poor devil.
Das wäre lecker. (*sl.*)	That would hit the spot.
Der hat den Löffel abgegeben. (*sl.*)	He's grounded for good, dead.
Der ist über den Jordan gegangen. (*coll.*)	(here) died, gone across the creek
Die hört den Kuckuck nicht mehr schrei'n. (*coll.*)	Kayoed for keeps.
die Radieschen von unten wachsen sehen (*coll.*)	to push up daisies, to be dead

JÜRGEN   She was such a pretty babe.

KONRAD   Well, she's done for. Kayoed for keeps.

JÜRGEN   And Herr Schulze?

KONRAD   You mean the poor devil with Montezuma's revenge?

JÜRGEN   I mean the old fart with the fat schnoz.

KONRAD   Gone across the creek.

JÜRGEN   Meeting his maker?

KONRAD   Pushing up the daisies.

JÜRGEN   Speaking of daisies, I could eat a horse.

KONRAD   Let's put on the feedbag. How about some booze?

JÜRGEN   That would hit the spot.

---

draufgehen (v. sl.)	to bite the dust
Dünnschißproblem (n. vulg.)	Montezuma's revenge, diarrhea
geliefert sein (v. coll.)	done for
Haste (hast du) Bock auf'n Köm? (sl.)	How about some booze? Are you in the mood for . . .
(sich) hochrappeln (v. coll.)	to pick oneself up
Ich hab' 'n (habe einen) Kohldampf (Kohldampf: ravenous hunger**) bis unter die Arme.** (coll.)	(here) I could eat a horse.
ins Gras beißen (v. coll.)	(here) to bite the dust, meet one's maker, kick the bucket, die
I wo! (coll.)	No way!
knackig sein (adj. coll.)	to be attractive, cute
Knolle (f. sl.)	(here) schnoz
Knülch (m. sl.)	guy; fart
Komm, laß uns was zwischen die Beißerchen schieben.	Come, let's put on the feedbag, let's get something to eat.

Lulatsch *(m. coll.)*	lamppost
nach Tannenholz riechen *(coll.)*	*(lit.)* to smell of pine (the coffin); (here) to be a goner
Puppe *(f. coll.)*	(here) old lady, wife, doll
Quengelfritze *(m. coll.)*	grouch
Tja! *(coll.)*	Well!
Weibsstück *(n. coll.)*	babe
wie Geist Leo *(sl.)*	like death warmed over

A Smidgen of Streetwise Grammar
Fun (?) with Idioms

☐ Sterben ist der schönste Tod.

There is an abundance of terms, all meaning to die. Here is a small selection:
abhauen, abkratzen, absterben, an die Reihe kommen, sich auflösen, sich davonmachen, eingehen, sich in den Himmel lachen, in die Gruft steigen, krepieren, den Löffel abgeben, den Löffel wegschmeißen, umkippen, veratmen, verrecken.

Also:
Den hat's erwischt, gefaßt, geholt.
Der schnauft nimmer.
Der ist gewesen.

☐ wie Geist Leo

Er geht mir auf den Geist.   He drives me nuts.
Sie ist ein dienstbarer Geist.   She is a domestic.

☐ Der pfeift aus'm letzten **Loch.**

Er hat ein Loch im Magen.   He's a glutton.
Man hat ihn ins Loch gesteckt.   They put him in the slammer.

Das ist ein elendes Loch.   That's a real dump.
Du hast ein Loch im Kopf.   You lost your marbles.
Er redet mir ein Loch in den Bauch.   He talks me blind.

☐   Die hört den **Kuckuck** nich' mehr schrei'n.

Das ganze Geld ist zum Kuckuck.   All the money went
    down the drain.
Da ist der Kuckuck los.   There's a screw-up.
Weiß der Kuckuck, wo er ist.   Goodness knows where he is.
Scher dich zum Kuckuck!   Go to hell!

☐   **Luder**

kleines Luder   little rascal
blödes Luder   jackass
freches Luder   smarty-pants
kaltes Luder   cold fish
süßes Luder   heartthrob

A Real Problem

DOCTOR   Sie müssen wissen, tiefes   You must know, deep
          Atmen vernichtet die   breathing destroys the
          Bakterien.   bacteria.

PATIENT   Aber Herr Doktor, wie kann   But, doctor, how can I force
          ich sie zwingen, tief zu   them to breathe deeply?
          atmen?

Exercises

A. Complete the phrase by filling in the appropriate word from the list:

Gras, hochrappeln, knackig, Knülch, Kohldampf, Köm, Leo, Löffel, Lulatsch, Tannenholz.

1. Der Kerl riecht nach ————————.

2. Wie Geist ————————.

3. Hat auch ins ———————— beißen müssen?

4. Er hat 'n ———————— bis unter die Arme.

5. Noch immer so ————————?

6. Der hat den ———————— abgegeben.

7. Und sein Bruder, der lange ————————?

8. Kann sich nicht mehr ————————?

9. Haste Bock auf'n ————————?

10. Ich mein' den ollen ————————.

B. True or False?

	T/F
1. Herr Schulze hat ein Verdauungsproblem.	————
2. Der hat ins Gras beißen müssen.	————
3. Jürgen ist überhaupt nicht hungrig.	————
4. Konrad hört den Kuckuck nicht mehr schreien.	————
5. Der lange Lulatsch ist draufgegangen.	————
6. Sie sieht aus wie Geist Leo.	————
7. Sie war immer ein häßliches Mädchen.	————
8. Wolfgang pfeift aus'm letzten Loch.	————

9. Herr Schulze hat eine schöne Nase. _____

10. Aber sonst ist er gesund. _____

C. Match the German with the English:

1. _____ Der hat den Löffel abgegeben.
2. _____ Der hat ins Gras beißen müssen.
3. _____ Der pfeift aus'm letzten Loch.
4. _____ Haste Bock auf'n Köm?
5. _____ War doch 'n schönes Weibsstück.
6. _____ Sieht aus wie Geist Leo.
7. _____ Die hört den Kuckuck nicht mehr schrei'n.
8. _____ Die ist geliefert.
9. _____ Das wäre lecker.
10. _____ Abgeschnappt?

A. Kayoed for keeps.
B. That would hit the spot.
C. Grounded for good.
D. She is done for.
E. Keeled over?
F. Gone across the creek.
G. How about some booze?
H. She was such a pretty babe.
I. He's on his last leg.
J. Looks like death warmed over.

D. Find the appropriate questions to the following answers:

1. _____

   Das wäre lecker.

2. _____

   Nee, sieht aus wie Geist Leo.

3. _____

   Tja, die ist geliefert.

4. _____

   Abgeschnappt.

5. _____

   Der pfeift aus'm letzten Loch.

6. _____

   Aber sicher. Dem wird kein Zahn mehr schmerzen.

7. _____

   I wo. Der Kerl riecht nach Tannenholz.

8. _____

   Der sieht jetzt die Radieschen von unten wachsen.

E. Translate the following into Streetwise German:

1. He's on his last leg.

   _____

2. Let's put on the feedbag.

   _____

3. I could eat a horse.

   _____

4. Grounded for good.

   _____

5. The guy's a goner.

   _____

6. She looks like death warmed over.

   _____

7. Can't he pick himself up?

   _____

8. How about some booze?

_____

9. You mean the poor devil with Montezuma's revenge?

_____

10. That would hit the spot.

_____

Dialog 14

Southern German

Bericht vom Land

Herr Witzlhuber, before returning to his farm from a business trip, is calling Seppl, his foreman, to find out how things were going in his absence. Please don't blame Seppl for sounding a bit confused. Given a similar situation, would you sound normal?

WITZLHUBER	Grüaß Gott, Seppl! Is' was passiert?
SEPPL	Nix, Herr Chef. Die Woch'n war fad. Das Hundsviech hat zum Hink'n ang'fangen.
WITZLHUBER	Der Fido, wo doch immer so rüstig war?
SEPPL	Ja, ja. Aber das Pferd. Das Pferd hätten's seh'n soll'n.
WITZLHUBER	Das Pferd?
SEPPL	Ich war grad dabei, den Zaun zu reparier'n, wia's mir's an'g'schafft hab'n, und was seh' ich? Das Pferd flitzt aus'm Stall raus—
WITZLHUBER	*(incredulously)* Flitzt?
SEPPL	Daß d' Fetz'n fliag'n, und halb versengt. Der Fido is' in sei'm Weg, da tritt's halt dem Hund in den Hax'n.

Report from the Sticks

WITZLHUBER	Good morning, Seppl. Anything new?
SEPPL	Nothing. It was a dull week. The dog started limpin'.
WITZLHUBER	Fido, who always was sound as a bell?
SEPPL	Yessir. But the horse. You should've seen the horse.
WITZLHUBER	The horse?
SEPPL	I was just repairin' the fence like you told me, an' what do I see? The horse boltin' out of the stable—
WITZLHUBER	Boltin', you say?
SEPPL	Like some big-assed bird, and half-burned. Fido is in the way, so it steps on the dog's foot.

WITZLHUBER   *(perplexed)* Halb versengt?

SEPPL   *(getting more animated)* Genau. Nämlich vom Feuer, Herr Witzlhuber. Also z'erscht hat's im Stall zum Brennen ang'fangen, die Küh' und die Kalbln, ja, die hat's alle derwischt. Und dann das Heu im Schupf'n, Kruzifix, wie Zunder hat's 'brannt, lichterloh, wie man sagt.

WITZLHUBER   *(flabbergasted)* Lichterloh — und — die Feuerwehr?

SEPPL   Hab' ich gleich ang'ruf'n. G'sperrt am Sonntag. *(Pause)* Herr Witzlhuber? San's noch dort? — Ah so. Aber des war noch garnix! Weil plötzlich hör' ich an Mordsradau, direkt aus Ihrem Haus, ein Gebrüll wie am Spieß, "Seppl, Seppl, Hilfe, Hilfe, 's brennt, 's Haus brennt!"

WITZLHUBER   *(stunned)* 's Haus auch?

SEPPL   No freilich. Aber machen's Ihna nix draus, Herr Witzlhuber. Weil mit die drei Faßln Most, da hab' ich noch ein Mordsschwein g'habt, die hab' ich noch rechtzeitig rauskriegt aus der Hütt'n hinter der Kuchl, i hab' mir halt denkt, unser Herr Witzlhuber, der hat eine sehr durschtige Leber, also das wird ihm eine helle Freude machen — aber dann war's bereits vorbei mit Ihrer werten Familie, der gnä' Frau, den drei Madeln, den zwa alten Herrschaften und'm Kanari auch. Also die war'n alle bereits arg versengt — no, das is' ja logisch. Aber der Most is' heil.

WITZLHUBER   *(half-paralyzed)* Heil, sagst? *(choking)* Sonst noch was?

SEPPL   Sonst nix, Herr Chef. Die Woch'n war fad.

WITZLHUBER   *(perplexed)* Half-burned?

SEPPL   You bet. *(getting more animated)* The fire, Herr Witzlhuber. First, the stable starts burnin', the cows and the calves, yeah, they all got caught, and then the hay in the barn, by gosh! It sure burned like tinder, 't was a real blaze, like they say.

WITZLHUBER   *(flabbergasted)* A real blaze—and—the fire department?

SEPPL   I called 'em. Closed on Sunday. *(Pause)* Herr Witzlhuber? You still there? O.K. But that was only half of it. 'Cuz suddenly there's a mean racket comin' direct from your home, a gosh-awful scream, "Seppl, Seppl, help, help, it's burnin', the house is burnin'!"

WITZLHUBER   *(stunned)* The house, too?

SEPPL   You bet. But don't worry, Herr Witzlhuber. I sure had a lucky break with them three little kegs of moonshine, gettin' 'em out of the shack behind the kitchen just in time. I just thought, our Herr Witzlhuber likes his booze a lot, so I figured he'd be overjoyed. But then it was too late for your esteemed family, the missus, the three little girls, the old man and his lady, and the canary bird, too. Well, sir, they all were already scorched bad, that's only logical. But the juice is O.K.

WITZLHUBER   *(half-paralyzed)* O.K., you say? *(choking)* Anything else?

SEPPL   That's it, boss. It was a dull week.

Vocabulary

Ah so. *(coll.)*	O.K.; I see
Das wird ihm eine (helle) Freude machen.	He'll be overjoyed.
daß d' Fetzn fliagn (daß die Fetzen fliegen) *(sl.)*	*(lit.)* that the rags are flying; (here) like some big-assed bird
Der hat eine sehr durschtige (durstige) Leber. *(coll.)*	(here) He likes his booze a lot.
Des (das) war noch garnix. *(coll.)*	That's only half of it.
Die hat's (hat es) alle derwischt (erwischt). *(sl.)*	They all got caught.
fad *(adj. coll.)*	boring, dull
Faßl *(n. coll.)*	little keg
(ein) Gebrüll wie am Spieß *(sl.)*	(a) gosh-awful scream
gnä' Frau (gnädige Frau) *(coll.)*	missus
Grüaß Gott! (Grüß Gott!)	Good morning!
Hax'n *(f. sl.)*	foot
Herr Chef (pronounced "sheff")	boss
Hundsviech *(n. sl.)*	(contemptuously) dog
Hütt'n (Hütte) *(f. coll.)*	shack
I (ich) hab' mir halt denkt (gedacht), . . . *(coll.)*	I just thought, . . .
Kalbln *(pl. n. coll.)*	calves
Kanari *(m. coll.)*	canary bird
Kruzifix! *(sl.)*	By gosh!
Kuchl (Küche) *(f. coll.)*	kitchen
Machen's (Machen sie) Ihna (Ihnen) nix draus! *(coll.)*	Don't worry!
Madln *(pl. n. sl.)*	girls
Mordsradau *(m. sl.)*	mean racket
Mordsschwein *(n. sl.)*	(here) a lot of luck
No freilich! *(coll.)*	You bet
rausflitzen *(v. sl.)*	to bolt
rauskriegen *(v. coll.)*	to get out
rüstig *(adj. coll.)*	healthy; (here) sound as a bell
San's (Sind Sie) noch dort? *(coll.)*	You still there?

Schupfen (Schuppen) *(m. sl.)*	barn
sei'm (seinem) *(pron. coll.)*	his
Sonst noch was? *(coll.)*	Anything else?
wia's mer's ang'schafft hab'n **(wie Sie es mir angeschafft haben)** *(sl.)*	like you told me
z'erscht (zuerst) *(adv. sl.)*	first
Zunder *(m. coll.)*	tinder
(die) zwa (zwei) alten Herrschaften	(here) the old man and his lady

A Smidgen of Streetwise Grammar
Fun with Idioms and Such

☐ Using **zum** or **mit** instead of the grammatical **zu:**

Das Hundsviech hat **zum** Hinken angefangen.
(Das Hundsviech hat zu hinken angefangen.)

Ich hab' **mit'm** Lesen aufgehört.
(Ich hab' zu lesen aufgehört.)

☐ The uses of **wo** in Streetwise German Grammar:

a. substituting **wo** for a relative pronoun:
Der Fido, **wo** doch immer so rüstig war
(Der Fido, der doch immer so rüstig war)

Der Mann, **wo** ich gesehn hab'
(Der Mann, den ich gesehn hab')

b. substituting **wo** for the conjunction *da:*
wo ich ihn doch nicht ausstehn kann
(da ich ihn doch nicht ausstehn kann
since I cannot stand him)

c. separating **wo** from its adverbial or prepositional
component:
Wo kommt das **her?**
(Woher kommt das?)

Wo gehst du **hin?**
(Wohin gehst du?)

d. expressing negation:
I (ach) **wo!**
(Keine Spur!   Nonsense! Oh no!)

☐ **Ihnen (Ihna)** is sometimes preferred to the reflexive pronoun
sich:

Machen's **Ihnen** nix draus.
(Machen Sie sich nichts draus.)

Tun's **Ihnen** nix an.
(Tun Sie sich nix an.   Don't show off.)

Tun's **Ihnen** nicht so aufblasen.
(Tun Sie sich nicht so aufblasen.   Don't brag so much.)

☐ Mordsradau, Mordsschwein

Other "Mords"-Wörter:
Er hat eine Mordsangst.   He's a 'fraidycat.
Das ist eine Mordsarbeit.   That's a heck of a job.
Sie hatte einen Mordsbeifall.   She brought down the house.
Ich hab' einen Mordsdurst.   I'm dry as dust.
Das war ein Mordsgewitter.   That was a doozie of a
thunderstorm.
Er ist ein Mordsrindvieh.   He don't know nothin' from
nothin'.

Life on the Farm

HERR BAUER   Auf einem Bauernhof zu leben, ist nicht leicht. Du gehst schlafen mit den Hühnern, du stehst auf mit den Hähnen, du arbeitest wie ein Pferd, du frißt wie ein Schwein, und dann behandelt man dich wie einen Hund.

Life on a farm is not easy. You go to sleep with the chickens, you get up with the roosters, you work like a horse, you eat like a pig, and then they treat you like a dog.

Exercises

A. Complete the phrase by filling in the appropriate word from the list:

derwischt, draus, durschtige, flitzt, garnix, Hax'n, Kuchl, Mordsradau, rüstig, Spieß.

1. Der Fido, wo doch immer so _____ war.

2. Da tritt's dem Hund in den _____.

3. Das Pferd _____ aus'm Stall raus.

4. Machen's Ihnen nix _____.

5. Plötzlich hör' ich an _____.

6. Der hat eine sehr _____ Leber.

7. Aber das war noch _____.

8. Die hat's alle _____.

9. Die Hütt'n hinter der _____.

10. ein Gebrüll wie am _____

B. True or False?

T/F

1. Die Feuerwehr war am Sonntag gesperrt.   ———

2. Das Pferd war immer so rüstig.   ———

3. Die Woch'n war fad, sagt Seppl.   ———

4. Seppl hat grad' den Zaun repariert.   ———

5. Den alten Herrschaften is' nix passiert.   ———

6. Fido hat das Pferd gebissen.   ———

7. Z'erscht hat's im Stall gebrannt.   ———

8. Seppl hat den Most rausgekriegt.   ———

9. Der Kanari war auch versengt.   ———

10. Die Küh' und die Kalbl'n sind am Leben.   ———

C. Match the German with the English:

1. ——— San's noch dort?

2. ——— Da hab' ich noch ein Mordsschwein g'habt.

3. ——— Da Pferd flitzt aus'm Stall raus.

4. ——— Des war noch garnix.

5. ——— daß d'Fetzen flieg'n

6. ——— die zwa alten Herrschaften

7. ——— ein Gebrüll wie am Spieß

8. ——— wia's mir's ang'schafft hab'n

9. ——— lichterloh, wie man sagt

10. ——— No freilich.

A. That was only half of it.
B. You bet.
C. a real blaze, like they say
D. You still there?
E. like some big-assed bird
F. like you told me
G. The horse bolting out of the stable
H. I sure had a lucky break.
I. the old man and his lady
J. a gosh-awful scream

D. Underline the English term that comes closest in meaning to the German word:

1. Hax'n

   a. hex   b. hackle   c. foot

2. flitzen

   a. to bolt   b. to flex   c. to belt

3. rüstig

   a. rusty   b. restive   c. sound

4. Zunder

   a. sand   b. tinder   c. sender

5. Schupf'n

   a. barn   b. cold   c. shop

6. Chef

   a. cook   b. boss   c. barber

7. fad

   a. boring   b. temporary   c. bleak

8. Kuchl

   a. cook   b. kitchen   c. cake

9. Madln

   a. madcaps   b. maggots   c. girls

10. Faßl

   a. little keg   b. little hat   c. little bag

E. Translate the following into Streetwise German:

1. I just thought . . .

   _____

2. He'll be overjoyed.

   _____

3. Don't worry!

   _____

4. They all got caught.

   _____

5. That's only half of it.

   _____

6. a gosh-awful scream

   _____

7. like some big-assed bird

   _____

8. Good morning!

   _____

9. By gosh!

_____

10. You bet!

_____

Dialog 15

Northern German

In der Disco

Björn and Rieke, two teenagers, at their first date.

BJÖRN Laß uns mal ordentlich einen fetzen gehen, Rieke. So richtig mal tanzen und so. Mit so 'nem süßen Püppchen wie dich im Arm, bin ich echt happy.

RIEKE Echt?

BJÖRN Nur mit dem Beat hab' ich meine Problems. Da wollen die Füße nicht so recht mit. Ich bin schon ganz döspaddelig von dem vielen Aufpassen.

RIEKE Ach Mönsch, Björn! Du tanzt ja wie deine alte Mutti zu den Schnulzen von Hans Albers. Stell' dich nicht an wie der letzte Macker! Der D.J. hat gerade die neueste Scheibe von Madonna aufgelegt.

BJÖRN Schuldigung, Rieke. Ich könnte mich selber übers Knie legen. Also den Song hab' ich dir gründlich versaut.

RIEKE Laß mal stecken, Björn! Schau dir die Tussi da an, die ist aufgetakelt wie 'ne alte Fregatte.

In the Disco

BJÖRN   Let's have some real fun, Rieke. Like dancing 'n stuff. With a sweet little cat like you on my arm, I'm real happy.

RIEKE   Honest?

BJÖRN   But I got problems with the beat. My feet won't cooperate. I get all crazy just watching 'em.

RIEKE   Man oh man, Björn! You're dancing like your old mom to the tearjerkers of Hans Albers. Don't act like a klutz! The d.j. just now put on the latest record of Madonna.

BJÖRN   Sorry, Rieke. I could kick myself. I sure loused that song up for you.

RIEKE   Forget it, Björn. Get a load of that dame there, decked out like a Christmas tree.

BJÖRN   Ja, die ist ganz schön knackig.

RIEKE   Knackig, sagste? Die hat man doch in ihre Fetzen direkt hineingegossen und dann vergessen, den Hahn abzudrehen.

BJÖRN   Ja, die ist zum Abgewöhnen. *(sniffing her)* Sag', ist das dein Parfüm oder du? Rieke, du törnst mich an.

RIEKE   Versuchst du, mich anzumachen, Alter? Tut mir leid, is' nix.

BJÖRN   Du bist nicht biege, Rieke. Aber frech und ulkig. Also, Ehrenwort, bevor ich dich traf, hatte ich null Bock auf nix, und mein Leben kam mir vor wie 'ne Wüste.

RIEKE   Tanzt du deshalb wie ein Kamel?

BJÖRN   Rieke, du bist zum Schießen! Wie wär's, wenn wir uns so'n richtig langsames Lied wünschen, du weißt schon, so 'ne richtige Schnulze. Dann können wir so richtig eng tanzen.

RIEKE   Mensch, du hast 'nen Vogel.

Vocabulary

Ach Mönsch! (Mensch) *(coll.)*	Man, oh man!
aufgetakelt wie 'ne (eine) alte Fregatte *(sl.)*	(lit.) rigged up like an old warship; (here) decked out like a Christmas tree
Beat *(m. sl.)*	beat, rhythm
biege (dumm) *(adj. sl.)*	stupid
Die ist zum Abgewöhnen. *(sl.)*	(here) She's a pest.
D.J. *(m. coll.)* (pronounced as in English)	d.j., disc jockey
direkt *(adj. coll.)*	straight
döspaddelig *(adj. sl.)*	strange, miserable
Du hast 'nen (einen) Vogel. *(sl.)*	You're outta your skull. You're crazy.
Du törnst mich an. *(sl.)*	You turn me on.
Echt? *(adj. coll.)*	Honest?
echt happy *(sl.)*	real happy

BJÖRN   Yea, she sure is hefty.

RIEKE   Hefty, you say? Someone poured her straight into her rags,
but she forgot to say when.

BJÖRN   Yes, she's a pest. *(sniffing her)* Say, is that your perfume or is
it you? Rieke, you turn me on.

RIEKE   D'you try to come on to me, man? Sorry, tough luck.

BJÖRN   You're not stupid, Rieke. But bitchy and funny. Honest, before
I met you, I felt out of it, like living in a desert.

RIEKE   Is that why you dance like a camel?

BJÖRN   You're a scream, Rieke. How about a real slow song? You
know, a real schmaltzy tune? Then we can dance real close.

RIEKE   Man, you're outta your skull.

Ehrenwort! *(n.)*	word of honor; (here) Honest!
eng tanzen *(coll.)*	to dance real close
frech *(adj.)*	fresh, bitchy
(etw.) gründlich versauen *(sl.)*	to louse up s.th.
Ich könnte mich selber übers Knie legen. *(sl.)*	(here) I could kick myself.
knackig (stramm) *(adj. sl.)*	muscular, hefty
Laß mal stecken! *(sl.)* **(Ist schon okay!)**	Forget it!
Laß uns mal ordentlich einen fetzen gehen! *(sl.)*	Let's have some real fun!
null Bock auf nix (nichts) haben *(sl.)*	to feel out of it
Problems haben *(sl.)* (noun pronounced as in English)	to have problems
Scheibe *(f. sl.)*	record
Schnulze *(f. coll.)*	schmaltzy tune
Schuldigung! (Entschuldigung!) *(f. coll.)*	Sorry!

süßes Püppchen *(coll.)*	sweet little cat
Stell' dich nicht an wie der letzte Macker! *(sl.)*	Don't act like a klutz!
Tussi (Püppchen, Torte, Sahneschnitte) *(f. sl.)*	chick, dame
Tut mir leid, is' nix (nichts). *(sl.)*	Sorry, tough luck.
ulkig *(adj. coll.)*	funny, a scream
Versuchst du, mich anzumachen, Alter? *(sl.)*	D'you try to come on to me, man?
Zum Schießen! *(sl.)*	A scream!

A Smidgen of Streetwise Grammar
More Fun with Idioms and Stylistic Oddities

☐ Du törnst mich an.

> **Antörnen,** pronounced as in English, takes its place alongside many other American-English imports that have been enriching the German language. Here are two more examples:
> **Frust hat viele frustrierte Menschen zum Selbstmord getrieben.**   Frustration drove many frustrated people into suicide.
> **Die Trimm-dich-Aktion** (keep-fit program) **hat vielen Menschen geholfen. Jetzt sind sie fit.**

☐ Die hat man in ihre Fetzen direkt hineingegossen.

> The word **direkt** can be used in many ways. Here are some examples:
> **Das ist ein direkter Zug nach Paris.**   This is a direct train to Paris.
> **Wir haben keinen direkten Schaden erlitten.**   We did not suffer any immediate injury.
> **Wir haben keine direkte Information.**   We don't have any first-hand information.
> **Er gab mir eine direkte Antwort.**   He gave me a plain answer.

Er rannte direkt gegen die Mauer.   He ran smack into the
   wall.
Das Haus schaut direkt nach Süden.   The home faces due
   south.
Das ist direkt lächerlich.   That's downright ridiculous.

☐   Disco

Disco-Fee   disco singer
Disco-Fieber   disco fever
Disco-Kätzchen   young female disco visitor
Disco-Mieze   disco lover
Disco-Muffel   disco hater
Disco-Typ   overdressed disco girl or guy

☐   Stell' dich nicht an wie der letzte Macker!

dufter Macker   favorite boy-friend
geschaffter Macker   enterprising young man
großer Macker   capable man
linker Macker   disagreeable fellow
reicher Macker   rich guy
schräger Macker   unreliable guy
zackiger Macker   very nice young man

☐   Hans Albers

was a very popular actor and singer on Hamburg's *Reeperbahn*
in the thirties and forties.

The Only Obstacle

SHE	Liebling, abgesehen von zwei Dingern wärst du ein großartiger Tänzer.	Darling, except for two things, you would be a wonderful dancer.
HE	Und was sind diese zwei Dinger?	And what are those two things?
SHE	Deine Füße.	Your feet.

Exercises

A. Complete the phrase by filling in the appropriate word from the list:

Aufgetakelt, Beat, biege, döspaddelig, eng, knackig, Macker, Schießen, Schnulzen, stecken.

1. Nur mit dem _____ hab' ich meine Probleme.

2. Stell' dich nicht an wie der letzte _____.

3. Du tanzt zu den _____ von Hans Albers.

4. Ich bin schon ganz _____.

5. Die ist ganz schön _____.

6. Dann können wir so richtig _____ tanzen.

7. Rieke, du bist zum _____.

8. Du bist nicht _____.

9. _____ wie 'ne alte Fregatte.

10. Laß mal _____, Björn!

B. True or False?

	T/F
1. Er will eng mit ihr tanzen.	_____
2. Das viele Aufpassen stört ihn überhaupt nicht.	_____
3. Er tanzt wie ein Bär.	_____
4. Sie glaubt, Björn hat 'nen Vogel.	_____
5. Er möchte sie gern übers Knie legen.	_____
6. Aber er glaubt, sie ist frech und ulkig.	_____
7. Allerdings mag er ihr Parfüm nicht.	_____
8. Sie möchte gern mit ihm schwimmen gehen.	_____

9. Er versucht, sie anzumachen, sagt er. _____

10. Man spielt eine Scheibe von Michael Jackson. _____

C. Match the German with the English:

1. _____ Laß mal stecken!

2. _____ Ich könnt' mich selber übers Knie legen.

3. _____ Du bist zum Schießen.

4. _____ Das hab' ich dir gründlich versaut.

5. _____ Tut mir leid, is' nix!

6. _____ Mensch, du hast 'nen Vogel!

7. _____ Du bist nicht biege.

8. _____ Laß uns mal einen Fetzen gehen.

9. _____ Versuchst du, mich anzumachen?

10. _____ Ich bin schon ganz döspaddelig.

A. I sure loused that up for you.
B. Let's have some real fun.
C. D'you try to come on to me?
D. You're not stupid.
E. I get all crazy.
F. You're a scream.
G. Forget it!
H. Sorry, tough luck!
I. Man, you're outta your skull!
J. I could kick myself.

D. Underline the synonym:

1. döspaddelig

   a. wunderbar   b. vergnügt   c. schwindlig

2. Macker

   a. Fisch   b. Klotz   c. Bandit

3. ulkig

   a. lustig   b. fett   c. klug

4. knackig

   a. stramm   b. gescheit   c. anständig

5. biege

   a. biegsam   b. dumm   c. beige

6. Tussi

   a. Husten   b. Püppchen   c. Wurf

7. versauen

   a. verderben   b. vernähen   c. versagen

8. Schnulze

   a. Schnupfen   b. Schuppen   c. Schlager

E. Translate the following into Streetwise German:

1. My feet won't cooperate.

   _____

2. Man, you're outta your skull!

   _____

3. I could kick myself.

   _____

4. You really ruined it for me.

   _____

5. Yes, she's a pest.

   _____

6. Forget it, Björn!

   _____

7. Let's have some real fun!

_____

8. Hefty, you say?

_____

9. I felt out of it.

_____

10. decked out like a Christmas tree

_____

Answers
Dialogs 11 through 15

Dialog 11

A.
1. Fatzke
2. reinlegen
3. achtkantig
4. Dreck
5. erlogen
6. Dämpfer
7. Saures
8. Bett
9. abgemeldet
10. Eisenbahn

B.
1. T	3. F	5. T	7. T	9. F
2. F	4. F	6. T	8. F	10. T

C.
1. G	3. F	5. H	7. J	9. C
2. D	4. B	6. I	8. A	10. E

D.
1. b	3. c	5. a	7. b	9. b
2. a	4. b	6. c	8. a	10. c

E.
1. Er ist ein ausgekochter Fatzke.
2. Sie wird ihn achtkantig hinausschmeißen.
3. Jemand sollte ihm gehörig aufs Dach steigen.
4. Er hat Geld wie Dreck.
5. Bei mir ist der abgemeldet.
6. Es ist zum Auswachsen.
7. Bei mir muß er da früher aufstehen.
8. Ich muß meine Wut in mich hineinfressen.
9. Es ist höchste Eisenbahn.
10. erstunken und erlogen

Dialog 12

A.
1. g'spaßig
2. Kreid'n
3. Jux
4. halt
5. Pump
6. Fressalien
7. Gaudi
8. Kasse
9. abstottern
10. spottbillig

B.
1. T   3. T   5. F   7. F   9. F
2. F   4. T   6. T   8. T   10. F

C.
1. B   3. G   5. A   7. E   9. F
2. D   4. H   6. I   8. J   10. C

D.
1. a   3. c   5. b   7. c
2. b   4. a   6. a   8. b

E.
1. You're always chipper, a real gas.
2. D'you want me to close up the joint?
3. You are a scream!
4. Don't ever say that!
5. The fresh carp would be a real delicacy.
6. The situation is no longer a laughing matter.
7. You're too deep in the red as is.
8. Nothing more on credit, ma'm!
9. And we are even.
10. I mean, in small installments.

Dialog 13

A.
1. Tannenholz
2. Leo
3. Gras
4. Kohldampf
5. knackig
6. Löffel
7. Lulatsch
8. hochrappeln
9. Köm
10. Knülch

B. 1. T   3. F   5. T   7. F   9. F
        2. T   4. F   6. T   8. T   10. F

C. 1. C   3. I   5. H   7. A   9. B
        2. F   4. G   6. J   8. D   10. E

D. 1. Haste Bock auf'n Köm?
        2. Und deine Puppe? Noch immer knackig?
        3. Geht's der so schlecht?
        4. Und sein Bruder, der lange Lulatsch?
        5. Und Wolfgang?
        6. Draufgegangen?
        7. Kann sich nicht hochrappeln?
        8. Hat auch ins Gras beißen müssen?

E. 1. Der pfeift aus'm letzt'n Loch.
        2. Komm, laß uns was zwischen die Beißerchen schieben.
        3. Ich hab' 'n Kohldampf bis unter die Arme.
        4. Dem wird kein Zahn mehr schmerzen.
        5. Der Kerl riecht nach Tannenholz.
        6. Sieht aus wie Geist Leo.
        7. Kann sich nicht hochrappeln?
        8. Haste Bock auf'n Köm?
        9. Du meinst das arme Luder mit dem Dünnschißproblem?
        10. Das wäre lecker.

Dialog 14

A. 1. rüstig   5. Mordsradau   8. derwischt
        2. Hax'n   6. durschtige   9. Kuchl
        3. flitzt   7. garnix   10. Spieß
        4. draus

B. 1. T   3. T   5. F   7. T   9. T
        2. F   4. T   6. F   8. T   10. F

C. 1. D   3. G   5. E   7. J   9. C
        2. H   4. A   6. I   8. F   10. B

D. 1. c   3. c   5. a   7. a   9. c
        2. a   4. b   6. b   8. b   10. a

E.   1. Ich hab' mir halt denkt, . . .
         2. Das wird ihm eine helle Freude machen.
         3. Machen's Ihnen nix draus!
         4. Die hat's alle derwischt.
         5. Das war noch garnix.
         6. ein Gebrüll wie am Spieß
         7. daß d' Fetzen fliegen
         8. Grüaß Gott!
         9. Kruzifix!
        10. No freilich!

Dialog 15

A. 1. Beat   5. knackig   8. biege
        2. Macker   6. eng   9. Aufgetackelt
        3. Schnulzen   7. Schießen   10. stecken
        4. döspaddelig

B. 1. T   3. F   5. F   7. F   9. T
        2. F   4. T   6. T   8. F   10. F

C. 1. G   3. F   5. H   7. D   9. C
        2. J   4. A   6. I   8. B   10. E

D. 1. c   3. a   5. b   7. a
        2. b   4. a   6. b   8. c

E. 1. Die Füße wollen nicht so recht mit.
    2. Mann, du hast 'nen Vogel!
    3. Ich könnte mich selber übers Knie legen.
    4. Das hast du mir gründlich versaut.
    5. Ja, die ist zum Abgewöhnen.
    6. Laß mal stecken, Björn!
    7. Laß uns mal ordentlich einen fetzen gehen!
    8. Knackig, sagste?
    9. Ich hatte null Bock auf nix.
   10. aufgetakelt wie 'ne alte Fregatte

Review
Dialogs 11 through 15

Exercises

A. Replace the words in parentheses with the Streetwise German synonyms from the right:

    1. Ich mein' den alten Knülch mit der dicken (Nase) ———.

    2. Hast (Lust) ——— auf'n Köm?

    3. Das Pferd (rennt) ——— aus'm Stall raus.

    4. Da tritt's dem Hund in den (Fuß) ———.

    5. Nur mit dem (Rhythmus) ——— hab' ich meine Probleme.

    6. Den Song hab' ich dir gründlich (verdorben) ———.

    7. Aber mich wird er nie mehr (betrügen) ———.

    8. Bei mir ist der (erledigt) ———.

    9. Aber die Situation ist kein (Spaß) ——— nicht mehr.

   10. Nix mehr auf (Kredit) ———.

A. Beat
B. Hax'n
C. reinlegen
D. abgemeldet
E. Jux
F. Knolle
G. Pump
H. Bock
I. versaut
J. flitzt

B. Underline the word in parentheses that makes sense in the context of a dialogue when the sentence is completed.

    1. Sie sieht aus wie Geist (Franz, Zacharias, Leo).

    2. War doch ein schönes (Weibsstück, Kind, Leben).

    3. und dann das Heu im (Garten, Schupfen, Keller)

4. Die Faßln hab' ich noch rechtzeitig (g'sehn, verkauft, rausgekriegt).

5. Stell' dich nicht an wie der letzte (Dieb, Macker, Freund).

6. Du bist zum (Schießen, Jagen, Rennen).

7. Er ist ein ausgekochter (Kalbsfuß, Feigling, Fatzke).

8. Sie steigt ihm gehörig aufs (Haus, Ohr, Dach).

9. Soll ich die Bud'n (aufmach'n, zuriegeln, anstreichen)?

10. Bei Ihnen gibt's immer a Hetz' und a (Gaudi, Trankl, Mehlspeis').

C. Fill in the blank with the letter indicating your best choice in reference to a dialogue that you read before:

1. Ich hab' 'n _____ bis unter die Arme.

   a. Durst   b. Kohldampf   c. Bock

2. Der Kerl riecht nach _____.

   a. Tannenholz   b. Parfüm   c. Radieschen

3. Der Fido, wo doch immer so _____ war?

   a. stark   b. rüstig   c. schnell

4. Die Faßln hat er noch rechtzeitig _____.

   a. rausgekriegt   b. g'fund'n   c. fortg'schickt

5. Ich hab' null _____ auf nix g'habt.

   a. Stier   b. Hund   c. Bock

6. Mensch, du hast 'nen _____.

   a. Fisch   b. Vogel   c. Kater

7. Es ist höchste _____.

   a. Eisenbahn   b. Ankunft   c. Abfahrt

8. Mit seinen finanziellen Projekten kann er _____ gehn.

   a. turnen   b. baden   c. eislaufen

9. Ein Hendl _____ auf'm Ei den ganzen Tag.

   a. liegt   b. hockt   c. bleibt

10. Die _____ sind gepfeffert heutzutag'.

   a. Getränke   b. Fische   c. Fressalien

D. Complete the following words:

1.	F										
2.	A										
3.	T										
4.	Z										
5.	K										
6.	E										

Wanted: the German equivalent for the following expressions:

1. eats; food
2. decked out
3. little by little
4. tinder
5. ravenous hunger
6. genuine; really

E. There are 12 Streetwise German words and other colloquialisms in this puzzle. Can you find them?

C	B	O	S	A	U	K	E	R	L	N
D	L	B	P	B	S	C	B	Z	G	M
E	G	H	O	C	K	E	N	K	O	A
A	B	S	T	O	T	T	E	R	N	L
U	E	L	T	M	N	L	I	E	G	C
S	A	N	B	T	S	G	M	I	P	A
G	T	M	I	G	G	F	A	D	R	S
E	N	I	L	L	E	H	P	N	K	L
K	Ö	M	L	U	L	A	T	S	C	H
O	G	G	I	O	I	X	R	K	O	P
C	D	X	G	N	E	N	V	L	A	N
H	F	S	O	A	F	L	X	A	G	S
T	L	O	M	V	E	I	O	M	B	A
M	A	L	B	C	R	A	G	S	D	S
E	C	N	H	L	T	P	W	A	I	K

Expressions for:

(horizontal):　sleazeball, to sit, to pay off in installments, boring, booze, lamppost (tall, lanky man)

(vertical):　tricky, rhythm, very cheap, done for, foot, (in the) red

Answers to Review

Dialogs 11 through 15

A. 1. F   3. J   5. A   7. C   9. E
    2. H   4. B   6. I   8. D   10. G

B. 1. Leo   5. Macker   8. Dach
    2. Weibsstück   6. Schießen   9. zuriegeln
    3. Schupfen   7. Fatzke   10. Gaudi
    4. rausgekriegt

C. 1. b   3. b   5. c   7. a   9. b
    2. a   4. a   6. b   8. b   10. c

D. 1. Fressalien   3. tröpferlweis   5. Kohldampf
    2. aufgetakelt   4. Zunder   6. echt

E. (horizontal):   Saukerl, hocken, abstottern, fad, köm,
                     Lulatsch
    (vertical):   ausgekocht, Beat, spottbillig, geliefert, Haxn,
                     Kreidn

E.

C	B	O	S	A	U	K	E	R	L	N
D	L	B	P	B	S	C	B	Z	G	M
E	G	H	O	C	K	E	N	K	O	A
A	B	S	T	O	T	T	E	R	N	L
U	E	L	T	M	N	L	I	E	G	C
S	A	N	B	T	S	G	M	I	P	A
G	T	M	I	G	G	F	A	D	R	S
E	N	I	L	L	E	H	P	N	K	L
K	Ö	M	L	U	L	A	T	S	C	H
O	G	G	I	O	I	X	R	K	O	P
C	D	X	G	N	E	N	V	L	A	N
H	F	S	O	A	F	L	X	A	G	S
T	L	O	M	V	E	I	O	M	B	A
M	A	L	B	C	R	A	G	S	D	S
E	C	N	H	L	T	P	W	A	I	K

Vocabulary

The vocabulary section, both the German-English and the English-German parts, was designed with students on the intermediate level in mind (after three to four units or semesters of German). Basic vocabulary items are not included. The list is intended *only* to help the student complete the exercises following each chapter. It is not meant to be a general guide to streetwise German. Also, since the dialogs are fully translated and streetwise expressions used in them are explained, there was no need to include in the list all vocabulary items occurring in the dialogs.

In rendering idioms, their literal meanings are disregarded and only idiomatic equivalents are given. For example, the expression "haste Spätzündung?" is rendered as "slow on the uptake?" No attempt is made to explain the literal meaning of "Spätzündung" ("delayed ignition"), although admittedly the origin and literal meaning of such idioms can be quite interesting and amusing. Listing them would have transcended the scope of a vocabulary section.

Idioms and expressions that are used predominantly in the north or in the south are marked N or S. The number in parentheses refers to the dialog(s) in which the word or phrase appears.

German-English

A

das Aas bastard (11)

die Abfahrt departure (R 11–15)

ab·geben, a, e to turn in (13)

ab·kratzen (sl.) to croak (5)

ab·melden; bei mir ist er abgemeldet (sl.) N he is sidelined in my book (11)

s. ab·regen (sl.) to knock it off, to calm down (8)

die Abreibung, -en; der kriegt 'ne saftige Abreibung (sl.) N I'll beat the living daylight out of him (4)

ab·schieben, o, o (coll.) to transfer (2)

ab·schnappen (sl.) to keel over, die (13)

ab·stauben to dust off (12)

ab·stecken to mark (12)

ab-stottern (sl.) to pay off in installments (12)

achtkantig; achtkantig hinaus·schmeißen, i, i (sl.) N to throw s.o. out on his ass (11)

die Ahnung, -en idea (9)

alle; nicht mehr alle haben (sl.) to be crazy (4)

allerdings to be sure (15)

allerhand; das ist allerhand! (coll.) this is really something, I'm all shook up (8)

die Alte, -n (coll.) (my) old lady (2)

an·betteln (jn.) to pester s.o. with requests for handouts (7)

an·geben, a, e to show off (7)

an·hau'n; jn. um Geld anhau'n (sl.) S to bug s.o. for money (7)

die Ankunft arrival (R 11–15)

s. an·lachen (jn.) (sl.) to make a catch (9)

an·machen (jn.) (coll.) to come on to s.o., to pester s.o. (7)

an·schaffen to tell s.o. to do something, order (14)

anständig decent (15)

s. an·stellen (coll.) to act, behave (15)

an·streichen, i, i to paint (5)

an·zeigen to report, to turn in (7)

der Anzuch (Anzug); dich stoß' ich aus'm Anzuch (sl.) N I'll squeeze you out of your suit, skin you alive (4)

aufgeschmissen sein (coll.) to be in a fix (2)

aufgetakelt (sl.) N rigged up (15)

auf·passen to watch out, be careful (15)

s. auf·pudeln (sl.) S to get snooty (8)

auf·reißen, i, i (sl.) to pick up (5)

auf·stehen, a, a; bei mir mußt du früher aufstehen (sl.) N don't play games with me (11)

auf·ziehen, o, o to wind (clock); wie aufgezogen ratschen (coll.) S to gab without a pause (7)

der Aufzug (coll.) funny outfit, getup (1)

aus·fressen, a, e; hast was ausg'fressen? (sl.) have you been up to some mischief? is your conscience bothering you? (10)

ausgekocht (coll.) shrewd, tricky (11)

aus·packen (coll.) N to spill the beans (6)

aus·schecken (sl.) to find out (12)

aus·wachsen, u, a; es ist zum
Auswachsen! *(coll.)* it drives me
up the wall (11)

B

baden; er kann damit baden
gehen *(sl.)* he can shove it (11)
der Balkon; da wackelt der
Balkon *(sl.)* N I'm all shook up
(8)
der Batzen, –; ein Batzen Geld
(sl.) S big bucks (10)
der Bauch, ̈e; ich tret' dir vor'n
Bauch *(sl.)* N I'll slam you in the
guts (4)
s. beherrschen; ich kann mich
beherrschen *(coll.)* count me out
(8)
beißen, i, i to bite (14)
der Beißkorb muzzle (7)
beknackt *(sl.)* rotten (2)
belemmert *(sl.)* N terrible, rotten (2)
beömmeln; das ist zum
Beömmeln *(sl.)* N that cracks me
up (8)
beruhigen to set at ease (12)
bescheuert *(coll.)* lousy, too bad,
tough (2)
das Bett, -en; sich ins gemachte
Bett legen *(coll.)* to look for (and
find) a cozy niche (11)
bettelarm poor as a church mouse
(7)
bewundern to admire (8)
die Beziehung; in der Beziehung
in this regard (5)
biege *(adj. sl.)* N stupid (15)
biegsam flexible, supple (15)
die Biene, -n (lit.: bee) *(sl.)* N girl
(6)
das Biest, -er *(coll.)* beast, bitch (2)
die Bißgurn, – *(sl.)* S battle ax,
bitch (7)
der Blaue, -en *(sl.)* N 100-mark note
(2)

blechen *(coll.)* to dish out, to pay (10)
bloß merely (6)
der Blubberheini, -s *(sl.)* N airhead
(4)
blühen; wie's blühende Leben
(coll.) alive and kicking (5)
die Blunz'n, – *(sl.)* S butterball (3)
der Bock, ̈e; Bock haben auf
etw. *(sl.)* to feel like having or
doing s.t. (13)
bockig *(coll.)* ornery (9)
die Bohne, -n; nich' die Bohne!
(sl.) N not a chance! you should
live so long! (8)
die Bohnenstange, -n beanpole (11)
braten, ie, a to roast (1)
der Buckel; er kann mir den
Buckel 'runterrutschen *(coll.)* he
can go to hell (Buckel lit.:
backside) (3)
die Bude, -n shop, joint (12)
das Bügelbrett, -er; flach wie ein
Bügelbrett *(coll.)* flat as a
pancake (3)
bunkern; Geld bunkern *(sl.)* to
stash money (2)
die Butter; in Butter sein *(sl.)* to
be OK (9)

C

der Chef, -s boss (14)

D

das Dach, ̈er; jm. aufs Dach
steigen *(coll.)* to bawl s.o. out, to
rake s.o. over the coals (11)
dafür können; er kann nichts
dafür *(coll.)* it's not his fault
(10)
der Dämpfer, –; jm. einen
Dämpfer aufsetzen *(coll.)* to tell
s.o. off, to take s.o. down a peg or
two (11)
die Dampfnudel, -n *(coll.)* S
dumpling (3)

der Depp, -en *(sl.)* S idiot, dope (7)

deppert *(sl.)* S nuts (3)

derwischen; die hat's alle derwischt (erwischt) *(sl.)* S they all got caught, took the last count (14)

dick; dickes Geld *(sl.)* lots of money (2)

s. dicktun, a, a *(sl.)* N to throw one's weight around (6)

Donner und Hagel! *(sl.)* N I'm flabbergasted! (8)

doof *(coll.)* N stupid (4)

döspaddelig *(sl.)* N strange, miserable (15)

dran; arm dran sein *(coll.)* to be badly off (6)

drauf·gehen, i, a *(sl.)* to bite the dust (13)

draus; er macht sich nichts draus *(coll.)* he doesn't worry about it (14)

der Dreck; Geld wie Dreck haben *(sl.)* to have money to burn (11)

dreizehn; nun schlägt's dreizehn! *(sl.)* now I've heard everything, this beats me (8)

dufte *(sl.)* N nifty (8)

dünne; s. dünne machen *(sl.)* N to do a vanishing act (2)

durchbrennen, a, a *(sl.)* to run off (2)

durschtig (durstig) *(sl.)* S thirsty (14)

duschen; es duscht *(coll.)* S it's raining cats and dogs (3)

dusselig *(coll.)* N dopey (9)

E

echt *(adv. coll.)* truly, wildly (2)

eh *(coll.)* S anyway (3)

der Eheschlamassel, – *(coll.)* marital mess, misery (9)

der Eimer, –; im Eimer *(coll.)* N on the rocks (3)

s. auf etw. ein·lassen, ie, a to agree to s.t. (2)

die Eisenbahn, -en; es ist höchste Eisenbahn *(coll.)* it's high time (11)

eng tight, close (15)

enttäuscht disappointed (7)

die Erfrischungen *(pl.)* refreshments (12)

erlogen; erstunken und erlogen *(sl.)* a lot of bull (11)

F

fad *(coll.)* S boring, dull (14)

der Fang; ein guter Fang *(coll.)* a good catch (9)

das Faßl, -n *(coll.)* S small keg (14)

der Fatzke, -s *(sl.)* N real hot shot (11)

das Faultierfilet, -s filet of sloth (1)

der Feigling, -e coward (R 11–15)

das Fell, -e; ein dickes Fell haben *(coll.)* to have a thick skin (11)

das Fett fat (9)

die Fettwanze, -n *(sl.)* S lard-ass (3)

fetzen; laß uns mal ordentlich einen fetzen gehen *(sl.)* N let's have some real fun (15)

die Fetzen *(pl. coll.)* rags (clothes) (6); **daß d'Fetzen fliag'n (fliegen)** *(sl.)* S like you wouldn't believe it (14)

fetzig *(sl.)* N super (2)

die Feuerwehr fire department (14)

finden, a, u; find' ich ja auch! *(coll.)* right you are! you got it! (7)

fix und fertig *(coll.)* all done in, pooped (10)

die Flamme, -n *(coll.)* flame, love (3)

das Fliegengewicht, -e *(coll.)* wimp (4)

flitzen; 'rausflitzen *(sl.)* S to bolt (14)

flöten gehen *(sl.)* to be gone, done in (2)

flott smart, fast (6)

flunkern *(coll.)* N to fib (6)

das Frauenzimmer, – *(coll.)* broad (6)

frech fresh, bitchy (15)

die Fregatte, -n; aufgetakelt wie 'ne alte Fregatte *(sl.)* N decked out like a Christmas tree (15)

freilich; no freilich *(coll.)* S you bet (14)

die Fressalien *(pl. coll.)* food, eats (12)

die Fresse, -n *(vulg.)* N mug (4)

das Freßproblem, -e *(coll.)* eating problem (3)

der Freßsack, ⁻e glutton (1)

die Frikadelle, -n hamburger (4)

die Füaß (Füße) *(pl.);* **kalte Füaß krieg'n** *(sl.)* S to get cold feet (3)

G

der Ganove, -n *(sl.)* N crook (9)

garnix *(coll.)* S nothing at all (14)

die Gaudi; immer a Hetz und a Gaudi *(sl.)* S always chipper (12)

das Gebrüll screaming, noise (14)

gehn's (gehen Sie) *(coll.)* S come on, go on! (8)

gehörig properly (11)

geil *(sl.)* terrific (lit.: horny) (2)

der Geizkragen, ⁻ *(coll.)* miser (11)

geliefert *(coll.)* done for (13)

gepfeffert *(coll.)* wild, outta sight (12)

das Gerücht, -e rumor (6)

gescheit smart, bright (15)

das Geselchte *(coll.)* S smoked meat (7)

s. g'fretten *(sl.)* S to do without (7)

das Gift poison (12); **da kannst du Gift drauf nehmen** *(coll.)* you can bet your sweet life (5)

die Giftnudel, -n *(sl.)* S bitch (3)

der Grabstein, -e tombstone (5)

das Gras; ins Gras beißen *(coll.)* to kick the bucket (13)

großzügig generous (1)

grüßen; grüß dich! *(coll.)* hi!

die Grütze; Grütze im Kopf haben *(coll.)* N to have horse sense (9)

g'schmalz'n *(sl.)* S expensive; **das ist ja g'schmalz'n** *(sl.)* S this is highway robbery (1)

g'schnallt (schnallen); er hat's g'schnallt *(sl.)* S he swallowed it (1)

g'spaßig; Sie sind so g'spaßig *(sl.)* you are a scream (12)

die Gurke, -n cucumber (7)

die Güte; ach du meine Güte! *(coll.)* holy Moses! (5)

H

die Haare *(pl.);* **Haare auf den Zähnen haben** *(coll.)* to have a mean temper (2)

das Hackfleisch; aus dir mach' ich Hackfleisch *(sl.)* I'll make mincemeat out of you (4)

der Hafen, ⁻; in den Hafen der Ehe einlaufen *(coll.)* to get hitched (2)

der Hallodri, -s *(sl.)* S jerk, rat (3)

der Hals; dann hast du die am Hals *(coll.)* then you have her on your back (5); **Hals über Kopf** *(coll.)* headlong, in a rush (9)

halt *(adv. particle);* **da kann ma (man) halt nix (nichts) machen** *(coll.)* S sorry, there's nothing one can do about it (12)

der Hampelmann, ⁻er *(coll.)* jellyfish (4)

die Hand, ⁻e; für jn. die Hand ins Feuer legen *(coll.)* to stick up for s.o., to stake one's life on s.o. (9)

häßlich ugly (13)
hauen to hit (4)
der Haufen, – heap, pile (10)
der Hausdrache, -n *(coll.)* shrew, nagging woman (7)
der (die) Hax'n *(sl.)* S foot, leg (14)
heikel sensitive, finicky (5)
helfen, a, o; ich kann mir net (nicht) helfen *(coll.)* S I can't help it (5)
das Hendl, -n *(coll.)* S chicken (12)
die Herrschaften *(pl.)* ladies and gentlemen (14)
her·schauen; da schau her! *(coll.)* S I'm bowled over! What do we have here! (8)
das Heu hay (14)
hinaus·schmeißen, i, i *(coll.)* to throw out (11)
hin·ballern *(sl.)* to belt (4)
der Hintern *(sl.)* ass; **ist dir's Gehirn in den Hintern gerutscht?** *(vulg.)* have you got your head up your ass? (10)
s. hoch·rappeln *(coll.)* N to pick oneself up (13)
hocken to sit, squat (12)
der Holzkopp (Holzkopf, ⁀e *(sl.)* N noggin (4)
das Honiglecken; es ist kein Honiglecken *(coll.)* it is no ball (2)
der Hopfen; an ihm ist Hopfen und Malz verloren *(coll.)* he's a lost cause (9)
die Hose, -n; die Hosen voll haben *(sl.)* to be scared, to have a guilty conscience (9)
der Husten cough (15)
die Hütte, -n cottage (14)

I

impfen to vaccinate (6)

J

Jessasna! *(sl.)* S I'm floored, you don't say (8)
der Jux *(coll.)* S joke, trick (12)

K

das Kalbl, -n (Kalb, ⁀er) *(coll.)* S calf (14)
der Kalbsfuß, ⁀e calf's foot (R 11–15)
der Karpfen, – carp (fish) (12)
die Kasse, -n cash register; **knapp bei Kasse sein** *(coll.)* to be broke (1); **das reißt ein Loch in die Kasse** *(coll.)* that's real steep (12)
der Kater, – tomcat; hangover (R 11–15)
der Kerl, -e *(coll.)* guy (11)
das Kiekerchen, – *(sl.)* N eye (4)
kiel·holen *(sl.)* N to beat the shit out of s.o. (4)
das Kittchen, – *(coll.)* jail (2)
die Klamotten *(pl. sl.)* clothes, duds (6)
die Klamüser *(pl. sl.)* N clothes, duds (6)
der Klotz, ⁀e *(coll.)* klutz (15)
klug clever (4)
knackig *(coll.)* N attractive, cute, hefty (13, 15)
knapp; knapp bei Kasse sein *(coll.)* to be broke (1)
die Knete *(sl.)* N money (2)
das Knie, -e; jn. übers Knie legen *(sl.)* to give s.o. a good licking (15)
die Kniekehlen *(pl.); mir hängt der Magen in den Kniekehlen** *(sl.)* I'm starved (1)
der Knochen, – bone (4)
die Knolle, -n *(sl.)* N nose (13)
knorke *(sl.)* N great, cool (8)
die Knospe, -n flower bud (12)
der Knülch, -e *(sl.)* N guy; fart (13)
ködern to bait, to catch (9)
der Koffer, – suitcase (9)

der **Kohldampf; Kohldampf haben** (*coll.*) N to be hungry (13)

Kokolores; so'n Kokolores! (*sl.*) N what a waste! what a grind! (8)

der **Köm** (*sl.*) N booze (13)

können; du kannst mich . . . (*vulg.*) you know what *you* can do (8)

der **Kotzbrocken, –** (*sl.*) piece of vomit (4)

die **Kreide; in der Kreid'n stecken** (*sl.*) S to be in the red (12)

kriegen to get (1)

die **Kröten** (*pl. sl.*) N money (2)

die **Kuchl (Küche), -n** (*coll.*) S kitchen (14)

der **Kuckuck; den Kuckuck nicht mehr schreien hören** (*sl.*) to be k.o.'d for keeps (13)

die **Kugel, -n** sphere (7)

die **Kuh, ̈e** cow (14)

das **Kunststück, -e; kein Kunststück** (*coll.*) piece of cake (3)

L

lachen; daß i' net lach'! (*sl.*) S thanks but no thanks (8)

der **Laden, ̈** store, shop (12)

der **Lauaffe, -n** (*sl.*) pushover (9)

der **Laufpaß, ̈sse; jm. den Laufpaß geben** (*coll.*) to send s.o. packing, to blow s.o. off (9)

die **Laus, ̈e** louse (4)

lausen; mich laust der Affe (*sl.*) N I'll be damned (8)

das **Leben; wie's blühende Leben** (*coll.*) alive and kicking (5)

die **Lebensmittel** (*pl.*) food (12)

die **Leber** liver (14); **ist dir was über die Leber gelaufen?** (*coll.*) what's come over you? (10)

lecker; das wäre lecker (*coll.*) N that would hit the spot (13)

ledig single, unmarried (2)

leiden, i, i; ich kann ihn nicht leiden I can't stand him (9)

die **Leine, -n; Leine ziehen** (*sl.*) N to take a hike, to beat it (9)

Leo; wie Geist Leo (*sl.*) N like death warmed over (13)

lichterloh (*adv.*) burning wildly (14)

das **Lied, -er; ich kann ein Lied davon singen** (*coll.*) I can tell you a thing or two about this (9)

die **Litfaßsäule, -n** large cylindrical billboard (6)

das **Loch, ̈er; aus'm letzten Loch pfeifen** (*coll.*) to be on one's last leg (13)

der **Löffel, –; den Löffel ab·geben, a, e** (*sl.*) N to be grounded for good (13)

der **Lulatsch, -e** (*coll.*) N lamppost (tall man) (13)

M

macht nix (nichts) (*coll.*) S it doesn't matter (1)

der **Macker, –** (*sl.*) N klutz (15)

das **Madl, -n (Mädchen)** (*coll.*) S girl (14)

der **Magen, ̈** stomach (1)

das **Malz; an ihm ist Hopfen und Malz verloren** (*coll.*) he's a lost cause (9)

die **Mammutkeule, -n** mammoth loin (1)

das **Männeken, – (Männchen)** (*sl.*) N little man, little guy (8)

die **Marille, -n; einen Wurm in der Marille haben** (*sl.*) S to be zonked out (8)

die **Mauldiarrhöe** (*sl.*) verbal diarrhea (6)

das **Mehl** flour (13)

die **Mehlspeis'** (*coll.*) S dessert (R 11–15)

die **Milch; da stockt mir die Milch** (*sl.*) N I'm bowled over (8)

der Mistkerl, -e *(sl.)* S slippery
louse, rat (3)
das Moos *(coll.)* N money (2)
das Mordsproblem, -e *(sl.)* huge
problem (10)
der Mordsradau *(sl.)* mean racket
(14)
**das Mordsschwein, -e; ein
Mordsschwein haben** *(sl.)* to get
all the breaks, to be very lucky (7,
14)
der Most *(coll.)* S hard cider,
moonshine (14)
Möwendreck! *(sl.)* N thunbs down!
like hell! (8)

N

**der Narr, -en; jn. zum Narr'n
halten** *(coll.)* S to rib s.o. (7)
narrisch; jn. narrisch machen
(sl.) S to drive s.o. nuts (8)
nebenraus hauen *(sl.)* S to fool
around (10)
nee nanu! *(sl.)* N I'm floored (8)
**'neinziehen, o, o (hineinziehen);
s. etw. 'neinziehen** *(sl.)* S to stuff
one's face (1)
nix (nichts) *(coll.)* S nothing (7); **is'
nix** *(sl.)* S nothing doing, tough
luck (15)
null; ich hab' null Ahnung *(sl.)*
search me (9)
nullkommanix (in . . .) *(coll.)* in
no time (4)
**die Nummer, -n; auf Nummer
sicher gehen** *(coll.)* to make
absolutely certain (5)
nummerieren to number (4)
die Nuß, ˙˙sse; in die Nüsse gehen
(sl.) N to kick the bucket (6)

O

**der Ochs, -en; wie der Ochs
vor'm Berg stehen** *(coll.)* S to be
stumped (10)

**das Ohr, -en; es faustdick hinter
den Ohren haben** *(coll.)* to be a
sly dog (11)
olle *(sl.)* N old (13)

P

pampig *(coll.)* N snotty (4)
passieren to happen (14)
patschnaß *(coll.)* dripping wet (3)
die Pause, -n; bei mir Pause *(sl.)*
N count me out (8)
das Pech *(coll.)* bad luck, bummer
(6)
**der Pfannkuchen, –; aufgehen
wie ein Pfannkuchen** *(coll.)*
swell up (get fat) like a balloon
(3)
**der Pfeifendeckel, –; ja,
Pfeifendeckel!** *(sl.)* N thanks, but
no thanks (8)
das Pfund pound (13)
der Piefke, -s *(sl.)* (derogatory term
applied to North Germans by
South Germans) "big mouth" (8)
piekfein; piekfein aussehen *(coll.)*
N to look spiffy, to look like a
straight arrow (9)
piepen *(coll.)* to chirp (4)
die Pille, -n pill (8)
die Plattenspielernadel, -n
phonograph needle (6)
die Pleite; Pleite machen *(coll.)* N
to go broke (2)
plietsch *(sl.)* N smart, clever (9)
polieren; jm. die Fresse polieren
(sl.) N to smack s.o. in the teeth
(4)
polstern; mit Geld gepolstert sein
(coll.) N to be well-heeled (2)
prima *(coll.)* great, tops (7)
**pudelwohl; ich fühl' mich
pudelwohl** *(coll.)* I feel like a
million bucks (5)
der Pump; auf Pump *(sl.)* on credit
(12)

pumperlg'sund *(coll.)* S fit as a fiddle (5)

das Püppchen, – *(coll.)* N little doll (15)

die Pupille, -n pupil (eye) (4)

Pustekuchen! *(sl.)* N rubbish! (8)

Q

quatsch! *(sl.)* no way! rubbish! (8)

quitt *(coll.)* even (12)

R

das Radieschen, – radish (13); **er sieht die Radieschen von unten wachsen** *(sl.)* N he is pushing up the daisies (13)

der Rand, ⸚er; außer Rand und Band sein *(coll.)* to be all shook up (10)

s. 'ran·machen an *(sl.)* to sidle up to s.o. (9)

ratschen *(sl.)* S to gab (7)

'raus·kriegen *(coll.)* to move s.t. out of s.t. (14)

rechtzeitig in time (14)

'rein·hauen; reinhauen wie ein Scheunendrescher *(sl.)* S to eat like a horse (1)

'rein·legen (jn.) *(coll.)* to cheat, sucker s.o. (11)

riechen to smell (13)

'rum·gondeln *(coll.)* to drive around aimlessly (3)

'rum·schnüffeln *(coll.)* to snoop around (7)

rüstig sound, healthy (14)

S

das Sabbermaul, ⸚er *(sl.)* N dweeb (4)

saftig juicy (4)

sagen; was d' net sagst! *(coll.)* S you don't say! (7)

san (sind) *(sl.)* S are (to be) (14)

saublöd; saublöd daher·reden *(sl.)* S to talk rubbish (5)

saudumm *(sl.)* S very dumb (3)

der Saukerl, -e *(vulg.)* sleazeball (11)

Saures; gib ihm Saures! *(sl.)* N let him have it (11)

das Schach chess (7)

die Scheibe, -n disk (15)

scheißegal; das is' mir scheißegal *(vulg.)* I couldn't care less (8)

der Scheißkerl, -e *(vulg.)* bastard (8)

der Scheunendrescher, –; 'reinhauen wie ein Scheunendrescher *(sl.)* S eat like a horse (1)

schießen, o, o; zum Schießen *(sl.)* a scream (15)

der Schimmer; keinen blassen Schimmer haben *(coll.)* to have no idea (7)

Schiß kriegen *(vulg.)* to get spooked, scared (7)

der Schlager, – hit (mus.) (1)

der Schlauberger, – *(coll.)* smartass (9)

der Schmarr'n; an (einen) Schmarr'n! *(sl.)* S like hell! thumbs down! (8)

die Schnalle, -n buckle (3)

der Schnellschritt, -e; dich vernasch ich im Schnellschritt *(sl.)* N I'll cream you in a sec (4)

die Schnulze, -n *(coll.)* schmaltzy tune, film, etc. (15)

der Schnupfen, – cold (15)

das Schnupptuch (Schnupftuch), ⸚er hankie (4)

schnurstracks *(coll.)* S immediately (5)

die Schnute, -n *(sl.)* N trap (mouth) (6)

der Schrank, ⸚e closet (6)

die Schuld debt (12)

der Schupfen (Schuppen), – *(sl.)* S barn, shed (14, 15)

die Schuppen *(pl.)* dandruff, scales (15) (s. also Schupfen)

der Schuß, ∹sse; einen Schuß haben *(sl.)* to be touched in the head (7)

schwafeln *(sl.)* S to yap, to gab (5, 6)

das Schwein, -e; mehr Schwein als Verstand haben *(coll.)* S to be a lucky dog (10)

der Schweinebraten, – pork roast (1)

schwummerig strange, miserable (15)

selig (lit.: blessed); **wer's glaubt, wird selig** *(coll.)* S my eye! (7)

die Sorgen *(pl.)* worries (12)

der Sozius *(coll.)* S back seat (of a bike) (3)

die Spätzündung; haste (hast du) Spätzündung? *(sl.)* N slow on the uptake? not all there? (8)

der Speck bacon (7)

sperren to close (14)

der Spezi, – *(sl.)* S friend, buddy (7)

der Spieß, -e; ein Gebrüll wie am Spieß *(sl.)* some gosh-awful screaming (14)

spottbillig *(coll.)* dirt-cheap (12)

die Spucke; mir bleibt die Spucke weg *(sl.)* N it boggles the mind (8)

die Spur, -en; ka (keine) Spur! *(sl.)* S rubbish! no way! (8)

das Stahlroß, ∹sser *(coll.)* (motor)bike (3)

der Stall, ∹e stable (14)

stecken; laß mal stecken! *(sl.)* N forget it! (15)

der Stein, -e; mir fallt (fällt) ein großer Stein vom Herzen *(coll.)* that's a big load off my chest (5)

der Stich, -e; einen Stich haben *(coll.)* to be not quite fresh (food) (1)

der Stiefel, –; Stiefel 'zam (zusammen) reden *(sl.)* S to talk nonsense (10)

stören to disturb (15)

stoßen, ie, o push, shove, squeeze (4)

stramm snappy, hefty (15)

der Streifen, –; da drüben laufen Streifen *(coll.)* N there's a cinema over there (8)

der Strizzi, – *(sl.)* S chum, rascal (10)

strohdumm *(sl.)* stupid, dumb as straw (7)

das Stückl, -n *(coll.)* S small piece (1)

s. stürzen (in) to rush (into) (9)

der Stuß; Stuß reden *(sl.)* to talk nonsense (3)

der Sündenbock, ∹e scapegoat (10)

süß *(adj.)*; **ein süßes Püppchen** *(sl.)* N a sweet little cat (15)

T

das Tannenholz; nach Tannenholz riechen *(coll.)* N to smell of pine used for coffins, to be a goner (13)

die Tasche, -n pocket (10)

taub deaf (3)

die Tinte; in der Tint'n sitzen *(coll.)* S to be in the soup (10)

toll *(coll.)* great, wonderful (9)

der Totschläger, – blackjack (7)

die Tour; in einer Tour *(coll.)* all the time (3)

der Traatschfimmel *(sl.)* N gabbing fit (6)

der Trabbel *(sl.)* N difficulties (2)

das Trankl *(sl.)* S drink (R 11–15)

tratschen *(coll.)* to gab, gossip (6)

die Traube, -n grape (12)

treten, a, e to step, kick (14)

der Tritt, -e kick (4)

tröpferlweis' *(sl.)* S little by little (12)

'tschuldigen (entschuldigen) Sie excuse me (1)

turnen to do gymnastics (R 11–15)

die Tussi, -s *(sl.)* N dame (15)

das Tuttchen, – *(coll.)* N dreamboat (6)

U

ulkig *(coll.)* N funny, a scream (15)

unlängst *(coll.)* the other day (1)

s. unterhalten, ie, a to have a good time (10)

V

verarschen *(vulg.)* to make fun of s.o. (1)

das Verdauungsproblem, -e digestive disorder (13)

verderben, a, o to ruin, spoil (3)

s. verdrücken *(coll.)* to beat it, to sneak out (2)

vergnügt happy, cheerful (15)

verhaften to arrest (3)

s. verkrümeln *(sl.)* N to do a vanishing act (2)

vermachen to hand down (3)

vermasseln *(sl.)* N to mess up (3)

vernaschen to waste (4)

s. verplappern *(coll.)* to open one's mouth too wide (6)

versauen; das hat er mir gründlich versaut *(sl.)* he really loused it up for me (15)

verschossen sein (in jm.) *(coll.)* to be nuts (about s.o.) (6)

verschütt' gehen *(sl.)* N to become lost (10)

verschwiegen discreet (6)

versengen to singe, scorch (14)

versetzen to pawn (12)

verspeisen to eat up (1)

der Verstand; da steht mir der Verstand still *(coll.)* I'm flabbergasted (8)

s. versündigen; versündigen Sie sich nicht! *(coll.)* S don't even say that! (12)

vertrauen to trust (11)

vertuckeln *(sl.)* N to stash away (2)

die Verwandten *(pl.)* relatives (1)

s. verziehen, o, o *(sl.)* to get lost (4)

die Verzweiflung despair (1)

der Vogel, ∸; einen Vogel haben *(sl.)* to be crazy (15)

vor·kommen, a, o to appear, seem (5)

W

der Wahnsinn; das ist ja Wahnsinn! *(coll.)* now I've heard everything (8)

das Waisenkind, -er orphan (11)

der Waschlappen, – *(coll.)* wimp (3)

der Wecker, –; jm. auf'n Wecker gehen *(sl.)* to go on s.o.'s nerves (7)

weg *(adv.)* away, gone (10)

das Weib, -er *(sl.)* woman (9)

das Weibsbild, -er *(coll.)* woman, wife (7)

das Weibsstück, -e *(coll.)* babe (13)

das Weichei, -er *(sl.)* sissy (9)

weit; wenn's so weit ist *(coll.)* at that point (3)

die Wiese, -n meadow (10)

der Wonneproppen, – *(coll.)* N idol, jewel, centerfold (6)

der Wurf, ∸e throw, cast (15)

der Würfel, – cube (12)

der Wurm, ∸er worm (8)

die Wurscht (Wurst), ∸e; es geht um die Wurscht *(coll.)* S it's do or die (3)

die Wut; seine Wut in sich hinein·fressen, a, e *(coll.)* to swallow one's anger (11)

Z

der Zahn, ⸚e; den schmerzt kein Zahn mehr *(sl.)* he is done for (13)

der Zaster *(sl.)* N money (2)

der Zaun, ⸚e fence (garden) (14)

die Zeit, -en; du liebe Zeit! *(coll.)* look at that! (12)

die Ziege, -n goat (3)

der Zunder *(coll.)* tinder (14)

ziehen, o, o; ich zieh' dir eine *(sl.)* N I'll thrash you (4)

die Zunge, -n; eine spitze Zunge haben *(coll.)* to have a malicious tongue (6)

zu·riegeln to lock up (12)

zusammen·kratzen *(coll.)* S to cough up (10)

zu·sperren to close (12)

zutzeln *(sl.)* S to suck (drink) (3)

der Zwirnsfaden, ⸚; dünn wie ein Zwirnsfaden *(coll.)* S skinny as a birdleg (3)

English-German

A

airhead der Blubberheini *(sl.)* N (4)

anyway eh *(coll.)* S (3)

arrow; he looks like a straight arrow er sieht piekfein aus *(coll.)* N (9)

ass der Hintern *(sl.)* N (4)

B

back; you got her on your back du hast sie am Hals *(coll.)* S (5)

bankruptcy die Pleite (Pleite machen) *(coll.)* (2)

to bark bellen (7)

to bawl out s.o. jm. aufs Dach steigen *(coll.)* (11)

beans; to spill the beans (mit etw.) aus·packen *(coll.)* N (6)

to beat; I'll beat the shit out of you kiel·holen müßte man dich *(sl.)* N; du kriegst 'ne saftige Abreibung *(sl.)* N (4)

to belt hin·ballern *(sl.)* N (4)

to bet; you bet! no freilich! *(coll.)* S (14); **you can bet your sweet life** da kannst du Gift drauf nehmen *(coll.)* (5)

billboard die Litfaßsäule, -n (6)

bird; like some big-assed bird daß d'Fetzen fliegen *(sl.)* S (14)

bitch die Giftnudl, -n *(sl.)* S (3)

to blast vertrimmen *(sl.)* N (4)

to blather ratschen *(coll.)* S (7)

booze der Köm *(sl.)* N; **how about some booze?** haste Bock auf'n Köm? *(sl.)* N (13)

boring fad *(sl.)* S (14)

boy; little boy das Bubi, -s *(coll.)* S (5)

to brag about (s.) dick·tun, a, a, mit *(sl.)* (6)

break; to get all the breaks (ein) Mordsschwein haben *(sl.)* (7)

broad das Frauenzimmer, – *(coll.)* (6)

bucket; to kick the bucket in die Nüsse gehen *(sl.)* N; ab·kratzen *(sl.)* (6)

bull; a lot of bull erstunken und erlogen *(sl.)* (11)

bum; he is a lazy no-good bum er ist ein stinkfaules Aas *(sl.)* (9)

bunk; don't give me that bunk reden's net so deppert daher *(sl.)* S (8)

to burn; it burns me up ich muß meine Wut in mich hinein·fressen, a, e *(coll.)* (11)

butterball die Blunz'n, – *(sl.)* S (3)

C

cause; he is a lost cause an ihm ist Hopfen und Malz verloren *(coll.)* (9)

cheap (very) spottbillig *(coll.)* (12)

Christmas tree; decked out like a Christmas tree aufgetakelt wie 'ne alte Fregatte *(sl.)* N (15)

chum der Spezi, – *(sl.)* S (7); der Strizzi, – *(sl.)* S (10)

to come; what's come over you? was is' dir über die Leber gelaufen? *(coll.)* (10)

conscience; is your conscience bothering you? hast was ausg'fress'n? *(sl.)* S (10)

cool geil *(sl.)* (2)

to cooperate; my feet won't
  cooperate die Füße wollen nicht
  so recht mit *(coll.)* (15)
corpse; this is wasting a corpse
  das ist Leichenschändung *(coll.)*
  (4)
to crack up; that really cracks me
  up das ist ja zum Beömmeln *(sl.)*
  N (8)
to cream (thrash) vernaschen *(sl.)*
  (4)
to croak ab·kratzen *(sl.)* (5)

D

damn you! Kruzitürken! *(sl.)* S
  (8)
death; he looks like death
  warmed over er sieht aus wie
  Geist Leo *(sl.)* N (13)
decked out aufgetakelt *(sl.)* N (15)
devil; the poor devil das arme
  Luder *(sl.)* (13)
difficulties Trabbel *(pl. sl.)* (2)
discreet verschwiegen (6)
to do; you know what *you* can do
  du kannst mich auch *(vulg.)* (8);
  he has to make do er muß sich
  g'fretten *(sl.)* S (7); done for
  geliefert *(sl.)* (13); do or die es
  geht um die Wurscht *(coll.)* S (3)
dope (idiot) der Depp, -en *(sl.)* S; to
  be a dope strohdumm sein *(coll.)*
  (7)
dopey dusselig *(sl.)* N; deppert *(sl.)* S
  (9)
double; on the double in
  nullkommanix *(coll.)* S (7)
dough (money) der Zaster, der
  Kies, die Knete, die Kröten *(pl.)*,
  das Moos, die Moneten *(pl.)*, das
  Pinkepinke *(all sl.)* N (2)

E

eye; my eye! wer's glaubt, wird selig
  (coll.) (7)

F

feedbag; let's put on the feedbag
  laß uns was zwischen die
  Beißerchen schieben *(sl.)* N (13)
to feel; I felt out of it ich hatte null
  Bock auf nichts *(sl.)* N (15); I feel
  like a million bucks ich fühl'
  mich pudelwohl *(coll.)* S (5)
to find out 'raus·kriegen *(coll.)* (10)
finicky heikel (5)
fit; fit as a fiddle pumperlg'sund
  (coll.) S (5)
food die Fressalien *(pl. sl.)* (12)
foot die (der) Hax'n, – *(sl.)* S (14)
to forget; forget it! laß mal stecken!
  (sl.) N (15)
fun; let's have some real fun laß
  uns mal ordentlich einen fetzen
  gehen *(sl.)* N (15)

G

to gab tratschen *(coll.)* (6); gabbing
  disease der Traatschfimmel *(sl.)*
  N (6)
game; he won't play games with
  me bei mir muß er da früher
  aufstehen *(coll.)* N (11)
to get; get outta here! red kan
  (keinen) Stuß! (lit.: don't talk
  nonsense) *(sl.)* S (3)
to get caught; they all got caught
  die hat's alle erwischt *(sl.)* S (14)
to get lost s. verziehen, o, o *(sl.)* N
  (4)
getup der Aufzug *(coll.)* (1)
goner; the guy's a goner der Kerl
  riecht nach Tannenholz *(sl.)* N (13)
gosh; by gosh! Kruzifix! *(sl.)* S (14)
grind; what a grind! so'n
  Kokolores! *(sl.)* N (8)
to ground; grounded for good den
  wird kein Zahn mehr schmerzen,
  der hat den Löffel abgegeben *(sl.)*
  N (13)
guy der Kerl, -e *(coll.)* (9)

H

half; that's not half of it das is' noch garnix *(sl.)* S (14)

hankie das Schnupptuch, ¨-er (Schnupftuch) *(coll.)* N (4)

heap; a heap of money ein Haufen Geld *(coll.)* (10)

heavy; a heavy problem ein Mordsproblem *(sl.)* (10)

heck; what the heck was der Geier, was zum Teufel *(coll.)* (10)

hefty knackig *(sl.)* (15)

hell; he can go to hell er kann mir den Buckl 'runter·rutschen *(sl.)* S (3)

to hike; to take a hike (beat it) Leine ziehen, o, o *(sl.)* N (9)

honest? no geh! *(coll.)* S (10)

horse; I could eat a horse ich hab'n Kohldampf bis unter die Arme *(sl.)* N (13)

hotshot; a tricky hotshot ein ausgekochter Fatzke *(sl.)* N (11)

hunger der Kohldampf *(sl.)* (13)

I

immediately schnurstracks *(coll.)* (5)

to inflict; to be inflicted with leiden, i, i an etw. (6)

J

jail das Kittchen, – *(coll.)* N (2)

jam (to be in) der Trabbel *(sl.)* N (2)

jumpy; to make s.o. jumpy jm. auf'n Wecker gehen *(sl.)* (7)

K

to kick; I could kick myself ich könnte mich selber übers Knie legen *(coll.)* (15)

to kill; you are killing me! du machst mich fix und fertig! *(coll.)* (10)

to knock it off s. ab·regen *(sl.)* (8)

L

lady; my old lady meine Alte *(coll.)* (2, 10)

lamppost (tall man) der Lulatsch *(sl.)* N (13)

leg; he's on his last leg er pfeift aus'm letzten Loch *(sl.)* (13)

line; to feed s.o. a line jm. an (einen) Kas (Käse) erzählen *(sl.)* S (7)

little; little by little tröpferlweis' *(sl.)* S (12)

load; this takes a big load off my mind mir fällt ein großer Stein vom Herzen *(coll.)* (5)

louse; slippery louse der Mistkerl, -e *(sl.)* S (3)

M

man; little man das Männeken (Männchen), – *(sl.)* N (8)

meathead der Hirnie, -s *(sl.)* (4)

to mess up vermasseln *(sl.)* (3)

mishap; marital mishap der Eheschlamassel, der Ehetrouble *(coll.)* (9, 10)

money das Moos *(coll.)* N (2) (see also "dough"); **to have money to burn** Geld wie Dreck haben *(sl.)* (11)

Montezuma's revenge das Dünnschißproblem, -e *(vulg.)* (13)

morning; good morning! grüaß (grüß) Gott! *(sl.)* S (14)

N

nerd der Depp, -en *(sl.)* S (3)

nothing nix (nichts) *(coll.)* S (1)

nuts; to be nuts about s.o. in jn. verschossen sein *(coll.)* (6)

O

obnoxious; did he seem that obnoxious to you? habt ihr ihn nicht verdauen können? *(sl.)* N (9)

old olle *(sl.)* N (8)
ornery bockig *(coll.)* (9)
overjoyed; he is overjoyed es macht ihm eine helle Freude *(coll.)* (14)

P

pants; now you got me with my pants down da soll mich der Klabautermann holen! *(sl.)* N (8)
to pay; to pay off in installments abstottern *(coll.)* (12)
pest; he's a pest der ist zum Abgewöhnen *(sl.)* (15)
to pick up; can't he pick himself up? kann er sich nicht hochrappeln? *(coll.)* N (13)
pussycat das Tuttchen, –, der Wonneproppen, –, das Schnackeduzchen, – *(all sl.)* N (6)

R

real(ly) *(adv.)* echt *(coll.)* (2)
red; in the red in der Kreid'n *(sl.)* S (12)
respect; in this respect in der Beziehung (5)
rotten beknackt *(sl.)* (2)
round; round the clock wie aufzog'n (aufgezogen) *(coll.)* S (7)
rubbish! Pustekuchen! *(sl.)* N (8)
to ruin; you've really ruined it for me das hast du mir gründlich versaut *(sl.)* (15)

S

to say; you can say that again! na und ob! *(coll.)* (7)
scarce; they are very scarce die kann man (sich) an einer Hand abzählen *(coll.)* (9)
scream; a gosh-awful scream ein Gebrüll wie am Spieß *(sl.)* (14)
second; in a sec im Schnellschritt *(sl.)* (4)

to see; what he sees is what he gets er kriegt, was er siacht (sieht) *(sl.)* S (3)
sense; makes sense Logo! *(sl.)* (7)
shnook; to be a poor shnook arm dran sein (6)
sick; are you sick? geht's dir net (nicht) gut? *(coll.)* S (5)
sideline; he is sidelined in my book bei mir ist er abgemeldet *(sl.)* (11)
to sit (in the pen) hocken (im Kittchen) *(coll.)* N (2)
skinny; skinny as a birdleg dünn wie ein Zwirnsfaden *(coll.)* S (3)
skull; you are outta your skull du hast 'nen Vogel *(sl.)* (15)
sleazeball der Saukerl, -e *(vulg.)* S (11)
to snoop around rum·schnüffeln *(coll.)* N (7)
snotty pampig *(sl.)* N (4); **don't get snotty with me** tun's Ihnen net (nicht) auf·pudeln *(sl.)* S (8)
to split (run off) durch·gehen, i, a *(coll.)* (2)
spot; this hits the spot (food) das ist lecker *(coll.)* N (13)
to squeeze; I'll squeeze you out of your suit (I'll skin you alive) dich stoß' ich aus'm Anzuch (Anzug) *(sl.)* N (4)
to steal; he stole it er hat es mitgehen lassen *(coll.)* (10)
to stick up for s.o. für jn. die Hand ins Feuer legen *(coll.)* (9)
stupid doof *(sl.)*; deppert *(sl.)* S (4)
to suck (drink) zutzeln *(sl.)* S (3)
super *(adj.)* fetzig *(sl.)* (2)
sweetie das Bubi, das Hasi, das Mausi, das Schatzi, Süßer *(m.)*, das Schnucki *(coll.)* (5)
to swell up (like a balloon) auf·gehen, i, a (wie ein Pfannkuchen) *(coll.)* S (3)

T

to think; I just thought ich hab' mir halt 'denkt (gedacht) *(sl.)* S (14)

to throw out; to throw s.o. out on his ass jn. achtkantig hinaus·schmeißen, i, i *(sl.)* N (11)

time; it's high time es ist höchste Eisenbahn *(coll.)* (11)

tinder der Zunder (14)

to transfer ab·schieben, o, o *(coll.)* (2)

tricky ausgekocht *(sl.)* (11)

turn; at every turn wo man geht und steht *(coll.)* (6)

W

waiter der Ober, –, der Kellner, – (1)

wall; this drives me up the wall es ist zum Auswachsen *(coll.)* (11)

wet; dripping wet patschnaß *(coll.)* S (3)

wimp der Waschlappen, – *(coll.)* N (3)

wonderful toll *(coll.)* N (2)

to worry; don't worry! machen's Ihnen nix (nichts) draus! *(sl.)* S (14)

Y

to yap klatschen *(coll.)* N (6); schwafeln *(sl.)* S (5)

Z

zonked out der hat an (einen) Wurm in der Marill'n *(sl.)* S (8)

Guide to Thesaurus

Thesaurus
Colloquial and Slang German

The following is a list of German expressions that can be used to express the concepts in each English heading. The standard German translation of each heading is given in parentheses. You will also find literal translations for most of the expressions. They should help you to determine their correct usage.

ADMIT, to *(zugeben)*

auspacken, *v. (coll.)* admit, *(lit.)* unpack.
ausspucken, *v. (coll.)* confess, *(lit.)* spit out the truth.
die Karten offen auf den Tisch legen, *exp.* to confess, *(lit.)* to lay one's cards open on the table.
die Katze aus dem Sack lassen, *exp.* to let the cat out of the bag.
eine Lippe riskieren, *exp.* to admit, *(lit.)* to risk a lip.
Farbe bekennen, *exp.* to show one's color.
klaren (or **reinen**) **Wein einschenken,** *exp.* to speak plainly, *(lit.)* to pour sb. clear wine.
mit offenen Karten spielen, *exp.* to confess, *(lit.)* to play with open cards.
verplappern, *v. (coll.)* make a slip of the tongue.
jm. nichts vormachen, *exp.* not to lie to sb.

ALCOHOL *(Alkohol)*
(See: **DRINK ALCOHOL, to**)

Dröhnung, *f. (coll.)* strong alcohol.
eine Buddel Rum, *exp. (sl.)* a bottle of rum.
ein guter Schluck, *exp.* good alcohol, *(lit.)* a good gulp.
ein guter Tropfen, *n.* good wine, *(lit.)* a good drop.
Fusel, *m. (coll.)* bad alcohol.
Gesöff, *n. (coll.)* alcohol.
Klarer, *m.* strong Northern German brandy.
Köm, *m.* strong Northern German brandy.
Kujambelwasser, *n. (sl.)* any kind of decent alcohol.
Rachenputzer, *m. (coll.)* strong alcohol, *(lit.)* throat cleaner.
Schnäpschen, *n.* a small glass of schnaps.
Schnapsdrossel, *f.* person who cares a lot about alcohol, *(lit.)* schnaps thrush.

Sprit, *m.* alcohol.
süffig, *adj.* sweet alcohol.
Wasser, *n.* weak alcohol, *(lit.)* water.
Zielwasser, *n. (sl.)* alcohol, *(lit.)* aiming water; *Note:* hunters' jargon.

AMUSING, to be *(lustig sein)*

Kanaille, *f.* funny person.
Kichererbse, *f.* person who giggles a lot, *(lit.)* giggle pea.
Knalltüte, *f.* funny person.
Nudel, *f.* funny person, *(lit.)* noodle.
schräger Vogel, *exp.* quite a character, *(lit.)* tilted bird.
ulkig, *adj.* funny.
Ulknudel, *f.* funny person.
zum Beömmeln sein, *exp. (sl.)* to be funny.
zum Kaputtlachen sein, *exp. (coll.)* to be funny, *(lit.)* to be breakingly funny.
zum Kringeln sein, *exp. (coll.)* to be funny, *(lit.)* to be curlingly funny.
zum Piepen sein, *exp. (coll.)* to be funny.
zum Schieflachen sein, *exp. (coll.)* to be funny, *(lit.)* to be crookedly funny.
zum Schießen sein, *exp. (coll.)* to be funny, *(lit.)* to be shootingly funny.
zum Schreien sein, *exp. (coll.)* to be funny, *(lit.)* to be screamingly funny.
zum Totlachen sein, *exp. (coll.)* to be funny, *(lit.)* to be dyingly funny.

ANGER *(Ärger)*

an die Decke gehen, *exp.* to be driven up the wall, *(lit.)* to go up to the ceiling.
jn. auf 180 bringen, *exp.* to get sb. mad, *(lit.)* to get sb. up to 180 (degrees).
jn. auf die Palme bringen, *exp.* to drive sb. up the wall, *(lit.)* to bring sb. up the palm tree.
aus der Haut fahren, *exp.* to get angry, *(lit.)* to drive out of one's skin.
ausflippen, *v. (sl.)* flip out, get very angry; *Note:* **ich glaub, ich flipp gleich aus!**/I'm about to get very angry.
ausrasten, *v. (sl.)* flip out, get very angry. *Note:* **ich glaub, ich raste gleich aus!**/I'm about to get very angry.
Dampf ablassen, *exp.* to steam, *(lit.)* to let off steam.
explodieren, *v.* explode.
sich fuchsen, *v.* get mad.
fuchsteufelswild werden, *exp.* to become furious.
jn. gefressen haben, *exp.* to be angry at sb., *(lit.)* to have eaten sb.
geladen, *adj.* be about to explode, *(lit.)* loaded.
sich giften, *v.* get furious, *(lit.)* to poison oneself.
hochgehen, *v.* explode.
sich in den Hintern beißen, *exp. (vulg.)* to get very mad at oneself, *(lit.)* to bite oneself in the behind. *Note:* **Arsch** *(vulg.)* can be substituted for **Hintern.**
in die Luft gehen, *exp.* to explode, *(lit.)* to go up in the air.
jm. läuft die Galle über, *exp. (coll.)* sb.'s blood is boiling, *(lit.)* sb.'s gallbladder is running over.

jm. läuft eine Laus über die Leber, *exp.* to be very angry, *(lit.)* a louse is running over sb.'s liver.

Luft ablassen, *exp.* to get very angry, *(lit.)* to let off air.

jm. platzt der Kragen, *exp.* sb. blew his top, *(lit.)* sb.'s collar burst.

jn. in Rage bringen, *exp.* to make someone mad, *(lit.)* to put sb. into a rage.

jm. reißt der Geduldsfaden, *exp.* sb.'s patience is wearing thin, *(lit.)* sb.'s "patience-thread" is ripping through.

sauer, *adj.* mad, *(lit.)* sour.

sich schwarzärgern, *v. (coll.)* get extremely angry, *(lit.)* get black with anger.

stinkesauer, *adj.* extremely mad, *(lit.)* stinking sour.

Tamtam machen, *exp. (coll.)* to get angry, *(lit.)* to make a to-do.

toben, *v.* rant and rave.

vor Wut kochen, *exp.* to foam at the mouth, *(lit.)* to boil with rage.

vor Wut rauchen, *exp.* to have steam coming out of one's ears, *(lit.)* to smoke with rage.

vor Wut rot werden, *exp.* to turn red with anger.

vor Wut schäumen, *exp.* to foam at the mouth, *(lit.)* to foam with rage.

Zoff machen, *exp. (sl.)* to become angry.

zum Kuckuck nochmal! *exp.* damn it, *(lit.)* to the cuckoo one more time.

jn. zum Mond schießen, *exp. (coll.)* to be mad at sb., *(lit.)* to shoot sb. to the moon.

ANNOYANCE *(Störung)*
(See: **CRAZY, to go**)

sich annerven, *v.* get on each other's nerves, *(lit.)* to nerve each other.

jm. auf das Dach steigen, *exp.* to cause annoyance to sb., *(lit.)* to climb onto sb.'s roof.

jm. auf den Docht gehen, *exp. (coll.)* to piss sb. off, *(lit.)* to step on sb.'s burner.

jm. auf die Eier gehen, *exp. (vulg.)* to piss sb. off, *(lit.)* to step on sb.'s eggs.

jm. auf den Keks gehen, *exp. (coll.)* to piss sb. off, *(lit.)* to step on sb.'s cookie.

auf jm. seinen Nerven herumtrampeln, *exp.* to get on sb.'s nerves, *(lit.)* to trample around on sb.'s nerves.

jm. auf den Schlips treten, *exp. (coll.)* to step on sb.'s toes, *(lit.)* to step on sb.'s tie.

sich aufregen, *v.* get upset; *Note:* **er regt mich auf**/he gets on my nerves.

jm. Beine machen, *exp. (coll.)* to cause sb. annoyance; *Note:* also to push sb.

jm. eins auf den Deckel geben, *exp. (coll.)* to cause annoyance to sb., *(lit.)* to hit a person on the lid (head).

jm. auf den Sender gehen, *exp. (coll.)* to bother sb., *(lit.)* to get on sb.'s broadcast.

auf den Wecker gehen, *exp. (coll.)* to bug sb., *(lit.)* to get on sb.'s alarm clock.

auf die Nerven gehen, *exp.* to get on sb.'s nerves.

jm. den letzten Nerv rauben, *exp.* to annoy sb., *(lit.)* to rob sb. of his last nerve.

sich fuchsen, *v.* be annoyed; *Note:* **das fuchst mich!**/that annoys me.

nerven, *v.* get on sb.'s nerves.

Nervensäge, *f.* pain in the neck, *(lit.)* nerve saw.
piesaken, *v.* pester.
jm. Saures geben, *exp.* to cause annoyance to sb., *(lit.)* to give sb. sth. sour.
Stunk machen, *exp.* *(coll.)* to make a fuss, *(lit.)* to make a stink.
zum Auswachsen, *exp.* to drive sb. up the wall, *(lit.)* to grow out; *Note:* **es ist zum Auswachsen**/it's enough to drive you up the wall.

ANXIETY *(Sorgen)*

das geht auf die Nieren! *exp.* *(coll.)* it gets to sb., *(lit.)* that goes to one's kidneys!
das schlägt auf die Galle! *exp.* *(coll.)* it gets to sb., *(lit.)* that hits the gallbladder!
sich graue Haare wachsen lassen, *exp.* *(coll.)* to worry, *(lit.)* to let oneself grow gray hair.
sein Kreuz zu tragen haben, *exp.* to have one's troubles, *(lit.)* to have to carry one's own cross.
sein Päckchen zu tragen haben, *exp.* to have one's troubles, *(lit.)* to have to carry one's own little package.

APPEASE, to *(beruhigen)*

eine Brücke zueinander finden, *exp.* to find each other, *(lit.)* to find a bridge to each other.
sich die Hand geben, *v.* reconcile, *(lit.)* to give (each other) one's hand.
das Kriegsbeil begraben, *exp.* to bury the hatchet.
ins reine bringen, *exp.* to clear things up, *(lit.)* to make things clean.
etw. unter einen Hut bringen, *exp.* to reconcile different interests of different people, *(lit.)* to bring sth. under one hat.
sich zusammenraufen, *exp.* *(coll.)* to pull oneself together.
sich zusammenreißen, *exp.* to pull oneself together.

ARREST, to *(verhaften)*
(See: **POLICE**)

auf freiem Fuß sein, *exp.* to be at large, *(lit.)* to be on free foot.
auf Nummer Sicher sitzen, *exp.* *(coll.)* to be arrested, *(lit.)* to sit securely on a number.
auf unbestimmte Zeit vereisen, *exp.* *(coll.)* to get arrested, *(lit.)* to go on a trip for an indefinite period of time.
brummen, *exp.* *(sl.)* to be arrested; *Note:* **zehn Jahre brummen**/to be in prison for ten years.
einbuchten, *v.* *(sl.)* arrest.
einbunkern, *v.* *(sl.)* arrest.
einlochen, *v.* *(sl.)* arrest.
gesiebte Luft einatmen, *exp.* *(sl.)* to be arrested, *(lit.)* to breath sieved air.
hinter Gitter stecken, *exp.* to put sb. behind bars.

hinter Schwedische Gardinen kommen, *exp.* to be behind bars, *(lit.)* to be behind Swedish curtains. *Note:* **Schwedische Gardinen** is a term for Gefängnis.

hocken, *v. (sl.)* to be arrested, *(lit.)* crouch.

Kittchen, *n. (sl.)* jail.

Knacki, *m. (sl.)* jailbird.

Knast, *m. (sl.)* jail.

Knast schieben, *exp. (sl.)* to be arrested, *(lit.)* to push jail.

Knastbruder, *m. (sl.)* jailbird.

Knastologe, *m. (coll.)* jailbird, *(lit.)* prisonologist.

sitzen, *v. (coll.)* to be arrested, *(lit.)* to sit.

Tüten kleben gehen, *exp. (coll.)* to be arrested, *(lit.)* to go and glue bags.

ARRIVE, to *(ankommen)*

angefegt kommen, *exp. (sl.)* to arrive at the last moment, *(lit.)* to be swept along.

angelatscht kommen, *exp. (sl.)* to arrive slowly.

auftauchen, *v. (coll.)* arrive, *(lit.)* to surface.

mit der Tür ins Haus fallen, *exp.* to arrive unexpectedly, *(lit.)* to fall into the house with the door.

reinschneien, *v. (coll.)* arrive unexpectedly, *(lit.)* to snow in.

ARROGANT, to be *(eingebildet sein)*

arroganter Affe, *exp. (coll.)* arrogant monkey.

auf einem hohen Roß sitzen, *exp.* to be conceited, *(lit.)* to sit on a high horse.

blasiert, *adj.* blasé.

die Nase hoch tragen, *exp.* to have one's nose in the air.

die Nase so hoch tragen, daß es reinregnet! *exp. (coll.)* to be conceited, *(lit.)* to carry one's nose so high that it rains into it.

eingebildet, *adj.* conceited.

eingebildeter Gockel, *exp. (coll.)* conceited rooster.

Snob, *m.* snob; *Note:* borrowed from English.

stolz wie ein Gockel sein, *exp.* to be as proud as a rooster.

stolzieren, *v.* flaunt.

BALD, to be *(glatzköpfig sein)*

blank wie ein Kinderpo sein, *exp. (coll.)* to be bald, *(lit.)* to be as shiny as a child's behind.

blanke Scheibe, *f. (sl.)* bald head, *(lit.)* blank disk.

breiten Scheitel, *m.* *(sl.)* bald head, *(lit.)* wide (hair) part.

fleischfarbene Badekappe, *exp.* *(sl.)* bald head, *(lit.)* skin-colored bathing cap.

geöffnetes Schiebedach, *exp.* *(sl.)* bald head, *(lit.)* open sunroof.

Platte, *f.* *(sl.)* bald head, *(lit.)* disk.

Polierscheibe, *f.* *(sl.)* bald head, *(lit.)* polished disk.

ratzekahl, *adj.* *(sl.)* completely bald.

BANKRUPT, to be *(bankrott sein)*

---

abstottern, *v.* pay off debts.

jn. anhauen, *exp.* *(coll.)* to borrow money from sb., *(lit.)* to hit on sb.

auf dem Trockenen sitzen, *exp.* to be broke, *(lit.)* to sit on the dry (spot).

bettelarm, *adj.* penniless, *(lit.)* begging poor.

blank, *adj.* broke.

das Geld ist zum Kuckuck! *exp.* the money is all gone, *(lit.)* the money is with the cuckoo; *Note:* **Kuckuck** refers to the bailiff's seal.

jm. den Geldhahn zudrehen, *exp.* to cut off sb.'s money, *(lit.)* to turn off the money faucet.

der Pleitegeier sitzt schon auf dem Dach! *exp.* *(coll.)* to be about to go bankrupt, *(lit.)* the bankruptcy vulture is already sitting on the roof. *Note: see* **Pleitegeier.**

der Rubel rollt nicht mehr! *exp.* *(coll.)* to be broke, *(lit.)* the Rubel does not roll anymore.

Ebbe im Portemonnaie haben, *exp.* *(coll.)* to be broke, *(lit.)* to have low tide in one's wallet.

ein Loch in der Tasche haben, *exp.* to be bankrupt, *(lit.)* to have a hole in one's pocket.

sich Geld pumpen, *v.* *(coll.)* borrow money; *Note:* **jn. anpumpen,** *v.* borrow money from sb.

in den Miesen sein, *exp.* *(coll.)* to be in the red.

jeden Pfennig dreimal umdrehen, *exp.* to pinch pennies, *(lit.)* to turn each penny over three times.

keine großen Sprünge mehr machen können, *exp.* to pinch pennies, *(lit.)* not to be able to make big jumps anymore.

keine Knete mehr haben, *exp.* *(coll.)* to be broke, *(lit.)* to be out of explosives.

keine müde Mark haben, *exp.* *(coll.)* to be bankrupt, *(lit.)* to not have a single tired Mark.

keinen Pfennig mehr in der Tasche (haben), *exp.* to be broke *(lit.)* to not have a single penny in one's pocket.

knapp bei Kasse sein, *exp.* to be poor, *(lit.)* to be tight at the cashier.

Miese haben, *exp.* *(coll.)* to be in the red; *Note:* **ich habe 1000 Miese/**I have 1000 in the red.

nackt dastehen, *exp.* *(coll.)* to be bankrupt, *(lit.)* to stand there naked.

nicht mehr flüssig sein, *exp.* *(coll.)* to have no liquid assets.

pleite, *adj.* bankrupt; broke.

Pleitegeier, *m.* specter of bankruptcy, *(lit.)* bankruptcy vulture.

vertuckeln, *v.* *(coll.)* waste money.

vom Pleitegeier geküßt sein, *exp. (coll.)* to be bankrupt, *(lit.)* to have been kissed by the bankruptcy vulture.

BEAT UP, to *(verprügeln)*

Abreibung, *f. (sl.)* thrashing, *(lit.)* rubbing off.
jn. aufmischen, *v. (sl.)* thrash sb., *(lit.)* mix sb. up.
jn. aus dem Anzug stoßen, *exp. (sl.)* to thrash sb., *(lit.)* to push sb. out of his suit.
aus jm. Frikassee machen, *exp. (sl.)* to make mincemeat out of sb.
aus jm. Hackfleisch machen, *exp. (sl.)* to make hamburger out of sb.
jm. den Hals umdrehen, *exp. (sl.)* to thrash a person, *(lit.)* to turn sb.'s neck.
jm. die Fresse polieren, *exp. (vulg.)* to thrash a person, *(lit.)* to polish sb.'s mouth.
jn. durchhauen, *v. (sl.)* thrash sb.
eine Abreibung kriegen, *exp. (sl.)* to get a thrashing.
jm. eine Naht verpassen, *exp. (sl.)* to give sb. a thrashing, *(lit.)* to give sb. a seam.
jm. eine Tracht Prügel verpassen, *exp. (sl.)* to give sb. a thrashing.
jm. eine Wucht verpassen, *exp. (sl.)* to give sb. a thrashing.
jm. ordentlich die Fresse polieren, *exp. (vulg.)* to really smash sb.'s face, *(lit.)* to thoroughly polish sb.'s mouth.
ordentliche Abreibung, *exp. (sl.)* real thrashing.
prügeln, *v. (coll.)* thrash.
saftige Abreibung, *f. (sl.)* thrashing, *(lit.)* juicy rubbing down.
Saures geben, *exp. (coll.)* to thrash sb., *(lit.)* to give sb. sth. sour.
jn. tüchtig vermöbeln, *exp. (sl.)* to really thrash sb.
jn. unangespitzt in den Boden stampfen, *exp. (sl.)* to give a person a thrashing, *(lit.)* to stamp sb. unsharpened into the ground.
jn. verdreschen, *v. (sl.)* thrash sb.
jn. verprügeln, *v. (coll.)* thrash sb.
jn. vertrimmen, *v. (sl.)* thrash sb.
jn. weich machen, *exp. (sl.)* to thrash sb., *(lit.)* to make sb. soft.
jn. weichklopfen, *v. (sl.)* beat the living daylights out of sb., *(lit.)* to knock sb. soft.
jn. weichprügeln, *v. (sl.)* beat the living daylights out of sb.
jn. windelweich schlagen, *exp. (sl.)* to beat the living daylights out of sb., *(lit.)* to hit sb. until they're as soft as a diaper.

BED *(Bett)*

Falle, *f.* bed, *(lit.)* trap. *Note:* **ab in die Falle!**/go to bed!
Federn, *f.pl.* bed, *(lit.)* feathers.
Flohkiste, *f. (coll.)* bed, *(lit.)* fleabox.
Klappe, *f.* bed, *(lit.)* trap.
Koje, *f. (sl.)* bed, *(lit.)* bunk.
Regal, *n. (sl.)* narrow bed, *(lit.)* shelf.

BELLY *(Bauch)*

Bierbauch, *m.* beer belly.

jm. ein Loch in den Bauch fragen, *exp.* to pester sb. with questions, *(lit.)* to ask a hole into sb.'s belly.

Fettwanst, *f.* pot belly.

Kartoffelbauch, *m.* potato belly.

Kugel, *f.* belly, *(lit.)* ball.

Kugelbauch, *m.* ball belly.

Schmierbauch, *m.* pot belly.

sie hat einen dicken Bauch! *exp.* she is pregnant, *(lit.)* she has a fat belly.

Vorderlade, *f.* pot belly.

Wampe, *f.* pot belly.

Wanst, pot belly.

BREASTS *(Busen)*

Apparate, *m.pl. (vulg.)* big breasts.

Balkon, *m. (vulg.)* big breasts.

flach wie ein Bügelbrett sein, *exp. (coll.)* to have small breasts, *(lit.)* to be as flat as an ironing board.

Holz vor der Hütte haben, *exp. (vulg.)* to have big breasts, *(lit.)* to have wood in front of the hut.

Lungenflügel, *m.pl. (vulg.)* big breasts, *(lit.)* lungwings.

Milchfabrik, *f. (vulg.)* big breasts, *(lit.)* milk factory.

Milchwirtschaft, *f. (vulg.)* big breasts.

Möpse, *m.pl. (vulg.)* big breasts.

Titten, *f.pl. (vulg.)* tits.

Vorbau, *m. (coll.)* big breasts, *(lit.)* porch.

Vorsteven, *m. (sl.)* big breasts, *(lit.)* stem.

CAR *(Auto)*
(See: **DRIVE, to**)

Benzin reden, *exp. (sl.)* to talk about cars and motorcycles, *(lit.)* to talk gasoline.

Benzinschleuder, *f.* car with high gas consumption, *(lit.)* gas catapult.

Brummi, *m. (sl.)* truck.

das Auto schluckt Benzin! *exp.* the car guzzles gas.

Ente, *f.* Citroën 2V, *(lit.)* duck; *Note:* the Citroën 2V is a French make of car.

es knallte! *exp. (coll.)* there was a crash.

Fahrgestell, *n. (coll.)* car, *(lit.)* chassis.

Feger, *m. (coll.)* fast car, *(lit.)* sweeper.

Flitzer, *m.* fast car.

Karre, *f. (coll.)* heap; *Note:* usually **alte Karre**/old heap.

Kiste, *f.* *(coll.)* old car.*(lit.)* crate.

Kutsche, *f.* *(coll.)* old car, *(lit.)* carriage.

Rostlaube, *f.* *(coll.)* rusty car.

Schlitten, *m.* *(coll.)* big car, especially American cars which are also referred to as **Amischlitten;** *(lit.)* sled.

Schnecke, *f.* slow car, *(lit.)* snail.

schnittig, *adj.* racy.

Schrottkiste, *f.* *(coll.)* piece of junk, *(lit.)* scrap crate.

Trabbi, *m.* short for the former East German **Trabant.**

CHILD *(Kind)*

Bagage, *pl,* *(coll.)* group of children.

Balg, *n.* *(coll.)* rascal.

Bürschchen, *m.* rascal.

Dreikäsehoch, *m.* *(coll.)* bold child, *(lit.)* three cheeses high.

Fratze, *f.* *(sl.)* rascal.

Frechdachs, *m.* rascal.

Früchtchen, *n.* rascal *(lit.)* little fruit.

Galgenstrick, *m.* rascal *(lit.)* gallow's rope.

Gör, *n.* *(sl.)* small child, brat; *Note:* **ein niedliches Gör**/a cute little thing.

Hamburger Deern, *f.* *(sl.)* girl from Hamburg.

Kids, *pl.* *(sl.)* teenager; *Note:* term borrowed from English.

Kieler Sprotte, *f.* *(sl.)* child born in Kiel.

kleines Würstel, *exp.* *(sl.)* little kid, *(lit.)* little sausage.

Klettermaxe, *m.* *(sl.)* child who loves to climb.

Kurzer, *m.* *(coll.)* little kid.

laufender Meter, *exp.* *(coll.)* little kid, *(lit.)* running meter.

Lausbengel, *m.* rascal.

Lausbub, *m.* rascal.

noch die Eierschalen hinter den Ohren haben, *exp.* *(coll.)* to be immature, *(lit.)* to still have eggshells behind one's ears.

noch feucht hinter den Ohren sein, *exp.* *(coll.)* to be immature, *(lit.)* to still be wet behind one's ears.

Pimpf, *m.* *(sl.)* little boy.

Pöks, *m.* *(sl.)* rascal; *Note:* usually **kleiner Pöks**/little rascal.

Racker, *m.* rascal; *Note:* usually **kleiner Racker**/little rascal.

Rotzlöffel, *m.* *(vulg.)* rascal, *(lit.)* snot spoon.

Rotznase, *f.* *(vulg.)* rascal, *(lit.)* snot nose.

Scheißer, *m.* *(vulg.)* rascal, *(lit.)* little shit; *Note:* often **kleiner Scheißer.**

Schlingel, *m.* rascal.

Schnotternase, *f.* *(coll.)* rascal, *(lit.)* snot nose.

Stinker, *m.* *(coll.)* rascal, *(lit.)* stinker.

CHIT-CHAT *(Gerede)*

babbeln, *v.* babble, chatter.

Gebabbel, *n.* chatter.

Gequatsche, *n.* gibberish.
Geschnatter, *n.* twaddle.
Geschwätz, *n.* twaddle.
Kauderwelsch, *n.* gibberish.
kauderwelschen, *v.* talk gibberish.
Klatsch, *m.* gossip.
klatschen, *v.* gossip.
klönen, *v.* talk at great length.
Klönschnack, *m.* gossip over a cup of tea.
papperlapapp! *Interj.* rubbish.
Plappermaul, *m.* blabbermouth.
Plaudertasche, *f.* blabbermouth.
plauschen, *v.* chat.
quasseln, *v.* prattle.
Quasselstrippe, *f.* prattler.
quatschen, *v.* blather.
ratschen, *v.* blather.
rumseibeln, *v. (sl.)* blather.
sabbeln, *v.* chatter.
schnacken, *v.* blather.
Schnatterliese, *f.* woman who blathers a lot.
schnattern, *v.* blather, chatter.
schwatzen, *v.* blather.

CIGARETTE *(Zigarette)*

Blätter, *n.pl. (coll.)* cigarette, *(lit.)* leaves.
Glimmstengel, *m. (coll.)* cigarette.
Hugo, *m. (coll.)* cigarette that was only half smoked and later finished.
Kiffe, *f. (sl.)* end of a cigarette.
kiffen, *v. (sl.)* smoke pot or grass.
Kiffer, *m. (sl.)* pot-head.
Kippe, *f.* cigarette end.
Kraut, *n.* bad cigarette, *(lit.)* cabbage.
Lungentorpedo, *exp. (coll.)* cigarette, *(lit.)* lung torpedo.
paffen, *v. (coll.)* smoke without inhaling.
Sargnagel, *m. (coll.)* coffin nail.
schmöken, *v. (sl.)* smoke.
Tabakröllchen, *n. (coll.)* cigarette, *(lit.)* little roll of tobacco.
Zigarettenstummel, *m.* end of a cigarette.

CLOTHING *(Kleidung)*

sich etwas anschmeißen, *v. (coll.)* dress quickly.
sich aufdonnern, *v. (coll.)* dress up in an exaggerated manner.
sich auftakeln, *v.* dress up in an exaggerated manner.
das kleine Schwarze, *exp.* a plain black dress that can be used for all
   occasions; *(lit.)* the little black one.

fesch, *adj.* fashionable.

Fetzen, *m.* *(coll.)* female clothing, *(lit.)* shreds.

flott, *adj.* nifty.

Fummel, *m.* *(coll.)* female clothing.

sich in Schale werfen, *exp.* *(coll.)* to dress elegantly.

in voller Montur sein, *exp.* to be dressed elegantly.

Klamotten, *f.pl.* *(sl.)* clothing.

knalleng, *adj.* skin-tight; *Note:* **es sitzt knalleng wie eine Leberwurst**/it fits as skin-tight as a liverwurst.

nullachtfuffzehn gekleidet sein, *exp.* to be dressed in a run of the mill way; *Note:* **nullachtfuffzehn = nullachtfünfzehn.**

out, *adj.* *(sl.)* out, out of fashion; *Note:* term borrowed from English.

passé, *adj.* out of fashion; *Note:* term borrowed from French.

piekfein, *adj.* posh.

raffiniert, *adj.* nifty.

sich rausputzen, *exp.* dress up.

schick, *adj.* fashionable.

schnieke, *adj.* *(coll.)* elegant.

sich etwas überschmeißen, *v.* get dressed quickly.

sich etwas überziehen, *v.* put on a sweater or coat.

COMPREHEND, to *(verstehen)*

auf den Trichter kommen, *exp.* *(coll.)* to get the message, *(lit.)* to come to the funnel.

bei jm. fallen die Groschen in Pfennigen, *exp.* *(coll.)* to be a little slow in understanding, *(lit.)* with sb. the dime falls in pennies.

da also liegt der Hase im Pfeffer! *exp.* *(coll.)* that's how it works, *(lit.)* that's where the rabbit lies in the pepper.

das ist der Kasus Knacktus! *exp.* *(coll.)* that is what was behind it.

das kommt mir Spanisch vor! *exp.* *(coll.)* that's Greek to me, *(lit.)* that seems Spanish to me.

das war der Pudels Kern! *exp.* *(coll.)* that's what was behind it, *(lit.)* that's the poodle's core.

den Durchblick haben, *exp.* *(coll.)* to know what is going on.

durchsickern, *v.* *(coll.)* grasp, *(lit.)* seep through.

jm. geht ein Licht auf, *exp.* *(coll.)* it dawns on sb., *(lit.)* a light goes on for sb.

jm. gehen die Augen auf, *exp.* the scales fall from sb.'s eyes.

kapieren, *v.* *(coll.)* understand.

Kapito? *exp.* *(coll.)* did you understand? *Note:* a term borrowed from Italian.

Knackepunkt, *m.* *(coll.)* the root of a problem.

raffen, *v.* *(coll.)* understand.

schnallen, *v.* *(coll.)* grasp.

verklartütteln, *v.* explain.

verklickern, *v.* *(coll.)* explain.

CORPULENT, to be *(dick sein)*

aus den Fugen gehen, *exp. (sl.)* to become fat, *(lit.)* to go out at one's joints.
auseinandergehen, *v.* become fat, *(lit.)* to draw apart.
Dampfnudel, *f. (sl.)* fat female, *(lit.)* steamed dumpling.
dicke Qualle, *exp. (sl.)* fat person, *(lit.)* fat jellyfish.
Dickerchen, *n. (sl.)* podge.
Elefantenbaby, *n. (sl.)* fat person, *(lit.)* elephant baby.
Elefantenkücken, *n. (sl.)* fat person, *(lit.)* elephant chick (as in baby chicken).
Fett ansetzen, *exp. (sl.)* to become fat, *(lit.)* to attach fat.
Fetter, *m. (sl.)* fat male.
Fettfleck, *m. (sl.)* fat person, *(lit.)* grease spot.
Fettsack, *m. (vulg.)* fat male, *(lit.)* fat sack.
Fettwanst, *m. (sl.)* fat male, *(lit.)* fat belly; *Note:* **Wanst,** *f.* belly.
füllig, *adj.* fat.
gut gepolstert, *adj. (sl.)* fat, *(lit.)* well upholstered.
gut wattiert, *adj.* fat, *(lit.)* well padded.
herausgefuttert, *adj. (sl.)* well fed.
Klops, *m. (sl.)* fat person, *(lit.)* meatball.
Klotz, *m. (sl.)* fat person, *(lit.)* block.
Kloß, *m. (sl.)* fat person, *(lit.)* dumpling.
kugelrund, *adj.* as round as a ball.
Mops, *m. (sl.)* fat person, *(lit.)* pug.
plump, *adj.* fat and clumsy.
Pummel, *m.* podge; *Note:* also used as a term of endearment.
Schwimmringe, *m.pl.* spare tires, *(lit.)* life rings.

CRAZY, to go *(verrückt werden)*
(See also: **STUPEFIED, to be**)

abdrehen, *v. (coll.)* go crazy, *(lit.)* twist off.
aus der Balance kommen, *exp.* to go insane, *(lit.)* to lose balance.
aus der Façon bringen, *exp.* to drive off balance.
ausflippen, *v. (sl.)* flip out; *Note:* often used when getting very angry.
aushaken, *v. (coll.)* go crazy; *Note:* often used when getting very angry.
ausrasten, *v. (coll.)* go crazy.
durchdrehen, *v. (coll.)* go crazy. *Note:* **durchgedreht**/to be crazy.
eine Krise kriegen, *exp. (coll.)* to have a crisis.
es ist zum Mäusemelken! *exp. (coll.)* I am going crazy, *(lit.)* it's like milking mice.
fummelig, *adj. (coll.)* impatient and fumbly.
im Carré springen, *exp.* to go crazy, *(lit.)* to hop in a square.
spinnen, *v.* go crazy.
überschnappen, *v.* go crazy.
vom wilden Affen gebissen sein, *exp. (coll.)* to be off one's rocker, *(lit.)* to have been bitten by a wild monkey.

CUTE, to be *(niedlich sein)*

entzückend, *adj.* charming.
goldig, *adj.* cute.
niedlich, *adj.* cute.
putzig, *adj.* cute.
schnuckelig, *adj.* charming.

DECEIVE, to *(betrügen)*

jn. an der Nase herumführen, *exp.* to pull the wool over sb.'s eyes, *(lit.)* to lead sb. by the nose.
jn. anschmieren, *v.* deceive sb.
jn. auf den Leim führen, *exp.* to deceive sb., *(lit.)* to lead sb. onto glue.
ausgekocht, *adj.* crafty, *(lit.)* to be cooked out.
Bauernfänger, *m.* swindler, *(lit.)* farmer catcher.
jn. behumpsen, *v.* *(sl.)* dupe sb.
jn. bescheißen, *v.* *(vulg.)* rip sb. off, *(lit.)* to shit someone.
jn. beschupsen, *v.* *(sl.)* deceive sb.
das Blaue vom Himmel herunterlügen, *exp.* to tell a lot of lies, *(lit.)* to lie the blue out of the sky.
ein krummes Ding drehen, *exp.* *(coll.)* to be up to sth. crooked.
einsacken, *v.* *(coll.)* profit by ripping sb. off.
er hat es faustdick hinter den Ohren! *exp.* he is a sly one, *(lit.)* he has it fist-thick behind his ears.
erstunken und erlogen, *adj.* *(coll.)* be a pack of lies, *(lit.)* stunk and lied.
etw. mitgehen lassen, *exp.* walk off with sth.
Flunkerei, *f.* story-telling.
flunkern, *v.* tell stories.
Ganove, *m.* crook.
Geldschneiderei, *f.* profiteering, *(lit.)* money tailoring.
Halsabschneider, *m.* swindler, cutthroat.
jn. hochnehmen, *v.* deceive sb.
klaufen, *v.* steal; *Note:* a compound of **kaufen**/buy and **klauen**/steal.
jn. lackmeiern, *v.* *(coll.)* deceive sb.; *Note:* **der Gelackmeierte sein,** *exp.* to be the deceived one.
lange Finger machen, *exp.* to steal, *(lit.)* to make long fingers.
Langfinger, *m.* thief, *(lit.)* long finger.
jn. leimen, *v.* *(coll.)* deceive sb.
mogeln, *v.* deceive.
mopsen, *v.* *(coll.)* steal.
jn. neppen, *v.* *(coll.)* rip sb. off.
jn. reinlegen, *v.* rip sb. off, *(lit.)* to lay sb. in (sth.).
schummeln, *v.* swindle.
jn. übers Ohr hauen, *exp.* to betray sb., *(lit.)* to hit sb. over the ear.

wie gedruckt lügen, *exp.* to lie like mad, *(lit.)* to lie as if it were being printed.

DIE, to *(sterben)*

---

abkratzen, *v. (sl.)* die, *(lit.)* scratch off.

abtreten, *v. (coll.)* die, *(lit.)* resign.

das Besteck hinwerfen, *exp. (sl.)* to die, *(lit.)* to throw the silverware.

den Arsch zukneifen, *exp. (vulg.)* to die, *(lit.)* to pinch one's ass shut.

die Radieschen von unten wachsen sehen, *exp. (coll.)* to die, *(lit.)* to see the radishes grow from underneath.

dran glauben müssen, *exp. (coll.)* to kick the bucket, *(lit.)* to believe in it.

draufgehen, *v. (sl.)* die, *(lit.)* perish.

einen Fuß im Grab haben, *exp. (coll.)* to have one foot in the grave.

einen kalten Arsch kriegen, *exp. (vulg.)* to die, *(lit.)* to get a cold ass.

ex und hops gehen, *exp. (sl.)* to die.

in die Bretter gehen, *exp. (sl.)* to kick the bucket, *(lit.)* to go into the boards.

in die ewigen Jagdgründe eingehen, *exp. (coll.)* to go to the happy hunting grounds.

in die Nüsse gehen, *exp. (sl.)* to kick the bucket, *(lit.)* to go into the nuts.

ins Gras beißen, *exp. (sl.)* to bite the dust, *(lit.)* to bite the grass.

krepieren, *v. (sl.)* to snuff it.

Löffel abgeben, *exp. (coll.)* to die, *(lit.)* to turn in one's spoon.

nach Tannenholz riechen, *exp. (sl.)* to be dead, *(lit.)* to smell like pine (of a casket).

sein (or **ihr**) **letztes Stündchen hat geschlagen,** *exp. (coll.)* his (or her) last hour has come, *(lit.)* his last hour has struck.

übern Jordan gehen, *exp. (coll.)* to die, *(lit.)* to cross the River Jordan.

verenden, *v. (sl.)* die a miserable death.

verrecken, *v. (sl.)* die a miserable death.

von der Bühne abtreten, *exp. (coll.)* to kick the bucket, *(lit.)* to get off the stage.

vor die Hunde gehen, *exp. (sl.)* to kick the bucket, *(lit.)* to go ahead of the dogs.

DIFFICULTIES *(Schwierigkeiten)*

---

alt aussehen, *exp.* to have difficulties, *(lit.)* to look old.

aufgeschmissen, *adj.* not to know what to do anymore.

bei jm. danebenliegen, *exp.* to have difficulties with sb.

das klappt wie am Schnürchen! *exp.* it works like clockwork.

jm. drückt der Schuh, *exp.* to have problems, *(lit.)* to be pinched by one's shoe; *Note:* du weißt nicht, wo mich der Schuh drückt/ you don't understand my problems.

Dünnschißproblem, *n. (vulg.)* Montezuma's revenge.

einen Haken haben, *exp.* to have a catch.

in Teufels Küche kommen, *exp. (coll.)* to get into trouble, *(lit.)* to come into the Devil's kitchen.

kein Honiglecken sein, *exp.* not to be easy, *(lit.)* not like licking honey.

Knatsch, *m.* trouble.

mit Ach und Krach, *exp.* with great difficulty.

mit Hängen und Würgen, *exp.* with difficulties, *(lit.)* with hanging and strangling.

mit etw. auf den Hintern fallen, *exp. (coll.)* to cause difficulties for oneself, *(lit.)* to fall on one's behind (with sth.).

Mordsproblem, *n.* huge problem.

nebenraus hauen, *exp. (sl.)* to have difficulties, *(lit.)* to hit next to it.

Probleme haben, *exp.* to have emotional problems.

Schlamassel, *m.* scrape, mess.

Trabbel, *m.* trouble.

übel auflaufen bei jm., *exp. (sl.)* not to be liked by someone anymore, *(lit.)* to run aground with sb.

verdaddeln, *v.* cause oneself difficulties by underestimating a situation.

verheddern, *v.* cause oneself difficulties by underestimating a situation.

vertüteln, *v.* cause oneself difficulties by underestimating a situation.

DISMISS FROM WORK, to *(entlassen)*

achtkantig rausschmeißen, *exp. (coll.)* to fire.

jn. an die frische Luft setzen, *exp. (coll.)* to fire sb., *(lit.)* to set sb. into the fresh air.

den Hut nehmen müssen, *exp. (coll.)* to be fired, *(lit.)* to have to take one's hat.

feuern, *v. (coll.)* fire.

jm. die Koffer geben, *exp. (coll.)* to fire sb., *(lit.)* to give sb. his suitcases.

rausschmeißen, *v. (coll.)* throw out.

jm. den Sack geben, *exp. (coll.)* to fire sb., *(lit.)* to give sb. the sack.

jn. vor die Tür setzen, *exp. (coll.)* to show sb. the door, *(lit.)* to put sb. in front of the door.

DOG *(Hund)*

Gejaule, *n.* howling.

Gekläffe, *n. (coll.)* barking.

Kalb, *n.* big dog, *(lit.)* calf.

Kläffer, *m. (coll.)* yapping dog.

Köter, *m.* cur, mongrel.

Mistvieh, *n. (vulg.)* damn dog.

Promenadenmischung, f, mongrel.

Straßenköter, *m. (sl.)* cur.

Streuner, *m.* dog without owner; *Note:* also tramp.

Töhle, *f. (sl.)* mongrel.

Viech, *n. (coll.)* beast.

DRINK ALCOHOL, to *(Alkohol trinken)*

absaufen, *v. (sl.)* be drunk, *(lit.)* drowned.

angetütelt, *adj.* be drunk.

ansetzen, *v.* drink.

auf die Swutsch gehen, *exp. (coll.)* to go out and drink.

auf ein Bierchen gehen, *exp.* to go out for a beer.

sich besaufen, *v. (sl.)* get drunk.

besäuselt, *adj.* tipsy.

beschwipst, *adj.* tipsy.

sich die Birne vollkippen, *exp. (sl.)* get drunk, *(lit.)* to fill the pear; *Note:* **Birne** is a colloquial term for Kopf.

blau, *adj. (coll.)* drunk, *(lit.)* blue.

blau wie ein Veilchen sein, *exp. (coll.)* to be drunk, *(lit.)* to be as blue as a violet.

den Kanal voll haben, *exp. (sl.)* to be drunk, *(lit.)* to have a full canal.

sich die Leber aus dem Leib saufen, *v. (vulg.)* get drunk, *(lit.)* to drink one's liver out of one's body.

die Leber befeuchten, *exp. (sl.)* to get drunk, *(lit.)* to moisten one's liver.

die Leber knistert schon! *exp. (sl.)* to be thirsty for alcohol, *(lit.)* one's liver is already crackling.

eine Sause machen, *exp. (sl.)* to go bar-hopping.

sich einen Affen kaufen, *exp. (sl.)* to get drunk, *(lit.)* to buy oneself a monkey.

einen Affen sitzen haben, *exp. (sl.)* to be drunk, *(lit.)* to have a sitting monkey.

sich einen fegen, *exp. (sl.)* to get drunk.

sich einen hinter den Schlips gießen, *exp. (sl.)* to get drunk, *(lit.)* to pour one behind one's tie.

sich einen hinter die Binde gießen, *exp. (sl.)* to get drunk, *(lit.)* to pour one behind one's tie.

einen in der Krone haben, *exp. (coll.)* to be drunk, *(lit.)* to have one in the crown.

sich einen in die Figur schütten, *exp. (sl.)* to get drunk, *(lit.)* to pour one into one's figure.

einen intus haben, *exp. (coll.)* to have had a few.

einen kippen, *exp. (sl.)* to drink alcohol.

sich einen schmettern, *exp. (sl.)* to drink alcohol.

sich einen schnasseln, *exp. (sl.)* to drink alcohol.

einen Schwips haben, *exp.* to be tipsy.

einen sitzen haben, *exp. (coll.)* to have had one too many.

sich einen zischen, *exp. (sl.)* to drink alcohol.

sich einen zur Brust nehmen, *exp. (sl.)* to drink alcohol, *(lit.)* to take one to one's chest.

sich einen zwitschern, *exp. (sl.)* to drink alcohol.

Fusel, *m. (sl.)* booze.

Gesöff, *n. (coll.)* booze.

granatenvoll, *adj. (sl.)* absolutely plastered.

hackedicht, *adj. (sl.)* wasted.

heben, *v. (sl.)* drink alcohol, *(lit.)* lift.

ins Glas gucken, *exp. (coll.)* to drink alcohol.

Karussel fahren, *exp. (sl.)* to be drunk, *(lit.)* to be driving a carousal.

knallvoll, *adj. (sl.)* wasted.

lallen, *v. (coll.)* speak when drunk.

lull und lall, *adj. (sl.)* wasted.

Öl auf die Lampe gießen, *exp. (sl.)* to get drunk, *(lit.)* to pour oil into the lamp.

saufen, *v. (vulg.)* drink a lot of alcohol.

Säufer, *m. (vulg.)* alcoholic.

Saufgelage, *n. (sl.)* drinking bout.

Saufkopf, *m. (vulg.)* alcoholic.

schnäpseln, *v.* booze.

schwere Schlagseite haben, *exp. (coll.)* to be rolling drunk, *(lit.)* to list heavily to one side.

sternhagelvoll, *adj. (coll.)* wasted.

stockbesoffen, *adj. (coll.)* wasted.

trinken wie ein Loch, *exp. (coll.)* to drink like a hole.

jn. unter den Tisch trinken, *exp.* to be able to drink more alcohol than another person, *(lit.)* to drink sb. under the table.

voll, *adj. (coll.)* completely wasted.

sich vollkippen, *v. (sl.)* get drunk.

voll wie ein Eimer sein, *exp. (sl.)* to be a wasted, *(lit.)* to be as full as a bucket.

voll wie Haubitze sein, *exp. (coll.)* to be as drunk as a newt.

weiße Mäuse sehen, *exp.* to be drunk, *(lit.)* to see white mice.

wie ein Fisch trinken, *exp.* to drink like a fish.

Zechgelage, *n.* drinking bout.

Zechgenosse, *m.* drinking companion.

Zechkumpan, *m.* drinking companion.

Zechprellerei, *f.* bill-dodging; *Note:* **Zechpreller,** *m.* person who leaves without paying.

Zechtour, *f.* bar hopping.

zu tief ins Glas geguckt haben, *exp. (coll.)* to be very drunk, *(lit.)* to have looked too deeply into one's glass.

zugekippt, *adj. (sl.)* drunk.

DRIVE, to *(fahren)*

---

abdampfen, *v. (coll.)* speed off, *(lit.)* to steam off.

abzischen, *v. (coll.)* speed off.

brettern, *v. (sl.)* drive fast.

davonbrausen, *v.* speed off.

dödeln, *v. (sl.)* drive slowly.

flitzen, *v.* drive fast.

herumeiern, *v. (coll.)* drive slowly, *(lit.)* egg about.

mit Vollgas fahren, *exp.* to go at high speed.

rasen, *v.* race.

sausen, *v.* speed.

schnecken, *v. (sl.)* drive slowly, *(lit.)* to snail.

EARS *(Ohren)*

auf den Ohren sitzen, *exp.* *(coll.)* to not listen, *(lit.)* to sit on one's ears.

sich aufs Ohr hauen, *exp.* *(coll.)* to lay down, *(lit.)* to hit oneself on the ear.

es faustdick hinter den Ohren haben, *exp.* *(coll.)* to be cunning, *(lit.)* to have it as thick as a fist behind the ears.

sich etw. hinter die Ohren schreiben, *exp.* *(coll.)* to remember sth. well, *(lit.)* to write sth. behind one's ears.

die Ohren hängen lassen, *exp.* *(coll.)* to be disappointed, *(lit.)* to let one's ears hang down.

jm. die Ohren lang ziehen, *exp.* *(coll.)* to read sb. the riot act, *(lit.)* to pull sb.'s ears until they're long.

die Ohren spitzen, *exp.* to listen, *(lit.)* to sharpen one's ears.

einen hinter die Löffel bekommen, *exp.* *(coll.)* to get hit, *(lit.)* to get one behind the spoons; *Note: see* **Löffel.**

einen Ohrwurm haben, *exp.* to have a catchy tune on one's mind, *(lit.)* to have an ear worm.

Horchmuscheln, *f.pl.* *(sl.)* big ears, *(lit.)* listening shells.

Löffel, *m.pl.* *(coll.)* ears, *(lit.)* spoons.

mit den Ohren schlackern, *exp.* *(coll.)* to be surprised, *(lit.)* to dangle by one's ears.

noch feucht hinter den Ohren sein, *exp.* *(coll.)* to be young and immature, *(lit.)* to be wet behind one's ears.

Segelohren, *n.pl.* prominent ears, *(lit.)* sail ears.

jn. übers Ohr hauen, *exp.* to betray sb., *(lit.)* to slap sb. over the ears.

E

EAT, to *(essen)*
(See: **HUNGRY, to be**)

da kommt einem der kalte Kaffee wieder hoch! *exp.* *(sl.)* I feel like puking, *(lit.)* the cold coffee comes up again.

jm. fällt das Essen aus dem Gesicht, *exp.* *(sl.)* to throw up, *(lit.)* the food is falling out of sb.'s face.

sich den Magen vollhauen, *exp.* *(coll.)* to eat a lot, *(lit.)* to fill one's belly.

sich den Wanst vollschlagen, *exp.* *(coll.)* to eat a lot, *(lit.)* to fill one's belly; *Note:* **Wanst** is a slang term for **Bauch.**

dem Mittag wieder guten Tag sagen, *exp.* *(sl.)* to vomit, *(lit.)* to say hello to one's lunch again.

dinieren, *v.* dine.

einfahren, *v.* *(sl.)* shove food (into oneself).

einkacheln, *v.* *(sl.)* eat fast.

Festmahl, *n.* feast.

Fische füttern, *exp.* *(sl.)* to vomit because of sea sickness, *(lit.)* to feed fish.

Fraß, *m.* *(vulg.)* grub.

fressen, *v.* *(vulg.)* eat like an animal.

Freßsack, *m. (vulg.)* glutton, *(lit.)* provender bag.

Fressalien, *f.pl. (vulg.)* food.

friß oder stirb! *exp. (vulg.)* eat or die.

futtern, *v. (sl.)* eat fast, *(lit.)* feed.

gefundenes Fressen, *exp.* (an edible) gift from the gods.

Gelage, *n.* much good food, *(lit.)* feast, banquet.

grasen, *v. (sl.)* gulp, *(lit.)* graze.

Hundefraß, *m. (vulg.)* bad food, *(lit.)* dogfood.

im Essen herumstochern, *exp.* to play with one's food, *(lit.)* to poke about in one's food.

in sich hineinspachteln, *exp. (sl.)* to eat fast, *(lit.)* to eat with a spatula.

kotzen, *v. (vulg.)* puke.

lecker, *adj.* yummy.

Leckerbissen, *m.* dainty morsel.

Leckermaul, *m.* sweet-tooth, *(lit.)* yummy snout.

Loch im Magen, *adj.* to be hungry, *(lit.)* to have a hole in one's stomach.

mampfen, *v. (sl.)* eat with one's mouth full.

Pampe, *f. (sl.)* bad food.

reinhauen wie ein Scheunendrescher, *exp. (sl.)* to eat like a horse, *(lit.)* to eat like a threshing machine.

sich reinziehen, *v. (sl.)* shove (food) down, *(lit.)* pull (the food) in.

runterwühlen, *v.* eat food which one doesn't like.

runterwürgen, *v. (sl.)* eat food which one doesn't like, *(lit.)* to choke down.

Schlanguri, *m. (sl.)* bad food; *Note:* comes from **salmagundi** which is a hearty meal made by pirates.

schwelgen, *v.* feast.

spachteln, *v. (sl.)* gorge.

Topfgucker, *m.* a person who looks in all pots to see what's cooking.

verdrücken, *v. (sl.)* devour.

verputzen, *v. (coll.)* gorge.

verschnabulieren, *v. (sl.)* gorge.

verspeisen, *v.* gorge.

vertilgen, *v. (sl.)* gorge.

Vielfraß, *m. (vulg.)* voracious eater.

sich vollstopfen, *v. (sl.)* eat a lot and fast., *(lit.)* stuff oneself.

wie ein Vogel picken, *exp.* to eat very little, *(lit.)* to pick like a bird.

etw. zwischen die Beißerchen schieben, *exp. (sl.)* to eat, *(lit.)* to push sth. between one's teeth; *Note:* **Beißerchen,** *n.pl.* teeth.

EFFORTLESS *(einfach)*

etw. auf die leichte Schulter nehmen, to take sth. lightly, *(lit.)* to take sth. on the light shoulder.

etw. aus dem Ärmel schütteln, *exp.* to do sth. with the greatest ease, *(lit.)* to shake sth. out of one's sleeve.

etw. aus dem Stand machen, *exp.* to do sth. easily, *(lit.)* to do sth. standing.

das klappt wie am Schnürchen! *exp.* that goes like clockwork.

das sind kleine Fische! *exp.* *(coll.)* those are small problems, *(lit.)* those are small fish.

echt easy! *exp.* *(sl.)* really easy; *Note:* **easy** is borrowed from English and also pronounced as such.

ein Kunststück sein, *exp.* to be easy, *(lit.)* to be a work of art.

etw. im Handumdrehen machen, *exp.* to do sth. quickly and easily, *(lit.)* to do sth. in a turn of the hand.

etw. im Schlaf machen, *exp.* to do sth. easily, *(lit.)* to do sth. in one's sleep.

kinderleicht, *adj.* very easy, *(lit.)* child's play.

Kinderspiel sein, *exp.* to be very easy, *(lit.)* to be child's play.

etw. mit dem kleinen Finger machen, *exp.* to do sth. with one's eyes shut, *(lit.)* to do sth. with one's pinky.

etw. mit geschlossenen Augen machen, *exp.* to do sth. with one's eyes shut.

etw. mit Links machen, *exp.* to do sth. easily, *(lit.)* to do sth. left-handed.

nichts ist leichter als das! *exp.* nothing is easier than that.

null Problemo! *exp.* *(sl.)* no problem.

etw. ohne Anlauf machen, *exp.* to do sth. without taking a running start.

pippifax, *adj.* *(sl.)* very easy.

puppig, *adj.* very easy, *(lit.)* doll-like.

etw. vor dem Frühstück machen, *exp.* *(coll.)* to do sth. before breakfast.

ENTERPRISING, to be *(tatkräftig sein)*

---

sich am Riemen reißen, *exp.* *(coll.)* to get a grip on oneself, *(lit.)* to pull oneself up by the belt.

andere Saiten aufziehen, *exp.* to become energetic and serious, *(lit.)* to draw up different strings.

anspornen, *v.* spur on.

jn. auf die Beine bringen, *exp.* to get sb. going, *(lit.)* to put sb. on their legs.

auf Draht sein, *exp.* *(coll.)* to be all there, *(lit.)* to be on the wire.

jn. auf Schwung bringen, *exp.* to get sb. going, *(lit.)* to get sb. swinging.

auf Zack sein, *exp.* *(coll.)* to be all there.

Bäume ausreißen, *exp.* to be energetic, *(lit.)* to rip out trees.

jm. Dampf machen, *exp.* *(coll.)* to put pressure on sb.

in Fahrt sein, *exp.* to be in gear, *(lit.)* to be on the drive.

in Schwung sein, *exp.* to be in gear, *(lit.)* to be in the swing.

mit der Faust auf den Tisch hauen, *exp.* to be energetic, to know what one wants, *(lit.)* to hit one's fist on the table.

mit Feuer unterm Hintern, *exp.* *(sl.)* to do sth. energetically, *(lit.)* with fire under one's behind.

mit Pfiff an die Sache gehen, *exp.* *(coll.)* to do sth. energetically, *(lit.)* to do sth. with a whistle.

schwer auf Draht sein, *exp.* *(coll.)* to be all there.

schwungvoll, *adj.* energetic.

EXAGGERATE, to *(übertreiben)*

an den Haaren herbeigezogen, *exp.* *(coll.)* to be far-fetched, *(lit.)* to be pulled by one's hair.

etw. auf die Spitze treiben, *exp.* *(coll.)* to carry sth. to extremes, *(lit.)* to push sth. to the tip.

Aufschneider, *m.* boaster.

aus einem Furz einen Donnerschlag machen, *exp.* *(vulg.)* to make a mountain out of a molehill, *(lit.)* to make thunder out of a fart.

aus einer Mücke einen Elefanten machen, *exp.* *(coll.)* to make a mountain out of a molehill, *(lit.)* to make an elephant out of a mosquito.

bluffen, *v.* *(coll.)* bluff.

dick auftragen, *exp.* *(coll.)* to lay it on thick.

sich dicktun, *v.* show off, *(lit.)* to make oneself fat.

dröhnen, *v.* *(sl.)* exaggerate.

ein Bimborium machen, *exp.* to exaggerate.

eine Nummer abziehen, *exp.* *(coll.)* to exaggerate, *(lit.)* to pull a number.

eine Schau abziehen, *exp.* to exaggerate, *(lit.)* to perform a show.

Farbe dick auftragen, *exp.* to exaggerate,*(lit.)* to paint it on thick.

große Bögen spucken, *exp.* *(coll.)* to exaggerate, *(lit.)* to spit big arches.

große Töne spucken, *exp.* *(coll.)* to exaggerate, *(lit.)* to spit big tones.

große Töne schwingen, *exp.* *(coll.)* to exaggerate, *(lit.)* to swing big tones.

mächtig ins Horn stoßen, *exp.* *(coll.)* to exaggerate, *(lit.)* to strongly hit one's horn.

Märchen erzählen, *exp.* to tell stories, *(lit.)* to tell fairy tales.

das Maul aufreißen, *exp.* *(vulg.)* to exaggerate, *(lit.)* to rip open one's snout.

das Maul vollnehmen, *exp.* *(vulg.)* to exaggerate, *(lit.)* to take one's snout full.

den Mund voll nehmen, *exp.* *(sl.)* to exaggerate, *(lit.)* to take one's mouth full.

nun bleib mal auf dem Teppich! *exp.* *(coll.)* keep your feet on the ground, *(lit.)* stay on the carpet.

rumtütern, *v.* exaggerate.

Schmu, *m.* big talk.

Seemannsgarn erzählen, *exp.* to tell stories, *(lit.)* to tell seamen's stories.

Sprüche klopfen, *exp.* *(coll.)* to talk big, *(lit.)* to knock out expressions.

die Story vom Pferd erzählen, *exp.* to exaggerate, *(lit.)* to tell the story about the horse.

Stories erzählen, *exp.* *(coll.)* to tell stories.

überspannen, *v.* exaggerate.

weit ausholen, *v.* exaggerate.

Wind machen, *exp.* *(coll.)* to exaggerate, *(lit.)* to make wind.

EXHAUSTED, to be *(ermattet sein)*

abgeschlafft, *adj.* *(coll.)* worn out.

alle, *adj.* *(sl.)* exhausted, *(lit.)* empty; *Note:* usually **völlig alle sein**/to be completely exhausted.

alles geht an jm. vorbei, *exp.* *(coll.)* to be tired, *(lit.)* everything goes past one.

alles plätschert an jm. vorbei, *exp.* to be tired, *(lit.)* everything patters past one.

am Ende sein, *exp.* to be exhausted, *(lit.)* to be at one's end.

auf dem letzten Loch pfeifen, *exp. (sl.)* to be exhausted, *(lit.)* to whistle out of the last hole.

auf dem Zahnfleisch kommen, *exp. (sl.)* to be exhausted, *(lit.)* to come up to one's gums.

ausgelaugt, *adj.* exhausted, *(lit.)* leached out.

ausgerungen, *adj.* exhausted, *(lit.)* wrung out.

ein Hund sein, *exp. (sl.)* to be tired, *(lit.)* to be a dog.

fertig, *adj. (coll.)* exhausted, *(lit.)* to be really done; *Note:* usually **völlig fertig/** really exhausted.

fix und fertig, *adj. (coll.)* exhausted.

fix und foxi, *adj. (coll.)* exhausted.

hundemüde, *adj. (coll.)* dog-tired.

kein Power mehr haben, *exp. (sl.)* to be unmotivated, *(lit.)* to have no power.

keinen Drive mehr haben, *exp. (sl.)* to be unmotivated, *(lit.)* to have no drive.

k.o., *adj.* exhausted.

neben der Mütze sein, *exp. (sl.)* to be fatigued, *(lit.)* to be next to the hat.

nicht auf Zack sein, *exp. (coll.)* to be exhausted.

nicht ganz drauf sein, *exp. (coll.)* to be tired, *(lit.)* not to be up to it anymore.

schlapp, *adj.* exhausted; *Note:* **eine Schlappe machen,** *exp.* to be exhausted, *(lit.)* to make a setback; **schlapp machen,** *exp.* to give up.

schwere Augen haben, *exp.* sleepy, *(lit.)* to have heavy eyes.

EYES *(Augen)*

---

jm. etw. aufs Auge drücken, *exp. (coll.)* to thrust a thing upon a person, *(lit.)* to press sth. against sb.'s eye.

Äuglein, *n.pl.* children's eyes.

aus den Augen sein, *exp.* to be out of sight, *(lit.)* to be out of one's eyes.

blauäugig, *adj.* naive, *(lit.)* blue-eyed.

blaues Auge, *exp.* black eye, *(lit.)* blue eye.

da bleibt kein Auge trocken! *exp. (coll.)* one has to laugh, *(lit.)* no eye is going to stay dry.

das geht ins Auge! *exp. (coll.)* it is going to go wrong, *(lit.)* it's going into one's eye.

ein Auge riskieren, *exp.* to take a peek, *(lit.)* to risk an eye.

ein Auge zudrücken, *exp.* to forgive, to overlook sth., *(lit.)* to close an eye.

jm. ein Dorn im Auge sein, *exp.* to be a thorn in one's side, *(lit.)* to be a thorn in sb.'s eye.

Fischaugen, *n.pl.* big eyes, *(lit.)* fish eyes.

Froschaugen, *n.pl.* big eyes, *(lit.)* frog eyes.

glotzäugig, *adj.* goggle-eyed.

Glupschaugen, *n.pl.* goggle eyes.

große Augen machen, *exp.* to open one's eyes in surprise, *(lit.)* to make big eyes.

ins Auge springen, *exp.* to be obvious, *(lit.)* to hop into one's eyes.

keine Augen im Kopf haben, *exp.* to be blind, *(lit.)* not to have eyes in one's head.

Kiekerchen, *n.pl.* *(sl.)* eyes.
Kuhaugen, *n.pl.* big eyes, *(lit.)* cow eyes.
Löcher in die Luft starren, *exp.* to be bored, *(lit.)* to stare holes into the air.
Schweinsaugen, *n.pl.* *(sl.)* small and narrow eyes, *(lit.)* pig eyes.
Sehschlitze, *m.pl.* *(sl.)* eyes, *(lit.)* sight slits.
Stielaugen, *n.pl.* *(sl.)* stalked eyes.
Veilchen, *n.* *(coll.)* black eye, *(lit.)* violet.
zwinkern, *v.* blink.

FACE *(Gesicht)*

Babyface, *n.* *(sl.)* cute face; *Note:* a term borrowed from English.
ein Gesicht wie sieben Tage Regenwetter machen, *exp.* to look unhappy,
   (lit.) to make a face as if it had rained for seven days.
ein langes Gesicht machen, *exp.* to make a long face.
ein saures Gesicht machen, *exp.* to look bad-tempered, *(lit.)* to make a sour
   face.
Fresse, *f.* *(vulg.)* ugly face; *Note:* this term is also used for mouth.
Gesicht verlieren, *exp.* to lose face.
Grimasse, *f.* *(sl.)* grimace.
Knutschgesicht, *n.* *(sl.)* cute face, *(lit.)* cuddle face.
Milchgesicht, *n.* young face, *(lit.)* milk face.
Mondgesicht, *n.* round face, *(lit.)* moon face.
Puppengesicht, *n.* cute face, *(lit.)* doll's face.
Visage, *f.* *(vulg.)* ugly face; *Note:* **Visage** is pronounced as in French but with a
   stressed "e."

FALL, to *(fallen)*

auf die Fresse fallen, *exp.* *(vulg.)* to fall on one's mouth.
auf die Nase fallen, *exp.* to fall on one's nose.
auf die Schnauze fallen, *exp.* *(vulg.)* to fall on one's mouth; *Note:* **Schnauze,** *f.*
   snout.
Bauchklatscher, *m.* *(coll.)* belly-flop.
Bauchlandung, *f.* *(coll.)* belly-flop; *Note:* also means failure.
damit ist er auf den Bauch gefallen! *exp.* he failed, *(lit.)* he fell on his belly
   with that.
jm. ein Beinchen stellen, *exp.* to trip sb.
plumpsen, *v.* fall with a bump.
sich langlegen, *v.* *(coll.)* fall, *(lit.)* lay oneself long.

FAST *(schnell)*

auf die Schnelle, *exp.* in a hurry.
auf die Tube drücken, *exp.* *(coll.)* to accelerate, *(lit.)* to squeeze the tube.

jn. Beine machen, *exp.* to urge sb. to hurry up, *(lit.)* to make sb. legs.

blitzschnell, *adj.* quick (as lightning).

das geht nicht so huschihuschi! *exp.* it can't be rushed.

einen Affenzahn draufhaben, *exp.* to move at high speed, *(lit.)* to have a monkey's tooth on it.

es ist höchste Eisenbahn! *exp.* it's high time, *(lit.)* it's highest train.

fix, *adj.* quick.

flink, *adj.* quick.

flott, *adj.* quick.

Hals über Kopf, *exp.* in no time, *(lit.)* neck over head.

huschen, *v.* slide quickly.

im Handumdrehen, *exp.* in no time at all, *(lit.)* in a turn of the hand.

in Null komma Nix, *exp.* in less than no time, *(lit.)* in zero comma nothing.

in Windeseile, *exp.* in next to no time, *(lit.)* in a wind's hurry.

mit einem Affenzahn, *exp. (coll.)* with high speed, *(lit.)* with a monkey's tooth.

mit Power, *exp. (sl.)* with power; *Note:* term taken from English and pronounced as such.

mit voller Karre, *exp. (coll.)* with high speed, *(lit.)* with full cart.

mit voller Pulle, *exp. (coll.)* with great speed, *(lit.)* with a full bottle.

pfeilschnell, *adv.* in a flash, *(lit.)* arrow fast.

rin in die Kartoffeln, raus aus die Kartoffeln! *exp. (coll.)* it's "do this" one minute, it's "do that" the next, *(lit.)* into the potatoes, out of the potatoes; *Note:* this expression is grammatically incorrect.

schnurstracks, *adv.* to go quickly and straight.

spritzig, *adj.* quick.

um die Ecke fegen, *exp.* to race around the corner, *(lit.)* to sweep around the corner.

wie aus der Pistole geschossen, *exp.* in a flash, *(lit.)* as if shot out of a pistol.

wie der Teufel, *exp.* in next to no time.

wie der Wind, *exp.* in next to no time.

wie vom wilden Affen gebissen, *exp. (coll.)* with high speed, *(lit.)* as if bitten by a wild monkey.

wie vom Teufel gejagt, *exp. (coll.)* in a daredevil fashion, *(lit.)* as if chased by the devil.

wie von einer Tarantel gestochen, *exp. (coll.)* quickly, *(lit.)* as if bitten by a tarantula.

FEAR *(Angst)*

Albträume bekommen, *exp.* to have nightmares.

ein Angsthase sein, *exp. (coll.)* to be a scaredy-cat, *(lit.)* to be a frightened rabbit.

Bammel haben (vor jm./etw.), *exp.* to be scared (of sb./sth.).

Bange, *f. (coll.)* fear; *Note:* **mir ist (ganz) bange!**/I am (very) afraid.

Blut und Wasser schwitzen, *exp.* to have intense fear, *(lit.)* to sweat blood and water.

Courage fehlen, *exp.* to lack courage; *Note:* **mir fehlt die Courage**/I lack the courage; **Courage** is spoken as in French but with a stressed "e."

das Fracksausen bekommen, *exp. (coll.)* to get the heebie-jeebies, *(lit.)* to get the tuxedo whistle.

ein Schißhase sein, *exp. (sl.)* to be a scaredy-cat, *(lit.)* to be a shit-rabbit; *Note:* **Schiß** is a commonly used term for **Angst.**

eine Heidenangst haben (vor jn./etw.), *exp.* to be scared stiff (of sb./sth.).

eine Schlotterhose sein, *exp. (sl.)* to be frightened, *(lit.)* to be a baggy pants.

die Hose voll haben, *exp. (vulg.)* to be afraid, *(lit.)* to have one's pants full.

die Pferde scheu machen *exp.* to get the jitters, *(lit.)* to frighten the horses.

feige, *adj.* afraid.

Feigling, *m.* coward.

Gänsehaut bekommen, *exp.* to get goose bumps, *(lit.)* to get goose skin.

sich in die Hose machen, *exp.* to wet one's pants.

sich ins Bockshorn jagen lassen, *exp.* to be frightened, *(lit.)* to let oneself get chased into the hartshorn.

sich ins Hemd machen, *exp.* to wet one's pants, *(lit.)* to wet one's shirt.

kalte Füße bekommen, *exp.* to get cold feet.

Manschetten (vor jm./etw.) haben, *exp. (sl.)* (sb./sth.) gives sb. the willies.

Memme, *f. (sl.)* coward.

Muffe, *f. (sl.)* fear.

jm. rutscht das Herz in die Hose, *exp.* to be frightened, *(lit.)* sb.'s heart slips into their pants.

Schiß haben (vor), *m. (sl.)* to be afraid (of sth.), *(lit.)* to be shit-scared (of sth.). *Note:* **Schiß** is a commonly used term for **Angst.**

Schisser, *m. (vulg.)* shit-scared person.

jm. schlottern die Knie, *exp.* sb.'s knees are shaking.

schwummerig, *adj.* frightened, *(lit.)* dizzy; *Note:* **mir ist ganz schwummerig**/I'm frightened.

sich verjagen, *v. (sl.)* frighten oneself, *(lit.)* to chase oneself away.

sich vor Angst die Hose naß machen, *exp. (sl.)* to be frightened, *(lit.)* to wet one's pants out of fear.

vom Mut verlassen werden, *exp.* to be deserted by courage.

weiche Knie bekommen, *exp.* to get frightened, *(lit.)* to get soft knees.

FED UP, to be *(genug haben)*

basta! *Interj.* enough; *Note:* borrowed from Italian; **jetzt aber basta!**/ that's enough.

bis (hier) oben stehen, *exp. (sl.)* to be fed up; *Note:* **es steht mir bis (hier) oben**/I'm fed up with it.

bis zum Hals stehen, *exp. (sl.)* to be fed up; *Note:* **es steht mir bis zum Hals.**

das Fass ist übergelaufen! *exp.* that's the limit, *(lit.)* the cask has run over.

das Fass ist voll! *exp.* that's the limit, *(lit.)* the cask is full.

das schlägt dem Faß dem Boden aus! *exp. (coll.)* that's the limit, *(lit.)* that knocks the bottom out of the cask.

die Koffer packen, *exp.* to have enough, *(lit.)* to pack one's suitcases.

die Nase voll haben, *exp. (coll.)* to have had enough, *(lit.)* to have one's nose full.

die Schnauze voll haben, *exp. (vulg.)* to be fed up, *(lit.)* to have one's snout full.

es kotzt mich an! *exp. (vulg.)* I'm fed up with it, *(lit.)* it makes me puke.

es langt! *exp.* that's enough.

es langt mir! *exp.* I am fed up with it.

es stinkt mir! *exp. (sl.)* that stinks (to me).

etw. gestrichen satt haben, *exp. (coll.)* to be really fed up with sth.; *Note:* **ich habe es gestrichen satt**/I am really fed up with it.

reichen, *v.* be enough; *Note:* **jetzt reichts!**/that's enough.

jm. zum Halse heraushängen, *exp. (sl.)* to be fed up *or* tired of sth., *(lit.)* to hang out of sb.'s throat; *Note:* **das hängt mir echt zum Halse heraus**/I'm tired of it.

etw. zum Kotzen satt haben, *exp. (vulg.)* to be fed up *or* tired of sth. (to the point of vomiting); *Note:* **ich hab das echt zum Kotzen satt**/I'm fed up with it.

FEEBLE, to feel *(sich schwach fühlen)*

---

alles dreht sich! *exp.* everything is turning.

sich ganz schwummerig fühlen, *exp.* to feel dizzy.

schwächeln, *v.* feel weak.

weichen Boden unter den Füßen bekommen, *exp. (coll.)* to feel dizzy, *(lit.)* to get soft ground underneath one's feet.

weiche Knie bekommen, *exp.* to feel dizzy, *(lit.)* to get soft knees.

FEET *(Füße)*

Entenfüße, *m.pl.* pigeon-toed feet, *(lit.)* duck feet.

Fuß fassen, *exp.* to gain footing, to reach a secure position.

gang und gebe sein, *exp.* to be customary.

Haxen, *m.pl.* feet.

kalte Füße kriegen, *exp. (coll.)* to get into a delicate situation, *(lit.)* to get cold feet.

latschen, *v. (sl.)* walk.

mit beiden Füßen fest auf dem Boden stehen, *exp.* to face reality, *(lit.)* to have both feet firmly on the ground.

sich mit Händen und Füßen wehren, *exp.* to reject strongly, *(lit.)* to protect oneself with hands and feet.

Plattfüße, *m.pl.* long and wide feet, *(lit.)* flat feet.

Quadratlatschen, *m.pl.* big feet; *Note:* also refers to casual shoes.

Quanten, *m.pl. (sl.)* big feet.

Quastenläufer, *m. (sl.)* person who walks funny.

FIGHT, to *(sich streiten)*

Note: in the following, **kriegen** can be substituted for **bekommen**.

sich die Haare ausreißen, *exp. (coll.)* to beat each other up, *(lit.)* to pull out each other's hair.

sich die Köpfe einhauen, *exp. (coll.)* to fight, *(lit.)* to smash each others heads in.

sich die Zähne zeigen, *exp. (coll.)* to show one's teeth.

es ist dicke Luft! *exp. (coll.)* we are fighting, *(lit.)* there is thick air.

sich in den Haaren legen, *exp. (coll.)* to lay into each other, *(lit.)* to lay into each other's hair.

sich in der Wolle legen, *exp. (coll.)* to fight, *(lit.)* to lay into each other's wool.

Kampfhahn, *m.* pugnacious fellow, *(lit.)* fighting cock.

jm. kein krummes Haar lassen, *exp. (coll.)* to thrash a person, *(lit.)* not to leave sb. with a crooked hair.

sich kloppen, *v. (sl.)* fight.

Klopperei, *f. (sl.)* fight.

mit jm. ein Hühnchen rupfen, *exp. (coll.)* to have a bone to pick with sb., *(lit.)* to pluck a chicken with sb.

jm. Pfeffer geben, *exp. (coll.)* to fight with sb., *(lit.)* to give sb. pepper.

sich um Kaisers Bart streiten, *exp. (coll.)* to fight, *(lit.)* to fight about the emperor's beard.

FIX, to be in a *(in einer schwierigen Lage sein)*

auf Grund laufen, *exp. (sl.)* to be in a difficult situation, *(lit.)* to run aground.

brenzlige Lage, *exp. (coll.)* dicey situation; *Note:* **jetzt wird's brenzlig!**/things are getting too hot now.

es wird eng! *exp.* now it's getting troublesome, *(lit.)* now it's getting tight.

festgeklemmt, *adj. (sl.)* to be stuck.

festsitzen, *v. (sl.)* be stuck, *(lit.)* to be sitting firmly.

haarige Angelegenheit, *exp.* hairy situation.

im Dreck sitzen, *exp. (vulg.)* to be up to the eyes in mud.

im Schlamassel sitzen, *exp. (coll.)* to be in a fix, *(lit.)* to sit in a mess; *Note:* **bis über beide Ohren im Schlamassel sitzen**/to be up to one's ear in a mess.

in der Klemme sitzen, *exp. (coll.)* to be in a fix, *(lit.)* to sit in the clamp.

in der Patsche sitzen, *exp. (coll.)* to be in a fix; *Note:* **bis über beide Ohren in der Patsche sitzen**/to be in a fix up to one's ears.

in der Scheiße sitzen, *exp. (vulg.)* to be in a fix, *(lit.)* to sit in the shit.

in der Scheiße stecken, *exp. (vulg.)* to be in a fix, *(lit.)* to be stuck in shit.

in der Tinte sitzen, *exp. (coll.)* to be in a fix, *(lit.)* to sit in ink; *Note:* **bis über beide Ohren in der Tinte sitzen**/to be in a fix up to one's ears.

ins Fettnäpchen treten, *exp. (coll.)* to put one's foot in one's mouth, *(lit.)* to step in a little bowl of fat.

jetzt hast du den Dreck in der Schachtel! *exp. (sl.)* now you're in a mess, *(lit.)* now you have the dirt in the box.

FLATTER, to *(schmeicheln)*

jm. Honig um den Bart schmieren, *exp. (coll.)* to say honeyed words to sb., *(lit.)* to smear honey around sb.'s beard.

jm. in den Hintern kriechen, *exp. (vulg.)* to brown-nose sb., *(lit.)* to crawl into sb.'s behind.

schöne Worte machen, *exp.* to flatter sb., *(lit.)* to make sb. nice words.

Speichelleckerei, *f. (coll.)* flattery.

jn. umgarnen, *v.* beguile sb.

jm. Zucker in den Hintern blasen, *exp. (vulg.)* to flatter sb., *(lit.)* to blow sugar into sb.'s behind.

Zucker reden, *exp. (coll.)* to flatter, *(lit.)* to speak sugar.

FORTUNATE, to be *(Glück haben)*

Bingo! *Interj.* bingo!

mit einem blauen Auge davonkommen, *exp.* to get away with little damage, *(lit.)* to get away with a blue eye. *Note:* **blaues Auge**/black eye.

Glück im Unglück haben, *exp.* to be lucky under the circumstances, *(lit.)* to have luck in one's bad luck.

Glückskind, *n.* person who was born under a lucky star, *(lit.)* lucky child.

Glückspilz, *m.* lucky devil, *(lit.)* lucky mushroom.

Glückssträhne, *f.* lucky streak.

Glückstreffer, *m.* lucky hit.

jm. Hals- und Beinbruch wünschen, *exp.* to wish sb. good luck, *(lit.)* to wish sb. a broken neck and leg.

mehr Glück als Verstand haben, *exp. (coll.)* to have more luck than common sense.

Schwein haben, *exp. (coll.)* to be lucky, *(lit.)* to have pig.

toi-toi-toi! *exp.* good luck.

Volltreffer, *m.* direct hit; *Note:* **das war ein Volltreffer!**/You hit the bull's eye!

FUN, to have *(Spaß haben)*
(See: **Party**)

---

bis die Fetzen fliegen, *exp. (coll.)* to have a lot of fun, *(lit.)* until the shreds fly; *Note:* **man feiert bis die Fetzen fliegen**/one parties until exhaustion.

da ist der Bär los! *exp. (sl.)* it's really fun there, *(lit.)* the bear is loose there.

da ist der Kuckuck los! *exp. (coll.)* it's really fun there, *(lit.)* the cuckoo is loose there.

echt gut abfahren, *exp. (sl.)* to have fun; *Note:* **die Party fährt echt gut ab**/the party is really fun.

eine Gaudi haben, *exp. (coll.)* to have fun.

eine Mordsgaudi haben, *exp. (coll.)* to have a lot of fun.

es ist tote Hose! *exp. (sl.)* nothing is going on, *(lit.)* it's dead pants.

Spaß in Dosen, *exp. (sl.)* funny thing, *(lit.)* fun in cans. *Note:* **auf der Party gab es Spaß in Dosen**/the party was really fun.

voll abgehen, *exp. (sl.)*to be fun; *Note:* **die Party geht voll ab**/the Party is fun.

GERMANS *(Deutsche)*

Bajuware, *m. (coll.)* Bavarian.

Bavare, *m. (coll.)* Bavarian.

Bazi, *m. (coll.)* Bavarian.

Besserwessi, *m. (coll.)* person from West Germany.

Fischkopf, *m. (coll.)* Northern German, *(lit.)* fish head.

Flachlandtiroler, *m. (coll.)* Northern German, *(lit.)* flatland Tyrolean; *Note:* a Tyrolean is a person from the Tyrol, a region in the Alps.

Häuslerbauer, *m. (coll.)* German who works hard in order to be able to buy a house and live an ordinary life.

Jodler, *m. (coll.)* Bavarian, *(lit.)* yodeler.

Juppie, *m.* Yuppie; *Note:* use a German pronunciation.

Muschelschupser, *m. (coll.)* Northern German, *(lit.)* shell shover.

Müslifresser, *m. (sl.)* Southern German, *(lit.)* granola muncher.

Nordlicht, *n.* Northern German, *(lit.)* northern light.

Nordstern, *m.* Northern German, *(lit.)* north star.

Null-Bock-Generation, *f. (coll.)* switch-off generation; *Note:* **Null-Bock haben,** *exp.* to feel like not doing anything at all.

Ossi, *m.* a person from former East Germany; *Note:* before the reunification this term was used for **Ostfriesen**/East Frisian.

Piefke, *m. (coll.)* Austrian term for Northern German.

Popper, *m.* young person dressed in a fashionable college style.

Preuße, *m. (coll.)* Northern German, *(lit.)* Prussian.

Preußenzipfel, *m. (coll.)* Northern German.

Quietscher, *m. (sl.)* Bavarian.

Quiddjes, *pl. (sl.)* Bavarians.

Schickimicki, *m.* Yuppie in Munich from the **Schickimicki-Szene.**

Wessi, *m.* West German.

Westhai, *m.* West German engaging in real estate speculation in the former East Germany, *(lit.)* west shark.

GIRL *(Mädchen)*

---

alte Schachtel, *exp. (sl.)* old woman, *(lit.)* old box.

Bißgurn, *f. (sl.)* unfriendly woman.

Deern, *f.* girl.

Dirndl, *n. (sl.)* girl; *Note:* also term for a traditional Bavarian dress.

Emanze, *f. (sl.)* emancipated woman.

flotte Biene, *exp. (sl.)* chic woman.

Frauenzimmer, *n. (sl.)* woman.

gute Frau, *f.* good woman.

Hexe, *f. (sl.)* witch.

junges Ding, *exp.* young inexperienced girl, *(lit.)* young thing.

Kuh, *f. (vulg.)* unfriendly woman, *(lit.)* cow; *Note:* often **dumme Kuh**/dumb woman.

Luder, *n. (vulg.)* bitch.

Mädel, *n.* young woman.

Mietze, *f. (vulg.)* sexy woman.

Miststück, *n. (vulg.)* bitch.

Pfundsweib, *n. (coll.)* really nice woman.

Puppe, *f. (sl.)* pretty woman.

Schickse, *f. (vulg.)* hussy.

Schlampe, *f. (vulg.)* slut.
Schlange, *f. (vulg.)* bitch, *(lit.)* snake; *Note:* often **falsche Schlange.**
schmucke Deern, *exp.* pretty girl.
schmucke Lady, *exp.* pretty girl.
Schnepfe, *f. (vulg.)* tart.
Schreckschraube, *f. (sl.)* ugly old woman.
Schrulle, *f. (sl.)* unfriendly old woman.
tolles Weib, *n. exp. (coll.)* great woman.
Torte, *f. (sl.)* dingbat.
Tulpe, *f. (sl.)* dingbat, *(lit.)* tulip.
Tunte, *f. (sl.)* hussy; *Note:* also refers to a homosexual man.
Tusse, *f. (sl.)* dingbat.
Tussie, *f. (sl.)* dingbat.
Vogelscheuche, *f.* ugly girl, *(lit.)* scarecrow.
Weibsstück, *n. (vulg.)* bitch.
Zicke, *f. (vulg.)* stupid woman, *(lit.)* nanny goat; *Note:* often **dumme** or **blöde Zicke.**
Ziege, *f. (vulg.)* mean woman, *(lit.)* goat; *Note:* often **dumme** or **blöde Ziege.**

GIVE, to *(geben)*

---

herhusten, *v.* give, *(lit.)* to cough up.
rausrücken, *v.* give.
rüberschieben, *v.* give, *(lit.)* slide (sth.) over.
rüberwachsen, *v.* give; *Note:* **laß mal rüberwachsen!**/hand it over.

GOSSIP *(Klatsch)*
(See: **CHIT-CHAT, to**)

---

jn. durch den Hechel ziehen, *exp. (coll.)* to gossip badly about sb., *(lit.)* to pull sb. through the flax comb.
ein schnodderiges Mundwerk haben, *exp. (coll.)* to have a big mouth, *(lit.)* to have a brash mouthpiece.
Gefasel, *n.* twaddle.
nicht auf den Mund gefallen sein, *exp.* to have a ready tongue, *(lit.)* not to have fallen on one's mouth.
kein Blatt vor den Mund nehmen, *exp.* to be plain-spoken, *(lit.)* not to take a leaf in front of one's mouth.
keinen guten Faden an jm. lassen, *exp.* to talk about sb. behind his back, (lit) not to leave a good thread on sb.
kein gutes Haar an jm. lassen, *exp.* to talk about sb. behind his back, *(lit.)* not to leave a good hair on sb.
klatschen, *v.* gossip, *(lit.)* to clap or applaud.
Klatschtante, *f.* woman who gossips a lot.
Klatschweib, *f. (coll.)* woman who gossips a lot.
Tratsch, *m.* gossip.
tratschen, *v.* gossip.
Tratschweib, *n.* woman who gossips a lot.

wie ein Wasserfall reden, *exp.* to speak constantly, *(lit.)* to speak like a waterfall.

verbal, *adj.* verbal.

GREAT *(toll)*

echt can be put in front of all the following adjectives for emphasis; *Note:* **echt** means *really* or *very.*

bombastisch, *adj.* great, *(lit.)* bombastic.

cool, *adj.* *(sl.)* cool; *Note:* taken from English.

dufte, *adj.* great.

fetzig, *adj.* *(sl.)* really mind-blowing, *(lit.)* shredded.

gehörig, *adj.* properly.

geil, *adj.* *(sl.)* superb; *(lit.)* horny; *Note:* even stronger terms are **affengeil, oberaffengeil,** *(lit.)* ape-horny, very ape-horny.

granatenmäßig, *adj.* *(sl.)* superb, *(lit.)* grenade-like.

höllisch, *adj.* *(sl.)* great.

irre, *adj.* superb, *(lit.)* crazy.

klasse, *adj.* superb, *(lit.)* classy.

knorke, *adj.* *(sl.)* great.

pfundig, *adj.* fantastic.

picobello, *adj.* great; *Note:* also means spick and span.

prima, *adj.* superb.

sahne, *adj.* *(sl.)* great, *(lit.)* cream.

saumäßig, *adj.* *(sl.)* great, *(lit.)* sow-like.

spitze, *adj.* tops.

spitzenmäßig, *adj.* top.

stark, *adj.* *(sl.)* great, *(lit.)* strong; *Note:* even stronger is **saustark.**

super, *adj.* superb.

superduper, *adj.* *(coll.)* great.

superturbo, *adj.* *(coll.)* great.

tierisch, *adj.* *(sl.)* terrific, *(lit.)* animal-like.

toll, *adj.* great.

ungeheuer, *adj.* unbelievable.

wahnsinnig, *adj.* terrific.

GUY *(Kerl)*

alter Strizzi, *m.* *(sl.)* pimp.

Aufreißer, *m.* *(sl.)* ladykiller.

Bubi, *m.* *(sl.)* fellow.

Bursche, *m.* chap; *Note:* **knallharter Bursche**/tough guy.

Don Juan, *m.* ladykiller.

Fatzke, *m.* *(coll.)* twit.

Flasche, *f.* *(sl.)* weakling, *(lit.)* bottle.

Fritze, *m.* chap.

geiler Bock, *m.* *(vulg.)* lecher, *(lit.)* lecherous goat.

Hampelmann, *m.* weakling, *(lit.)* jumping jack.
Hanswurst, *m.* stupid guy.
Heini, *m.* half-wit; *Note:* also refers to an idiot.
Kerl, *m.* chap.
Knaller, *m.* *(sl.)* chap.
Knilch, *m.* *(sl.)* bastard.
Koloß, *m.* hunk.
Kotzbrocken, *m.* *(vulg.)* filthy jerk.
Lackaffe, *m.* *(sl.)* dandy, *(lit.)* lacquered ape.
Luftikus, *m.* unreliable man.
Lutscher, *m.* *(sl.)* wimp, *(lit.)* lollipop licker.
Macho, *m.* macho; *Note:* taken from English and pronounced as such.
Macker, *m.* *(sl.)* guy.
Milchbubi, *m.* callow youth, *(lit.)* milk boy.
Mistkerl, *m.* *(sl.)* jerk, *(lit.)* manure guy.
Niete, *f.* weak, unsuccessful man, *(lit.)* failure.
Penner, *m.* *(sl.)* loser, *(lit.)* sleeper; *Note:* usually **alter Penner**/old loser.
Pfeife, *f.* wimp, *(lit.)* pipe.
Saukerl, *m.* jerk.
Schlaffi, *m.* weakling.
Schlägertyp, *m.* tough guy.
Schlappschwanz, *m.* *(sl.)* wimp, *(lit.)* limp tail.
Schnösel, *m.* young whippersnapper.
Schürzenjäger, *m.* womanizer, *(lit.)* apron hunter.
Schwächling, *m.* weakling.
Softie, *m.* softie; *Note:* term taken from English.
Typ, *m.* *(sl.)* guy; *Note:* **mieser Typ**/rotten guy.
Waschlappen, *m.* wimp, *(lit.)* washcloth.
Weiberheld, *m.* ladykiller.
Weichei, *n.* weakling, *(lit.)* soft egg.
Weichling, *m.* weakling.
Witzbold, *m.* jokester.

HANDS *(Hände)*

auf der Hand liegen, *exp.* to be obvious, *(lit.)* to lie on one's hand.
sich etw. aus den Fingern saugen, *exp.* *(coll.)* to think sth. up on the spot, *(lit.)* to suck sth. out of one's fingers.
aus zweiter Hand, *exp.* second-hand; *Note:* **das Auto ist aus zweiter Hand**/ this is a second-hand car.
Baggerschaufeln, *f.pl.* *(sl.)* huge hands, *(lit.)* digger shovels.
die Hand im Spiel haben, *exp.* to be involved in sth., *(lit.)* to have one's hands in the game.
(für jn. or etw.) die Hand ins Feuer legen, *exp.* to be honest, *(lit.)* to lay one's hand into the fire (for sb. or sth.).
eine grüne Hand haben, *exp.* to have a green thumb, *(lit.)* to have a green hand.

eine Hand wäscht die andere, *exp.* you scratch my back and I'll scratch yours, *(lit.)* one hand washes the other.

Flossen, *f.pl. (sl.)* hands, *(lit.)* flippers; *Note:* **Flossen weg!**/hands off.

fummeln, *v. (coll.)* fiddle (with).

Gichtgriffel, *m.pl. (sl.)* fingers, *(lit.)* gouty pencil.

grabbeln, *v. (coll.)* grope about; *Note:* **Grabbeltische,** *m.pl.* bargain tables.

grabschen, *v. (sl.)* snatch; *Note:* also refers to the molestation of women.

Grabscher, *m.pl. (sl.)*hand; *Note:* also means a molester of women.

Hand anlegen, *exp.* to help.

Hand aufs Herz! *exp.* cross my heart!

Hand und Fuß haben, *exp.* to make sense, *(lit.)* to have hand and foot.

jm. in die Hände fallen, *exp.* fall into sb.'s hands.

jn. um den (kleinen) Finger wickeln, *exp.* to wrap sb. round one's (little) finger.

Klauen, *f.pl. (coll.)* ugly big hands, *(lit.)* claws.

Krallen, *f.pl. (coll.)* hands with long fingernails, *(lit.)* claws.

öffentliche Hand, *exp.* the government, *(lit.)* public hand.

Pfoten, *f.pl. (sl.)* hands, *(lit.)* paws; *Note:* **Pfoten weg!**/hands off.

Schaufeln, *f.pl. (sl.)* big hands, *(lit.)* shovels.

sich die Finger verbrennen, *exp.* to burn one's fingers.

sich in den Finger schneiden, *exp.* to be mistaken *(lit.)* to cut oneself in the finger.

Spinnenfinger, *m.pl. (coll.)* long thin fingers, *(lit.)* spider fingers.

Würstchenfinger, *m.pl.* fat fingers, *(lit.)* sausage fingers.

zwei linke Hände haben, *exp.* to be clumsy, *(lit.)* to have two left hands.

HAPPY, to be *(glücklich sein)*

aus dem Häuschen sein, *exp.* to go wild because of happiness, *(lit.)* to be out of one's little house.

ausflippen, *v. (coll.)* get all excited, *(lit.)* to flip out.

sich freuen wie ein Schneekönig, *exp.* to be very happy, *(lit.)* to be as happy as a snow king.

happy, *adj. (sl.)* happy; *Note:* term taken from English and pronounced as such.

HEAD *(Kopf)*

Ballon, *m. (sl.)* big head, *(lit.)* balloon.

Birne, *f. (sl.)* head, *(lit.)* pear; *Note:* extremely popular nickname for the German Chancellor, Helmut Kohl.

den Kopf verlieren, *exp.* to lose one's head.

Döz, *m. (sl.)* head.

einen dicken Kopf haben, *exp.* to be stubborn, *(lit.)* to have a thick head.

einen schweren Kopf haben, *exp.* to have a hangover, *(lit.)* to have a heavy head.

Gipskopf, *m. (sl.)* head, *(lit.)* plaster head.

Globus, *m. (sl.)* head, *(lit.)* globe.

Glocke, *f.* *(sl.)* head, *(lit.)* bell.

Glumpskopf, *m.* *(coll.)* big head.

große Rosinen im Kopf haben, *exp.* to have big ideas, *(lit.)* to have big raisins in one's head.

Holzkopf, *m.* *(coll.)* blockhead, *(lit.)* wooden head; *Note:* expression often used for a stupid person.

Kürbis, *m.* *(sl.)* head, *(lit.)* pumpkin.

Mostschädel, *m.* *(sl.)* big head, *(lit.)* cider skull.

nicht auf den Kopf gefallen sein, *exp.* to be intelligent, *(lit.)* not to have fallen on one's head.

Poller, *m.* *(sl.)* head, *(lit.)* bollard.

Quadratschädel, *m.* *(sl.)* big, ugly head, *(lit.)* square skull.

Rübe, *f.* *(sl.)* head *(lit.)* beet.

Schädel, *m.* head, *(lit.)* skull.

Stroh im Kopf haben, *exp.* *(coll.)* to be stupid, *(lit.)* to have straw in one's head.

Wasserkopf, *m.* *(sl.)* big head, *(lit.)* water head.

HIT, to *(schlagen)*

---

jn. am Schlafittchen fassen, *exp.* *(coll.)* to rough up sb.

Backpfeife, *f.* slap in the face, *(lit.)* cheek pipe.

jm. den Hals umdrehen, *exp.* to hit sb., *(lit.)* to wring sb.'s neck.

jm. ein paar hinter die Löffel geben, *exp.* *(coll.)* to give sb. a slap on the ear; *Note:* **Löffel,** *m.pl.* ears, *(lit.)* spoons.

jm. eine Backpfeife zukommen lassen, *exp.* *(coll.)* to slap sb. in the face.

jm. eine ballern, *exp.* *(sl.)* to slap sb.

eine fangen, *exp.* *(sl.)* to be hit, *(lit.)* to catch one.

jm. eine funken, *exp.* *(sl.)* to hit sb.

eine in die Visage kriegen, *exp.* *(vulg.)* to be hit, *(lit.)* to get one in the face; *Note:* **Visage** is pronounced as in French, but with a stressed "e."

jm. eine klatschen, *exp.* *(sl.)* to slap sb. in the face; *Note:* **ich klatsch dir eine/** I'll slap you in the face.

jm. eine kleben, *exp.* *(coll.)* to hit sb., *(lit.)* to glue one onto sb.

jm. eine knallen, *exp.* *(sl.)* to hit sb.; *Note:* **sei ruhig oder es knallt!/**be quiet or you'll get a good slap.

jm. eine Kopfwäsche geben, *exp.* *(coll.)* to wash sb.'s head.

jm. eine langen, *exp.* *(coll.)* to hit sb.

jm. eine latschen, *exp.* *(sl.)* to hit sb.

jm. eine Ohrfeige verpassen, *exp.* to box sb.'s ears; *Note: see* **Ohrfeige.**

jm. eine runterhauen, *exp.* to hit sb.

jm. eine saftige Watschen geben, *exp.* *(coll.)* to slap sb. in the face.

jm. eine schallern, *exp.* *(sl.)* to hit sb.

jm. eine scheuern, *exp.* *(coll.)* to hit sb.

jm. eine schnalzen, *exp.* *(sl.)* to hit sb.

jm. eine verabreichen, *exp.* *(coll.)* to hit sb.

jm. eine winken, *exp.* *(sl.)* to hit sb.

jm. eine ziehen, *exp.* *(sl.)* to hit sb.

jm. einen Knopf an die Backe nähen, *exp.* to hit sb., *(lit.)* to sew a button on sb.'s cheek.

eins an die Glocke kriegen, *exp. (sl.)* to get a thrashing, *(lit.)* to get one on the bell.

jm. eins auf die Nuß geben, *exp. (sl.)* to bash sb., *(lit.)* to bash sb. on the nut.

jm. eins auf die Rübe geben, *exp. (sl.)* to bash sb., *(lit.)* to bash sb. on the beet; *Note:* **du kriegst eine auf die Rübe!**/you'll get a bash on the beet.

jm. eins über die Rübe ziehen, *exp. (sl.)* to bash sb.

es setzt was! *exp.* you'll get a slap.

jm. in die Schnauze schlagen, *exp. (vulg.)* to smack sb. in the nose, *(lit.)* to hit sb. on the snout.

Klaps, *m.* smack.

Kopfnuß, *f.* rap on the head with the knuckles; *Note:* **eine Kopfnuß kriegen**/to get a rap on the head.

Ohrfeige, *f.* slap in the face.

ohrfeigen, *v.* box sb.'s ears

jm. vorn Bauch treten, *exp. (sl.)* to kick sb. in the stomach.

Watschen, *f.* slap in the face.

HOSTILITY *(Feindseligkeit)*

fauchen, *v. (coll.)* react aggressively, *(lit.)* hiss.

frech, *adj.* fresh.

giftig, *adj.* aggressive, *(lit.)* poisonous.

Giftnudel, *f. (coll.)* bitch, *(lit.)* toxic noodle.

Giftzwerg, *m. (coll.)* bastard, *(lit.)* toxic dwarf.

Händelsucht, *f.* quarrelsomeness; *Note:* **er sucht Händel**/he wants to quarrel.

händelsüchtig, *adj.* quarrelsome.

keifig, *adj.* scolding.

kiebig, *adj.* scolding.

Knatsch, *m. (coll.)* trouble; *Note:* **sie haben Knatsch miteinander**/they are fighting.

Krach, *m.* trouble.

sich mit jm. anlegen, *exp.* to fight with sb.

pampig, *adj.* scolding.

patzig, *adj.* scolding.

schnippisch, *adj.* stinging, biting, snippy.

störrisch, *adj.* stubborn.

Streithammel, *m.* quarreler, *(lit.)* fighting mutton.

Streithansel, *m.* quarreler.

Stunk, *m. (coll.)* trouble.

zickig, *adj.* bitchy, *(lit.)* goatish.

Zoff, *m.* trouble with another person.

HOUSE *(Haus)*

Absteige, *f. (sl.)* rundown place.

Baracke, *f.* barrack.

Bude, *f.* student dorm room.
Hütte, *f.* shack.
in der Bude hocken, *exp. (coll.)* to stay at home, *(lit.)* to squat in one's room.
Kaninchenstall, *m. (sl.)* small rundown place, *(lit.)* rabbit hutch.
Loch, *n.* hole.
Mietskaserne, *f.* huge residential complex usually without parks, *(lit.)* rental (military) base.
Schuppen, *m. (sl.)* bar, discotheque, *(lit.)* barn.
Stall, *m. (sl.)* rundown place, *(lit.)* stall.

HOW'S IT GOING? *(Wie geht's?)*

alles klar? *exp.* how is it going? *(lit.)* everything clear?
gut (or schlecht) drauf sein, *exp.* to be doing well (or badly).
was'n los? *exp.* what's up?
was macht das Leben? *exp.* how is life?
wie läuft's? *exp.* how's it going?
wie geht's wie steht's? *exp.* how is it going?, *(lit.)* how's it going, how's it standing?

HUBBUB *(Krach)*

Geklapper, *n.* rattling.
Geklöter, *n.* rattling.
Geknalle, *n.* banging.
Geknatter, *n.* clattering.
Gekreische, *n.* shrieking, squealing.
Gepolter, *n.* thumping about; *Note:* **Polterabend,** *n.* evening before a wedding when friends break porcelain at the couple's door.
Getöse, *n.* roaring.
klappern, *v.* rattle.
klötern, *v.* rattle.
knallen, *v.* bang.
knattern, *v.* clatter (of a motor vehicle).
Krawall, *m.* rowdy.
kreischen, *v.* shriek.
poltern, *v.* thump about.
Rabatz machen, *exp. (coll.)* to kick up a fuss.
Rowdy, *m.* rowdy; *Note:* term taken from English.
tosen, *v.* roar.

HUNGRY, to be *(Hunger haben)*

da läuft einem das Wasser im Mund zusammen! *exp.* my mouth is watering.
ein Loch im Magen haben, *exp. (coll.)* to be very hungry, *(lit.)* to have a hole in one's stomach.

jm. hängt der Magen in den Kniekehlen, *exp. (coll.)* to be very hungry, *(lit.)* one's stomach is hanging in the hollow of one's knees.

Kohldampf, *m. (coll.)* hunger, *(lit.)* coal steam.

Kohldampf haben, *exp. (coll.)* to be ravenously hungry.

Kohldampf schieben müssen, *exp. (coll.)* to go hungry, *(lit.)* to have to push coal steam.

Leeregefühl, *n.* hunger, *(lit.)* empty feeling.

jm. knurrt der Magen, one's tummy is grumbling.

Mordshunger, *m. (coll.)* huge hunger, *(lit.)* murderous hunger.

IDIOT *(Idiot)*

Arschi, *m. (vulg.)* idiot, *(lit.)* little ass.

an dem ist Hopfen und Malz verloren! *exp. (coll.)* he is a hopeless case, *(lit.)* hops and malt are lost on him.

Blödmann, *m. (sl.)* stupid idiot, fool.

Daddelkopp, *m. (sl.)* idiot.

Depp, *m. (sl.)* twit.

Doofi, *m. (sl.)* twit.

Doofkopp, *m. (sl.)* dummy.

Doofmann, *m. (sl.)* dummy.

Dösbaddel, *m. (sl.)* dozy twit.

Döskopp, *m. (sl.)* dozy twit.

Dussel, *m. (sl.)* idiot.

ein Fall für die Klappsmühle sein, *exp. (coll.)* to be a case for the loony-bin.

Esel, *m.* idiot, *(lit.)* donkey, ass; *Note:* **so ein dummer Esel!**/what a stupid ass.

Hallodri, *m.* idiot.

Hirnie, *m. (sl.)* idiot.

hirnverbrand, *adj. (coll.)* idiotically, *(lit.)* brain-burned.

hoffnungsloser Fall, *exp. (coll.)* hopeless case.

Hornochse, *n. (sl.)* stupid idiot, *(lit.)* horned ox.

Kamel, *n.* fathead, *(lit.)* camel.

Knaller, *m. (sl.)* idiot.

Knallkopp, *m. (sl.)* idiot.

Rindvieh, *n.* stupid fool, *(lit.)* cow.

Schafskopf, *m.* idiot, *(lit.)* sheep's head.

Schussel, *m.* scatter-brain.

Schwachkopf, *m.* bonehead, dimwit, *(lit.)* weak head.

steh nicht da, wie Klein Doofi mit Plüschohren! *exp.* stop looking so stupid, *(lit.)* don't stand there like a little dummy with plush ears.

Töffel, *m.* fool.

Tölpel, *m.* fool.

Torfkopf, *m.* fool, *(lit.)* peat head.

Torfnase, *f.* fool, *(lit.)* peat nose.

Trottel, *m.* fool.

Vollidiot, *m.* complete idiot.

INDIFFERENCE *(Gleichgültigkeit)*

abstumpfen, *v.* become indifferent.

alle fünf gerade sein lassen, *exp.* to be indifferent, *(lit.)* to leave all five straight.

auf etw. pfeifen, *exp. (coll.)* to be indifferent about sth., *(lit.)* to whistle at sth.

auf etw. scheißen, *exp. (vulg.)* to be indifferent, *(lit.)* to shit on sth.

Banane sein, *exp. (sl.)* not to care, *(lit.)* to be a banana; *Note:* **das ist mir völlig Banane**/I don't care; **das ist doch totale Banane**/it doesn't matter.

das berührt mich soviel als ob in Hongkong ein Fahrrad umfällt! *exp.* I don't give a damn, *(lit.)* it concerns me as much as if a bike fell over in Hong Kong.

jm. den Buckel runterrutschen, *exp. (coll.)* not to care what sb. thinks, *(lit.)* to slide down sb.'s hump; *Note:* **der** (or **die**) **kann mir mal den Buckel runterrutschen**/he (or she) can go and chase himself (or herself).

jm. gestohlen bleiben, *exp.* not to care about sb.; **der kann mir mal gestohlen bleiben**/I don't give a damn about him.

das juckt mich nicht! *exp. (coll.)* I don't care, *(lit.)* it doesn't give me an itch.

das kann man sich an den Hut stecken! *exp. (coll.)* just forget about it (because it doesn't make a difference), *(lit.)* pin it to your head,

du kannst mich mal am Arsch lecken! *exp. (vulg.)* you can kiss my ass, *(lit.)* you can lick my ass.

sich einen Dreck draus machen, *exp. (vulg.)* not to care a bit, *(lit.)* to make oneself dirt out of sth.

Hose wie Jacke sein, *exp. (coll.)* it makes no difference, *(lit.)* pants are like a jacket.

kackegal, *adj. (vulg.)* all the same. *Note:* **das ist mir kackegal**/I don't give a shit.

kalt lassen, *exp.* not to care, *(lit.)* to leave cold, *(lit.)* **das läßt mich kalt**/I don't care about it.

keinen Finger für etw. (or **jn.**) **krumm machen,** *exp.* not to care about sth. (or sb.), *(lit.)* not to bend a finger for sth. (or sb.).

sich nicht die Bohne um etw. kümmern, *exp. (coll.)* not to care a bit about sth., *(lit.)* not to care a bean for sth.

nicht mit der Wimper zucken, *exp.* without turning a hair, *(lit.)* not to twitch an eyelash.

ob man das macht, oder in München fällt 'ne Schaufel um! *exp.* it makes no difference, *(lit.)* (it's the same) whether one does sth. or a shovel falls over in Munich; *Note:* this can be adjusted by taking a city as far away as possible from where one is.

ob man das macht, oder in China fällt ein Ascheimer um! *exp.* it makes no difference, *(lit.)* (it's the same) whether one does sth. or a garbage can falls over in China.

piepschnurzegal, *adj. (sl.)* all the same; *Note:* **das ist mir piepschnurzegal**/I couldn't care less.

etw. sausen lassen, *exp.* not to care about sth.

scheißegal, *adj. (vulg.)* all the same; *Note:* **das ist mir scheißegal**/I don't care.

schnurzegal, *adj. (sl.)* all the same; *Note:* **das ist mir schnurzegal**/I don't care.

schnorze, *adj.* *(sl.)* all the same; *Note:* **das ist mir schnorze**/I don't care.

Wurst sein, *exp.* *(coll.)* not to care, *(lit.)* to be sausage; *Note:* **das ist mir völlig Wurst**/I don't care; **das ist mir Wurst wie sonst noch was**/I don't give a damn.

INTELLIGENT, to be *(intelligent sein)*

Besserwisser, *m.* know-it-all.

clever, *adj.* clever; *Note:* a term borrowed from English.

den Faden für etwas haben, *exp.* to have the hang of sth., *(lit.)* to have a thread for sth.

den Hänger haben, *exp.* *(sl.)* to have the hang of sth.

einen schnellen Raffer haben, *exp.* *(sl.)* to grasp sth. fast.

fix drauf sein, *exp.* *(coll.)* to be intelligent, *(lit.)* to be on top of sth.

sich kein X für ein U vormachen lassen, *exp.* not to be able to be fooled, *(lit.)* not to allow oneself to be shown an X for a U.

sich nicht an der Nase herumführen lassen, *exp.* not to allow the wool to be pulled over one's eyes, *(lit.)* not to allow oneself to be led around by one's nose.

nicht auf den Kopf gefallen sein, *exp.* to be intelligent, *(lit.)* not to have fallen on one's head.

jm. nichts verkaufen können, *exp.* *(coll.)* to be unable to fool sb., *(lit.)* to be unable to sell sth. to sb.

plietsch, *adj.* witty.

Schlauberger, *m.* *(coll.)* witty person.

schlauer Fuchs, *exp.* cunning devil, *(lit.)* witty fox.

Schlaumeier, *m.* *(coll.)* witty person.

voll den Raffer haben für etw., *exp.* *(sl.)* to have the hang of sth.

J

JUNK *(wertlose Ware)*

ausmisten, *v.* clear out, *(lit.)* to clear out the manure.

Gelumps, *n.* junk.

Graffel, *m.* junk.

keinen roten (or lumpigen) Heller wert sein, *exp.* not to be worth a red cent.

Kinkerlitzchen, *pl.* knick-knacks.

Kitsch, *m.* kitsch.

kitschig, *adj.* kitschy.

Mist, *m.* *(sl.)* junk, *(lit.)* manure.

Nippes, *pl.* knick-knacks.

Plunder, *m.* *(coll.)* junk.

Ramsch, *m.* *(coll.)* junk.

Schnickschnack, *m.* knick-knacks.

Schnuddelwutz, *m.* *(sl.)* knick-knacks.

Schund, *m.* trash; *Note:* **Schundliteratur,** *f.* trashy literature, **Schundroman,** *m.* trashy novel.

Trödel, *m.* trinkets; *Note:* **Trödelladen,** *m.* trinket-shop.
Zeug, *n.* stuff.

KILL, to *(töten)*

jn. abmurksen, *v. (sl.)* do sb. in.
jn. alle machen, *exp. (sl.)* to do sb. in; *Note:* **den mach ich alle/**I'll do him in.
jm. die Luft abdrehen, *exp. (sl.)* to kill sb., *(lit.)* to cut off sb.'s air.
dran glauben müssen, *exp. (coll.)* to be killed *(lit.)* to have to believe in it.
jn. erledigen, *v. (sl.)* take care of sb.
jm. den Garaus machen, *exp. (coll.)* to do sb. in.
jm. den Hals umdrehen, *exp. (sl.)* to wring sb.'s neck.
jn. kaltmachen, *v. (sl.)* ice sb.; *Note:* **den mach ich kalt/**I'll ice him.
jn. killen, *v. (sl.)* bump sb. off.
Killer, *m. (sl.)* killer; *Note:* term taken from English.
jn. lahmlegen, *v. (sl.)* deactivate sb.
jn. um die Ecke bringen, *exp. (sl.)* to bump sb. off, *(lit.)* to bring sb. around the corner.
jn. umlegen, *v. (coll.)* bump sb. off.
Zeit totschlagen, *exp. (coll.)* to kill time.

KISS, to *(küssen)*

sich ablecken, *v. (sl.)* kiss, *(lit.)* lick each other.
sich abschmatzen, *v. (sl.)* kiss noisily.
Busserl, *n.* kiss.
busserln, *v.* kiss.
Bussi, *m.* kiss.
Cacooning, *n.* cuddling.
knutschen, *v. (sl.)* smooch.
Knutschfleck, *m.* hickie.
Küßchen, *m.* little kiss.
Schmatzer, *m.* kiss, *(lit.)* smack.
schmusen, *v.* cuddle and kiss.
schnäbeln, *v. (coll.)* kiss, *(lit.)* bill.
Zungenkuß, *m.* French kiss.

KIT AND CABOODLE, the whole *(alles)*

die ganze Chose, *exp.* the whole thing; *Note:* the French term **Chose** is pronounced as Schose.
mit Kind und Kegel, *exp.* with the whole kit and kaboodle, *(lit.)* with child and ninepins.

mit Mann und Maus, *exp.* with the whole kit and kaboodle, *(lit.)* with man and mouse.

mit Sack und Pack, *exp.* with the whole kit and kaboodle, *(lit.)* with sack and pack.

L

LAUGH, to *(lachen)*

sich beömmeln, *v. (sl.)* laugh hard.

da bleibt kein Auge trocken! *exp.* to laugh hard, *(lit.)* no eye stays dry there!

gackern, *v.* giggle, *(lit.)* cluck.

Gegacker, *n.* giggling.

Gekicher, *n.* giggling.

gut lachen haben, *exp.* to have a good laugh; *Note:* **nichts zu lachen haben**/to have nothing to laugh about.

kichern, *v.* giggle.

sich kringeln, *v. (coll.)* laugh one's head off, *(lit.)* to curl oneself.

platzen vor Lachen, *exp.* to laugh one's head off, *(lit.)* to burst from laughing.

sich scheckig lachen, *exp. (coll.)* to laugh oneself silly.

Schenkelklopfer, *m. (coll.)* joke *(lit.)* thigh-slapper.

sich schief lachen, *exp.* to laugh oneself silly, *(lit.)* to laugh oneself crooked.

sterben vor Lachen, *exp.* to laugh one's head off, *(lit.)* to die from laughing.

sich totlachen, *exp.* to laugh one's head off, *(lit.)* to laugh oneself to death.

sich vor Lachen den Bauch halten, *exp.* to split one's sides with laughter.

sich vor Lachen krümmen, *exp.* to double up with laughter.

vor Lachen wiehern, *exp. (coll.)* to roar with laughter, *(lit.)* to whinny from laughter.

wieherndes Gelächter, *exp. (coll.)* uproarious laughter.

LEAVE, to *(weggehen)*

ab durch die Mitte! *exp.* let's beat it, *(lit.)* go right through the middle.

abblitzen, *v. (sl.)* beat it; *Note:* **blitz ab!**/get lost.

abdampfen, *v. (sl.)* beat it, *(lit.)* steam off; *Note:* also means to drive fast.

abhauen, *v. (sl.)* beat it; *Note:* **hau ab!**/get lost.

absocken, *v. (sl.)* beat it.

abziehen, *v. (sl.)* beat it; *Note:* zieh ab!/beat it.

abzischen, *v. (sl.)* shoot off; *Note:* **zisch ab!**/beat it.

abzotteln, *v. (sl.)* trot off.

sich auf die Beine machen, *exp. (coll.)* to get going, *(lit.)* to get on one's legs.

sich auf die Socken machen, *exp. (coll.)* to get going, *(lit.)* to get on one's socks.

sich aus dem Staub machen, *exp. (coll.)* to make oneself scarce.

den Abflug machen, *exp. (sl.)* to leave,*(lit.)* to make a flying departure.

die Beine unter die Arme nehmen, *exp. (coll.)* to take to one's heels, *(lit.)* to take one's legs underneath one's arms.

die Koffer packen, *exp.* to leave, *(lit.)* to pack one's suitcases.

die **Kurve kratzen,** *exp. (sl.)* to manage to leave, *(lit.)* to scratch the curve.
eine **Fliege machen,** *exp. (sl.)* to shove off, *(lit.)* to make a fly.
eine **Mücke machen,** *exp. (sl.)* to shove off, *(lit.)* to make a mosquito.
sich **empfehlen,** *v. (coll.)* take one's leave, *(lit.)* to recommend oneself.
sich **fortstehlen,** *v.* steal away.
sich **in Luft auflösen,** *exp.* to vanish into thin air.
langsam gehen, *exp.* to leave soon, *(lit.)* to go slowly.
Leine ziehen, *exp. (sl.)* to clear off.
packen, *v.* leave; *Note:* **packen wir's**/lets go.
sich **schleichen,** *v. (sl.)* steal away; *Note:* **schleich dich!**/take off.
verduften, *v. (sl.)* clear off.
sich **verdünnisieren,** *v. (sl.)* clear off.
sich **verkriechen,** *v. (sl.)* creep away.
sich **verkrümeln,** *v. (sl.)* slip off.
sich **verpissen,** *v. (vulg.)* piss off; *Note:* **verpiss dich!**/piss off!
sich **verziehen,** *v. (sl.)* take oneself off; *Note:* **verzieh dich!**/clear off.
sich **wegscheren,** *v. (sl.)* clear off; *Note:* **scher dich weg!**/clear off.
sich **wegschleichen,** *v.* creep away.
sich **zum Teufel scheren,** *exp. (sl.)* to go to hell.

LEGS *(Beine)*

auf eigenen Beinen stehen, *exp.* to stand on one's own feet, *(lit.)* to stand on one's own legs.
jm. Beine machen, *exp. (coll.)* make sb. get a move on, *(lit.)* to make sb. legs.
Kackstelzen, *f.pl. (vulg.)* legs, *(lit.)* poop stilts.
Krautstampfer, *m.pl. (sl.)* short fat legs, *(lit.)* kraut stomper.
lange Haxen, *f.pl. (coll.)* long legs.
sich **kein Bein ausreißen,** *exp.* not to exert oneself, *(lit.)* not to rip one's legs out.
O-Beine, *n.pl.* bowlegs.
Stelzen, *f.pl. (coll.)* long skinny legs, *(lit.)* stilts.
Storchenbeine, *f.pl.* long skinny legs, *(lit.)* stork legs.
Stampfer, *m.pl.* fat short legs, *(lit.)* stompers.
X-Beine, *n.pl.* knock-knees.

LOOK, to *(schauen)*

äugeln, *v.* cast secret glances at sb.
sich **die Augen ausgucken,** *exp. (coll.)* to stare, *(lit.)* to stare one's eyes out.
die **Augen in die Hand nehmen,** *exp. (coll.)* to stare, *(lit.)* to take one's eyes in one's hands.
ein Auge riskieren, *exp.* to steal a peek at sth., *(lit.)* to risk an eye.
gaffen, *v. (sl.)* stare.
glotzen, *v. (sl.)* stare, *(lit.)* to goggle; *Note:* **Glotze** or **Glotzkiste,** *m.* TV, goggle box.
kieken, *v. (sl.)* look; *Note:* **mal kieken!**/let's see.

schielen, *v.* not see sth. correctly, *(lit.)* look at sth. cross-eyed.
starren, *v.* stare.
stieren, *v. (sl.)* stare.

LOVE *(Liebe)*

---

jn. abschleppen, *v. (sl.)* pick sb. up, *(lit.)* to tow sb. away.
jn. anbaggern, *v. (sl.)* attempt to pick sb. up, *(lit.)* to scoop sb. up.
jn. angraben, *v. (sl.)* attempt to pick sb. up, *(lit.)* to dig sb. up.
sich jn. anlachen, *exp. (sl.)* to pick sb. up, *(lit.)* to laugh in sb.'s direction.
jn. anmachen, *v. (sl.)* attempt to pick sb. up.
jn. anquatschen, *v. (sl.)* attempt to pick sb. up.
jn. antörnen, *v. (sl.)* turn sb. on.
jn. aufreißen, *v. (sl.)* pick sb. up.
jn. auftun, *v. (sl.)* pick sb. up.
Beziehungskiste, *f. (coll.)* romantic relationship, *(lit.)* relationship-crate.
bis über beide Ohren verliebt sein, *exp.* to be head over heels in love, *(lit.)* to be over both ears in love.
jm. den Hof machen, *exp.* to court sb.
jm. den Kopf verdrehen, *exp. (coll.)* to steal sb.'s heart away, *(lit.)* to turn sb.'s head.
ein Auge auf jn. werfen, *exp.* to have taken a liking to sb., *(lit.)* to throw an eye on sb.
einen Affen an jm. gefressen haben, *exp. (sl.)* to be attracted to sb., *(lit.)* to have eaten a monkey with sb.
einen guten Fang gemacht haben, *exp. (sl.)* to have made a good catch.
es kribbelt, *exp. (coll.)* to be excited when seeing one's lover.
es voll erwischt haben *exp. (coll.)* to have fallen madly in love.
Feuer fangen, *exp. (coll.)* to fall in love, *(lit.)* to catch fire.
Flamme, *f.* flame.
Flugzeuge im Bauch haben, *exp. (coll.)* to be madly in love, *(lit.)* to have airplanes in one's stomach.
Hals über Kopf verliebt sein, *exp.* to fall head over heels in love.
Händchen halten, *exp.* to hold hands.
im siebten Himmel sein, *exp.* to be in seventh heaven.
sich jn. ködern, *v. (sl.)* pick up sb., *(lit.)* lure sb.
liebestoll, *adj.* love-crazy.
liebestrunken, *adj.* drunk from love.
jm. schöne Augen machen, *exp.* to steal sb.'s heart away, *(lit.)* to make beautiful eyes at sb.
sterben vor Liebe, *exp.* to be badly in love, *(lit.)* to die from love.
Streß haben (mit jm.), *exp. (sl.)* to have difficulties in a relationship (with sb.).
Turteltaube, *f.* lovebird, *(lit.)* love dove.
um die Hand anhalten, *exp.* to ask for sb.'s hand (in marriage).
sich verknallen (in jn.), *v. (sl.)* fall head over heels in love (with sb.).
verknallt (in), *adj. (sl.)* be in love (with sb.).
verschossen (in), *adj. (sl.)* be in love (with sb).
jm. zu Füßen liegen, *exp. (coll.)* to adore sb., *(lit.)* to lie at sb.'s feet.

M

MATRIMONY *(Ehe)*

Eheschlamassel, *m.* matrimonial problems.
Gatte, *m.* husband; *Note:* old term, used ironically today.
Gattin, *f.* wife; *Note:* old term, used ironically today.
Habbi, *m.* husband.
Hausdrachen, *m. (sl.)* despotic wife, *(lit.)* house dragon.
mein Alter, *exp. (sl.)* my old man; *Note:* also means father.
mein Ex, *m.* my ex-husband.
mein Mann, *exp.* my husband.
mein mir Angetrauter, *exp.* my better half, *(lit.)* my to me wedded (husband).
mein Oller, *exp. (sl.)* my husband.
mein Olscher, *exp. (sl.)* my husband.
mein Spezie, *exp.* my husband; *Note:* also means good friend.
meine Alte, *exp. (sl.)* my old lady; *Note:* also means mother.
meine bessere Hälfte, *exp.* my better half.
meine Frau, *exp.* my wife.
meine mir Angetraute, *exp.* my better half, *(lit.)* my to me wedded (wife).
meine Olle, *exp. (sl.)* my wife.
meine Olsche, *exp. (sl.)* my wife.
Pantoffelheld, *m. (coll.)* henpecked husband, *(lit.)* slipper hero.
Pascha, *m.* chauvinistic husband, *(lit.)* pasha.
Scheich, *m.* chauvinistic husband, *(lit.)* sheik.
unter der Haube sein, *exp.* to be married, *(lit.)* to be under the hood.
Weib, *n. (sl.)* wife.

MESS UP, to *(Fehler machen)*

baden gegangen sein, *exp. (sl.)* to have taken a bath.
Beinchen stellen, *exp. (coll.)* to throw things into a person's path.
die Karre in den Dreck setzen, *exp. (vulg.)* to goof up, *(lit.)* to put the cart in the mud.
durchfallen, *v.* fail; *Note:* **ich bin durch die Prüfung gefallen**/I failed the exam.
jm. eins auswischen, *exp. (coll.)* to damage sb.'s work.
jn. fertig machen, *exp. (sl.)* to ruin sb.
flöten gegangen sein, *exp. (coll.)* to be in a jam, *(lit.)* to have gone to play the flute.
futschikato, *adj.* lost.
hops gegangen sein, *exp. (sl.)* to goof up.
im Arsch sein, *exp. (vulg.)* to have messed up, *(lit.)* to be in the ass.
im Eimer sein, *exp. (sl.)* to have messed up, *(lit.)* to be in the bucket.
in die Binsen gehen, *exp. (coll.)* to go down the drain.
etw. in den Sand setzen, *exp. (coll.)* to goof up sth., *(lit.)* to put sth. into the sand.

jm. Knüppel zwischen die Beine schmeißen, *exp.* *(coll.)* to make sb. goof up, *(lit.)* to throw pieces of wood between sb.'s legs.

Mist bauen, *exp.* *(sl.)* to goof up, *(lit.)* to build manure.

Murks machen, *exp.* *(coll.)* to goof up.

pfuschen, *v.* *(coll.)* mess up.

Pfuscher, *m.* *(coll.)* bungler.

jm. Sand ins Getriebe werfen, *exp.* to ruin sb., *(lit.)* to throw sand into sb.'s engine.

Scheiße bauen, *exp.* *(vulg.)* to goof up, *(lit.)* to build shit.

verhunzen, *v.* *(coll.)* mess up.

vermasseln, *v.* mess up.

vermurksen, *v.* *(coll.)* goof up.

verschütt gehen, *exp.* to get lost.

voll daneben liegen, *exp.* *(sl.)* to have goofed up, *(lit.)* to lie next to it.

MISCHIEF *(Unglück)*

da haben wir den Salat! *exp.* *(coll.)* that's a fine mess we're in, *(lit.)* there we have the salad.

ein Schlag ins Kontor sein, *exp.* *(coll.)* to be a real blow, *(lit.)* to be a hit in the office.

ins Auge gehen, *exp.* to go wrong, *(lit.)* to go into the eye.

mit dem linken Bein zuerst aufstehen, *exp.* to get up on the wrong side of the bed, *(lit.)* to get up with the left leg first.

Pechmarie, *f.* unlucky female, *(lit.)* unlucky Marie.

Pechsträhne, *f.* run of bad luck.

Pechvogel, *m.* unlucky person, *(lit.)* unlucky bird.

schiefgehen, *v.* go crooked.

Unglück am laufenden Band, *exp.* run of bad luck.

Unglückssträhne, *f.* run of bad luck.

voll in den Dreck gelangt haben, *exp.* *(vulg.)* to have had bad luck, *(lit.)* to have reached into the mud.

MONEY *(Geld)*

Blauer, *m.* *(coll.)* 100-Mark bill.

blechen, *v.* *(coll.)* pay.

Blüte, *f.* counterfeit paper money, *(lit.)* blossom.

Diridari, *n.* *(coll.)* dough.

Geizhals, *m.* miser, *(lit.)* miser-neck.

Geizkragen, *m.* miser, *(lit.)* miser-collar.

Groschen, *m.* 10-Pfennig piece; *Note:* **Groschenroman,** *m.* dime novel.

Heiermann, *m.* *(sl.)* 5-Mark piece.

Kies, *m.* *(sl.)* dough, *(lit.)* gravel.

Klötze, *m.pl.* *(sl.)* dough, *(lit.)* logs.

Knete, *f.* *(sl.)* dough.

Knöpfe, *m.pl.* *(sl.)* dough, *(lit.)* buttons.

Kohle, *f. (sl.)* dough, *(lit.)* coal; *Note:* **Hauptsache, die Kohle stimmt!**/as long as the money is right.

Kröten, *f.pl. (sl.)* dough, *(lit.)* toads.

Lappen, *m. (sl.)* bill, *(lit.)* rag.

Leim, *m. (sl.)* dough, *(lit.)* glue.

Mäuse, *f.pl. (coll.)* dough, *(lit.)* mice.

Mille, *f. (coll.)* 1000-Mark bill.

Moneten, *pl.* dough.

Moos, *n. (sl.)* dough, *(lit.)* moss.

ohne Moos nichts los! *exp. (coll.)* you can't get far without money.

Patte, *f. (sl.)* dough.

Pinkepinke, *f. (coll.)* dough.

Pulver, *n. (sl.)* dough, *(lit.)* powder.

quitt sein mit jm., *exp.* to be even with sb.

Riese, *m. (coll.)* 1000-Mark bill.

sauteuer, *adj.* extremely expensive, *(lit.)* sow expensive.

Schotter, *m. (sl.)* dough, *(lit.)* gravel.

spottbillig, *adj.* extremely cheap.

Steine, *m.pl. (sl.)* dough, *(lit.)* stones.

Stroh, *n. (sl.)* dough, *(lit.)* straw.

verbraten, *v. (sl.)* spend money aimlessly, *(lit.)* fry up.

Zaster, *m. (sl.)* dough.

MUCH *(viel)*

ein Batzen, *m. (coll.)* a heap, a pile; *Note:* **einen Batzen Geld haben**/to have a pile of money.

ein Haufen, *m. (coll.)* a heap, a pile; *Note:* **einen Haufen Arbeit haben** /to have a pile of work.

eine Menge, *f.* a large amount; *Note:* **eine Menge Arbeit** /a great amount of work.

massig, *adj. (coll.)* a lot; *Note:* **massig Arbeit**/a lot of work.

schrecklich viel, *adv.* too terribly much.

Stange, *f.* pole, stake; *Note:* **eine Stange Geld haben**/to have a lot of money.

tierisch viel, *adv.* too much; *Note:* **tierisch viel Arbeit haben**/*(lit.)* to have a beastly amount of work.

NAG, to *(mäckeln)*

bekritteln, *v. (coll.)* find fault.

herumhacken, *v. (coll.)* nag.

Lästermaul, *m.* a person who complains constantly.

lästern, *v.* slander.

mäckeln, *v.* nag.

maulen, *v.* nag.

meckern, *v.* nag, *(lit.)* bleat.

mosern, *v.* nag.

motzen, *v.* nag; *Note:* **Motzki** is the German Archie Bunker.

nörgeln, *v.* nag.

quaken, *v. (coll.)* nag.

quengeln, *v.* nag.

NASTY, to be *(gemein sein)*

Aas, *n. (vulg.)* asshole.

abgebrüht, *adj. (coll.)* mean and hardened.

Arschloch, *n. (vulg.)* asshole.

auf die (ganz) krumme Tour, *exp. (sl.)* in a nasty way.

auf die ganz linke Tour kommen, *exp. (sl.)* to do sth. in a very nasty way.

auf die miese Tour, *exp. (sl.)* in a nasty way.

jm. das Messer von hinten reinhauen, *exp. (coll.)* to stab sb. in the back.

Dreckskerl, *m. (vulg.)* meanie, *(lit.)* filthy guy.

ein linkes Ding drehen, *exp. (sl.)* to pull a dirty trick.

er hat es faustdick hinter den Ohren! *exp.* he is a sly one, *(lit.)* he's got it fist-thick behind the ears.

fies, *adj. (coll.)* nasty; *Note:* **das ist fies!**/that is mean.

fiese Matenten, *exp. (coll.)* nasty ways of doing sth.

fieser Kerl, *exp. (coll.)* nasty man.

fieses Weibsstück, *exp. (coll.)* nasty woman.

Fiesling, *m.* meanie.

gemein, *adj.* mean.

Halunke, *m.* jerk.

häßlich, *adj.* nasty, *(lit.)* ugly.

Knallkopf, *m.* jerk.

link, *adj.* mean.

mies, *adj. (coll.)* mean.

miese Nummer, *exp. (coll.)* lousy way of doing sth.

Miesmacher, *m.* party pooper.

Schuft, *m. (coll.)* swine.

Schwein, *n. (vulg.)* swine.

Schweinerei, *f. (coll.)* dirty trick.

schweinisch, *adj. (sl.)* mean.

übel, *adj.* nasty; *Note:* **das sieht übel aus!**/that's a nasty one.

unfair, *adj.* unfair; *Note:* term taken from English. **un-** is pronounced as in a regular German word.

von übelster Sorte sein, *exp.* to be of a bad sort.

NEVER *(nie)*

---

da kannste drauf warten! *exp. (coll.)* you can wait until Hell freezes over.

warten bis man graue Haare kriegt, *exp. (coll.)* to wait until hell freezes over, *(lit.)* to wait until one gets gray hair.

warten bis man schwarz wird, *exp. (coll.)* to wait till Hell freezes over, *(lit.)* to wait until one becomes black.

NONSENSE *(Unsinn)*

---

absurd, *adj.* absurd.
Blech, *m.* nonsense, *(lit.)* sheet metal.
Blödsinn, *m.* nonsense.
das kannste deiner Oma erzählen, aber nicht mir! *exp. (coll.)* don't talk such nonsense, *(lit.)* you can tell that to your grandmother, but not to me.
jm. einen Bären aufbinden, *exp.* to tell sb. nonsense, *(lit.)* to tie a bear to sb.
einen Stiefel zusammenreden, *exp. (coll.)* to talk nonsense., *(lit.)* to talk a boot together.
Firlefanz, *m.* nonsense.
Geschwafel, *n. (coll.)* nonsense.
Humbug, *m.* humbug.
Kacke, *f. (vulg.)* nonsense, *(lit.)* shit.
Kacke erzählen, *exp. (vulg.)* to speak nonsense, *(lit.)* to speak shit.
kalten Kaffee erzählen, *exp. (coll.)* to speak nonsense.
kalter Kaffee, *exp. (coll.)* nonsense, *(lit.)* cold coffee.
Käse, *m. (coll.)* nonsense, *(lit.)* cheese.
Klamauk, *m.* nonsense.
Kokolores, *m.* nonsense.
Mist erzählen, *exp.* to speak nonsense, *(lit.)* to speak manure.
Mumpitz, *m.* nonsense.
Nonsense, *m.* nonsense; *Note:* term taken from English.
ohne Sinn und Verstand sein, *exp.* to be nonsensical, *(lit.)* to be without sense and intelligence.
Quark, *m.* nonsense.
Quatsch, *m.* nonsense.
Quatsch machen, *exp.* to do sth. stupid.
Quatsch mit Soße sein, *exp. (coll.)* to be complete nonsense, *(lit.)* to be nonsense with gravy.
Rumgesülze, *n.* nonsensical speech.
rumsülzen, *v.* speak nonsense.
saublöd daherreden, *exp.* to speak nonsense.
Scharlatan, *m.* charlatan.
Schaumschläger, *m.* charlatan.
Schmarrn, *m.* nonsense.
Schrott, *m.* nonsense, *(lit.)* scrap metal.
schwafeln, *v.* speak nonsense.
Stuß, *m.* nonsense.
sülzen, *v. (sl.)* speak nonsense.
(herum-) tütern, *v.* speak nonsense.
Tütelkram, *m.* nonsense.
Unfug, *m.* nonsense.

NOSE (Nase)

alles aus der Nase ziehen, *exp.* *(coll.)* to suck sb. dry, *(lit.)* to pull everything out of one's nose.

jn. an der Nase herumführen, *exp.* to pull the wool over sb.'s eyes, *(lit.)* to lead sb. around by the nose.

jm. auf der Nase herumtanzen, *exp.* to play sb. for a fool, *(lit.)* to dance around on sb.'s nose.

jm. etw. auf die Nase binden, *exp.* to let sb. know sth., *(lit.)* to tie sth. on sb.'s nose.

die Nase hoch tragen, *exp.* to be conceited, *(lit.)* to carry one's nose up high.

die Nase in alles stecken, *exp.* to stick one's nose into everything.

Dobas, *m.* *(sl.)* schnozzle.

Haken, *m.* *(sl.)* hook nose, *(lit.)* hook.

Hauer, *m.* *(coll.)* schnozzle, *(lit.)* hitter.

Kartoffelnase, *m.* wide nose, *(lit.)* potato nose.

Klopper, *m.* *(coll.)* huge nose.

Knolle, *f.* *(coll.)* schnozzle, *(lit.)* tuber.

Nüstern, *f.pl.* *(sl.)* big nostrils, *(lit.)* nostrils of a horse.

jn. nicht riechen können, *exp.* *(coll.)* to be unable to stand sb., *(lit.)* to be unable to smell sb.

Rotznase, *f.* *(sl.)* rascal, *(lit.)* snot-nose.

Schnotternase, *f.* *(sl.)* runny nose, *(lit.)* snot-nose.

schnüffeln, *v.* busybody, *(lit.)* sniff; *Note:* **Schnüffler,** *m.*/snooper or sniffer of drugs.

schnuppern, *v.* sniff; *Note:* **frische Seeluft schnuppern**/to get some fresh sea air.

Schweinsnase, *f.* *(sl.)* nose that looks like a pig's nose with high nostrils.

Stupsnase, *f.* snub-nose.

Zinken, *m.* *(sl.)* conk.

NOTHING (nichts)

alles ist im Eimer! *exp.* *(coll.)* for peanuts, *(lit.)* everything is in the bucket.

für die Katz, *exp.* *(coll.)* for peanuts, *(lit.)* for the cat.

für ein Butterbrot und ein Ei, *exp.* for next to nothing, *(lit.)* for buttered bread and an egg.

fürn Appel und ein Ei, *exp.* for next to nothing, *(lit.)* for an apple and an egg.

in den Wind sprechen, *exp.* to speak in vain, *(lit.)* to talk into the wind.

nix, *adv.* nothing.

O

OKAY (in Ordnung)

alles roger! *exp.* *(coll.)* everything (is) okay.

echt sauber sein, *exp.* *(coll.)* to be perfect; *Note:* **das hat er sauber hingekriegt**/he did a fine job.

gepongt, *adj. (coll.)* okay.
in Butter sein, *exp.* to be fine, *(lit.)* to be in butter.
klar Schiff sein, *exp.* to be in order, *(lit.)* to be clear ship.
klar sein, *exp.* to be okay, *(lit.)* to be clear.
o.k., *adj.* as in English.

OLD PERSON *(alte Person)*

Alte, *f. (sl.)* old woman.
alte Herrschaften, *exp.* old ladies and gentlemen; *Note:* also means parents.
alte Oma, *exp. (sl.)* old woman, *(lit.)* old grandma.
alte Schachtel, *exp. (sl.)* old woman, *(lit.)* old box.
Alter, *m. (sl.)* old man.
alter Knacki, *m. (sl.)* old man.
alter Opa, *exp. (sl.)* old man, *(lit.)* old grandpa.
altes Wrack, *exp. (sl.)* old woman, *(lit.)* old wreck.
bei dem (or **der**) **sind die Tage gezählt,** *exp.* his (or her) days are numbered.
der Olle, *exp. (sl.)* old fart.
die Olle, *exp. (sl.)* old hag.
Gramusel, *m. (coll.)* grumpy old man.
Greis, *m.* senile old man.
Grufti, *m. (sl.)* old man; *Note:* also a term for a group of young devil worshippers.
hutzelig, *adj.* shriveled.
Hutzelmännchen, *n. (sl.)* shriveled old man.
in den Karton gehören, *exp. (sl.)*to write sb. off as being too old, *(lit.)* to belong in the box (meaning coffin).
je oller je doller! *exp. (coll.)* the older the madder.
Komposti, *m. (sl.)* very old man, *Note:* **Kompost,** *m.* compost.
Moos ansetzen, *exp. (sl.)* to get old, *(lit.)* to gather moss.
Omi, *f.* old woman, *(lit.)* granny.
Opi, *m.* old man, *(lit.)* grandpa.
Schrulli, *m. (sl.)* old fart.
schrumpelig, *adj.* shriveled.
Tattergreis, *m.* shaky old man.
tatterig, *adj.* old and shaky.
tütelig, *adj.* senile; *Note:* **ganz tütelig**/very senile.
verkalkt, *adj.* senile, *(lit.)* calcified.
Zombie, *m. (sl.)* old person, *(lit.)* zombie.
jn. zum alten Eisen zählen, *exp. (coll.)* to write sb. off as being too old, *(lit.)* to count a person as being old iron.

PANTS *(Hose)*

Baggerbeutel, *m. (coll.)* big wide pants, *(lit.)* digging bag.
Beinkleider, *n.pl.* pants.

Boxbeutel, *m. (coll.)* big wide pants.
Buchsn, *f.pl. (coll.)* pants; *Note:* **Lederbuchsn,** *f.pl.* leather pants.
Büxs, *f. (coll.)* pants; *Note:* term from Danish.
Karottenhose, *f.* fashionable, tapered pants shaped like a carrot.
Leggings, *pl.* tight pants.
Puffhose, *f.* puffy pants.
Schlapperhose, *f. (coll.)* baggy pair of pants.

PARENTS *(Eltern)*

mein Alter, *exp. (sl.)* my old man.
meine Alte, *exp. (sl.)* my old lady.
meine Alten, *exp. (sl.)* my old man and old lady.
meine alten Herrschaften, *exp.* my parents, *(lit.)* my old lady and gentleman.

PARTY *(Party)*

auf die Pauke hauen, *exp. (coll.)* to party like mad, *(lit.)* to beat the kettledrum.
da brummt der Bär! *exp. (sl.)* they party like mad, *(lit.)* the bear growls there.
da fliegen die Fetzen! *exp. (coll.)* they party like mad, *(lit.)* the shreds are flying there.
da steigt die Sause! *exp. (sl.)* they party like mad.
eine Feier steigen lassen, *exp.* to have a party, *(lit.)* to let a celebration rise.
Feierei, *f.* endless parties.
Feiermeier, *m. (coll.)* party-goer.
Fete, *f.* party.
feten, *v.* party.
fetzig, *adj. (sl.)* fun; *Note:* **das fetzt echt!** *exp.* that's really fun.
Highlife, *n. (coll.)* fun party; *Note:* **da war Highlife!**/there was a fun party going on; term taken from English.
lau, *adj.* no fun, *(lit.)* lukewarm.
Mordsradau, *m.* fun party.
Party, *f.* as in English.
Partylöwe, *n.* party-goer, *(lit.)* party lion.
Partytier, *m.* party-goer, *(lit.)* party animal.
Ratzifatzi, *m.* fun racket.

POLICE *(Polizei)*

anzeigen, *v.* report to the police.
Bulle, *m. (sl.)* cop, *(lit.)* bull.
Bullen aufhetzen, *exp. (sl.)* to inform the police, *(lit.)* to get the bulls heated up.
das Auge des Gesetzes, *exp.* police, *(lit.)* the eye of the law.

Knöllchen, *m. (coll.)* parking ticket.
Krimi, *m.* thriller.
Polente, *f. (sl.)* cops; *Note:* **der ist von der Polente**/he is a cop.
Polyp, *m. (sl.)* cop, *(lit.)* polyp.
rumballern, *v. (sl.)* shoot out.
verpfeifen, *v. (coll.)* inform the police, *(lit.)* whistle blow.

RAIN *(Regen)*

es duscht! *exp. (coll.)* it's pouring, *(lit.)* it's showering.
es gießt in Strömen! *exp.* it's raining cats and dogs.
es pieselt! *exp.* it's spitting.
es pinkelt! *exp. (coll.)* it's spitting, *(lit.)* it's tinkling.
es regnet wie aus Eimern! *exp.* it's coming down in buckets.
es schüttet! *exp.* it's pouring.
es strömt! *exp.* it's pouring.
Friesennerz, *m.* raincoat, *(lit.)* Frisian mink.
friesische Ballettschuhe, *m.pl.* rubber boots, *(lit.)* Frisian ballet shoes.
Pieselregen, *m.* drizzle.
plätschern, *v.* patter.
platschnaß, *adj.* soaking wet.
Sauwetter, *n. (sl.)* lousy weather, *(lit.)* sow weather.
Scheißwetter, *n. (sl.)* lousy weather, *(lit.)* shit weather.
Schietwetter, *n. (sl.)* lousy weather, *(lit.)* shit weather.
schiffen, *v.* chucking it down.
Schmuddelwetter, *n.* lousy weather, *(lit.)* shit weather; *Note:* People in
   Hamburg speak of **Schmuddelwetter** for the typical drizzle in their city.
vom Regen in die Traufe kommen, *exp.* to jump out of the frying-pan into the
   fire, *(lit.)* to come from the rain into the gutter.
Waschküche, *f.* drizzle and fog, *(lit.)* washing-kitchen/laundry room.

REJECT, to *(ablehnen)*

jn. abblitzen lassen, *exp. (coll.)* to give sb. the brush-off.
bleiben, wo der Pfeffer wächst, *exp. (coll.)* to get lost, *(lit.)* to stay where the
   pepper grows.
das kommt nicht in die Tüte! *exp. (coll.)* that's out of the question, *(lit.)* that
   doesn't come into the bag.
jm. den Buckel runterrutschen, *exp. (coll.)* to get lost, *(lit.)* to slip down sb.'s
   hump; *Note:* **der kann mir mal den Buckel runterrutschen!**/he can get
   lost.
jm. den Korb geben, *v. (coll.)* turn sb. down, *(lit.)* to give sb. a basket; *Note:*
   einen Korb bekommen/to be turned down.
jn. den Laufpaß geben, *exp. (coll.)* to break up a relationship, *(lit.)* give
   someone their walking papers.

jm. die kalte Schulter zeigen, *exp.* to give sb. the cold shoulder.

die (or der) kann mich mal! *exp.* she (or he) can get lost!

jm. eine Abfuhr erteilen, *exp.* to turn sb. down, *(lit.)* to give sb. a departure.

jn. gefressen haben, *exp.* to hate sb.'s guts, *(lit.)* to have eaten sb; *Note:* **den habe ich gefressen!**/I hate his guts.

jm. gestohlen bleiben, *exp. (coll.)* to get lost; **der kann mir mal gestohlen bleiben**/he can get lost.

jm. was husten, *exp. (coll.)* to get lost, *(lit.)* to cough a person sth.; *Note:* **ich huste dir was**/get lost!

keine zehn Pferde bringen jn. dazu, etw. zu tun, *exp. (coll.)* wild horses wouldn't make sb. do sth.

keinen Bock haben, etw. zu tun, *exp. (sl.)* not to fancy doing sth.*(lit.)* to have no goat to do sth.; *Note:* **ich habe keinen Bock, heute zu kochen**/I don't want to cook today.

jm. nicht abkönnen, *exp.* to be unable to stand a person.

null Bock auf etw. haben, *exp. (sl.)* not to want to do sth.; *Note:* **ich hab null Bock auf Kochen**/I don't want to cook.

null Bock auf nichts haben, *exp. (sl.)* to have no desire to do anything.

jn. zum Teufel schicken, *exp. (sl.)* to send sb. to Hell.

RICH, to be *(reich sein)*

absahnen, *v. (coll.)* make a good deal; *Note:* **eine Millionen absahnen**/to have made one million marks as a good deal.

auf großem Fuß leben, *exp.* to live in style, *(lit.)* to live on a big foot.

Bonze, *m. (coll.)* rich and influential man.

eine (ganze) Stange Geld haben, *exp.* to have a (whole) bunch of money, *(lit.)* to have a big bar of money.

Geld raffen, *exp. (coll.)* to rake in money.

Geldraffer, *m. (coll.)* money raker.

Geld wie Heu haben, *exp.* to be rolling in money, *(lit.)* to have as much money as hay.

gut bei Kasse sein, *exp.* to be well off; *Note:* **knapp bei Kasse**/to be short of cash.

im Geld schwimmen, *exp.* to be rolling in money, *(lit.)* to swim in money.

knauserig, *adj.* greedy.

Krösus, *m.* rich person, *(lit.)* Croesus.

mit dem goldenen Löffel im Mund geboren sein, *exp.* to be born with a silver spoon in one's mouth, *(lit.)* to be born with a golden spoon in one's mouth.

reich wie ein Krösus, *exp.* to be made of money, *(lit.)* to be as rich as a Croesus; *Note:* **ich bin doch kein Krösus!**/I'm not made of money.

scheffeln, *v. (coll.)* rake in (the money).

steinreich, *adj.* stinking rich, *(lit.)* stone rich.

stinkreich, *adj. (sl.)* stinking rich.

schwer beladen, *adj. (coll.)*to be heavily loaded down (with money).

vor Geld stinken, *exp. (coll.)* to be very rich, *(lit.)* to stink of money.

ROOM (*Zimmer*)

Bruchbude, *f.* *(coll.)* rundown room or house.
Bude, *f.* room of a university student.
Höhle, *f.* *(coll.)* dark and small room, *(lit.)* cave.
Kammer, *f.* small room, closet.
Loch, *n.* *(coll.)* rundown room, *(lit.)* hole.

RUMMAGE THROUGH, to (*durchsuchen*)

auf den Kopf stellen, *exp.* to turn upside down, *(lit.)* to turn onto the head.
ein Tohuwabohu machen, *exp.* to create chaos.
(herum-) kramen, *v.* rummage (about); *Note:* **durchwühlen**/rummage through, **hervorkramen**/pick out.
(herum-) stöbern, *v.* rummage (about); *Note:* **durchstöbern**/rummage through.
wühlen, *v.* rummage; *Note:* **Wühltische** or **Grabbeltische**/bargain counters, *(lit.)* rummage tables.

S

SAD, to be (*traurig sein*)

den Kopf hängen lassen, *exp.* to hang one's head.
ein Gesicht wie sieben Tage Regenwetter machen, *exp.* to have a long face, *(lit.)* to make a face like seven days of rain.
ein langes Gesicht machen, *exp.* to look disappointed, *(lit.)* to make a long face.
ein Stein auf dem Herzen haben, *exp.* to have a weight on one's mind, *(lit.)* to have a stone on one's heart.
ein Trauergesicht machen, *exp.* to look sad, *(lit.)* to make a face of mourning.
fix und fertig sein, *exp.* *(coll.)* to be sad; *Note:* also exhausted.
Frust haben, *exp.* *(coll.)* to be frustrated; *Note:* **Frust** is short for **Frustrationen.**
völlig down sein, *exp.* *(sl.)* to be really down; *Note:* down is pronounced as in English.
was ist dir über die Leber gelaufen? *exp.* what do you have on your mind? *(lit.)* what ran across your liver?
wo drückt denn der Schuh? *exp.* what's bugging you, *(lit.)* where does the shoe pinch.

SCOLD, to (*schimpfen*)

jn. anblöken, *v.* *(coll.)* scold sb., *(lit.)* to bleat at sb.
jn. anbrüllen, *v.* *(coll.)* scold sb., *(lit.)* to roar at sb.
jn. anfegen, *v.* *(coll.)* scold sb.

jn. anmachen, *v.* *(coll.)* scold sb.

jn. anpfeifen, *v.* *(coll.)* scold sb., *(lit.)* to whistle at sb.

jn. anpöbeln, *v.* *(coll.)* scold sb.

jn. anschnauzen, *v.* *(vulg.)* scold sb., *(lit.)* to blow one's nose at sb.

jn. anstauchen, *v.* *(coll.)* scold sb.

jn. anzischen, *v.* *(coll.)* scold sb.

jn. auf den Topf setzen, *exp.* *(sl.)* to read sb. the riot act, *(lit.)* to put sb. on the pot.

jm. den Kopf waschen, *exp.* to read sb. the riot act, *(lit.)* to wash sb.'s head.

jm. den Marsch blasen, *exp.* to read sb. the riot act, *(lit.)* to blow sb. the march.

jm. den Zahn ziehen, *exp.* to read sb. the riot act, *(lit.)* to pull sb.'s tooth.

jm. die Flötentöne beibringen, *exp.* *(coll.)* to read sb. the riot act, *(lit.)* to teach sb. the tones of the flute.

jm. die Hammelbeine langziehen, *exp.* *(coll.)* to read sb. the riot act, *(lit.)* to pull sb.'s mutton legs long.

jm. die Leviten lesen, *exp.* to read sb. the riot act.

jm. die Meinung geigen, *exp.* to read sb. the riot act, *(lit.)* to fiddle sb. one's opinion.

jm. die Ohren lang ziehen, *exp.* to give sb. a good talking to, *(lit.)* to pull sb.'s ears long.

jm. eine Gardinepredigt halten, *exp.* to give sb. a curtain-lecture; *Note:* **eine Gardinepredigt bekommen**/to get a curtain lecture.

jm. eine (heftige) Standpauke halten, *exp.* to give sb. a (good) dressing down.

jm. eine verpassen, *exp.* *(coll.)* to scold sb.

jm. eine Zigarre verpassen, *exp.* *(coll.)* to read sb. the riot act, *(lit.)* to give sb. a cigar.

jm. einen Anpfiff geben, *exp.* *(coll.)* to bawl sb. out; *Note:* **einen Anpfiff bekommen**/to get bawled out.

jm. einen Anschiß verpassen, *exp.* *(vulg.)* to bawl sb. out; *Note:* **einen Anschiß bekommen**/to get bawled out.

jm. einen Rüffel verpassen, *exp.* *(coll.)* to scold sb.; *Note:* **einen Rüffel bekommen**/to be scolded.

jm. etwas zeigen, *exp.* to scold sb., *(lit.)* to show sb. something.

jn. in die Pfanne hauen, *exp.* *(coll.)* to scold sb., *(lit.)* to throw sb. into the frying pan.

jm. Pfeffer geben, *exp.* *(coll.)* to scold sb., *(lit.)* to give sb. pepper.

jm. richtig die Meinung sagen, *exp.* to give sb. a piece of one's mind, *(lit.)* to tell sb. one's opinion.

jn. rüffeln, *v.* *(coll.)* scold sb.

jn. runtermachen, *v.* *(coll.)* scold sb.

sein Fett abkriegen, *exp.* to be scolded, *(lit.)* to get one's fat.

jn. vom Platz verweisen, *exp.* to scold, *(lit.)* to expel sb. from the court.

jn. zur Minna machen, *exp.* *(coll.)* to bawl sb. out.

jn. zur Sau machen, *exp.* *(vulg.)* to scold sb., *(lit.)* to make sb. into a sow.

jn. zur Schnecke machen, *exp.* *(coll.)* to scold sb., *(lit.)* to make sb. into a snail.

jn. zusammenputzen, *v.* *(coll.)* scold sb., *(lit.)* to clean sb. together.

jn. zusammenscheißen, *v. (vulg.)* scold, *(lit.)* to shit sb. together.
jn. zusammenstauchen, *v. (coll.)* scold sb.

SHOES *(Schuhe)*

jm. die Schuld in die Schuhe schieben, *exp.* to put the blame on sb. else, *(lit.)* to shove the blame into sb. else's shoes.
Galoschen, *f.pl.* casual shoes, *(lit.)* galoshes.
Gamaschen, *m.pl.* casual shoes, *(lit.)* gaiters.
Knobelbecher, *m.pl. (coll.)* boots, *(lit.)* dice cups.
Latschen, *f.pl.* old shoes, *(lit.)* slippers.
Pantinen, *f.pl.* big shoes, *(lit.)* clogs.
Pantoffeln, *m.pl.* big shoes, *(lit.)* slippers; *Note:* **Pantoffelheld,** *m.* henpecked husband, *(lit.)* slipper hero; **unterm Pantoffel stehen,** *exp.* to be henpecked, *(lit.)* to be under the slipper; **Pantoffelkino,** *n.* video recorder, *(lit.)* slipper cinema.
Puschen, *f.pl.* slippers.
Quadratlatschen, *f.pl. (coll.)* casual shoes, *(lit.)* square clogs.
Schlappen, *f.pl.* casual shoes.
Treter, *f.pl. (coll.)* casual shoes.

SHUT UP, to *(schweigen)*

das Maul halten, *exp. (vulg.)* to keep one's mouth shut; *Note:* **halts Maul!**/shut up.
jm. das Maul stopfen, *exp. (vulg.)* to shut sb. up, *(lit.)* to stuff sb.'s snout.
den Mund halten, *exp.* to keep one's mouth shut.
den Mund verbieten, *exp.* to shut sb. up, *(lit.)* to forbid sb.'s mouth.
die Fresse halten, *exp. (vulg.)* to shut up; *Note:* **halt die Fresse!**/shut up.
die Klappe halten, *exp. (sl.)* to keep one's trap shut; *Note:* **halt die Klappe!**/ shut up.
die Schnauze halten, *exp. (vulg.)* to keep one's snout shut; *Note:* **halt die Schnauze!**/shut up; **Schnauze!** /shut up.
jn. mundtot machen, *exp.* to silence sb., *(lit.)* to make sb. mouth-dead.
ruhig, *adj.* to be quiet, *(lit.)* to be calm; *Note:* **sei ruhig!**/be quiet.

SLEEP, to *(schlafen)*

sich aufs Ohr hauen, *exp. (coll.)* to hit the sack, *(lit.)* to hit oneself on the ear.
Augen pflegen, *exp.* to sleep, *(lit.)* to take care of one's eyes.
eine Mütze (voll) Schlaf nehmen, *exp.* to take a nap, *(lit.)* to take a hat (full) of sleep.
jn. einlullen, *v.* lull sb. to sleep.
einnicken, *v.* doze off.
die Matratze abhorchen, *exp. (sl.)* to sleep, *(lit.)* to listen to the mattress.

der Matratzenhorchdienst, *exp.* to sleep, *(lit.)* mattress-listening duty; *Note:* especially used among military draftees.

sich hinhauen, *v. (coll.)* go to bed, *(lit.)* to throw oneself down.

in die Horizontale legen, *exp. (coll.)* to hit the sack, *(lit.)* to lie down in the horizontal.

kein Auge zutun, *exp.* to be unable to sleep, *(lit.)* to not close an eye.

knacken, *v. (coll.)* snooze.

nicht alt werden, *exp.* to go to bed early, *(lit.)* not to become old.

Nickerchen, *n.* nap.

pennen, *v. (sl.)* snooze; *Note:* **Penner,** *m.* tramp.

pofen, *v. (sl.)* snooze.

ratzen, *v. (sl.)* snooze.

sägen, *v. (coll.)* snore, *(lit.)* to saw.

Schlafmütze, *f.* sleepy head, *(lit.)* sleeping cap.

schlafmützig, *adj.* sleepy.

schlummern, *v.* slumber.

Schönheitsschlaf, *m.* beauty sleep.

Siesta machen, *exp.* to take a nap.

über eine Sache schlafen, *exp.* to think sth. over, *(lit.)* to sleep on sth.

sich von innen begucken, *exp. (coll.)* to sleep, *(lit.)* to look at oneself from inside.

sich zwischen die Kissen hauen, *exp. (coll.)* to go to sleep, *(lit.)* to hit between the pillows with oneself.

SLOW, to be *(langsam sein)*

(herum-) bummeln, *v.* stroll (about).

ohne Drive, *exp. (sl.)* without drive, *Note:* as in English.

ohne Power, *exp. (sl.)* without power; *Note:* pronounced as in English.

pö a pö, *adv.* little by little; *Note;* from the French *peu à peu.*

schnecken, *v.* go slowly, *(lit.)* to snail.

Schnepfe, *f. (sl.)* slow person, *(lit.)* snipe; *Note:* also means hussy.

tranig, *adj.* drowsy.

Transuse, *f.* drowsy woman.

trödeln, *v.* stroll.

SLUGGISH, to be *(faul sein)*

auf der faulen Haut liegen, *exp.* to take it easy, *(lit)* to lay on one's lazy skin.

sich auf die faule Haut legen, *exp.* to sit back and do nothing, *(lit.)* to lie down on one's lazy skin.

auf Sparflamme arbeiten, *exp.* to work slowly, *(lit.)* to work on a low flame.

dem lieben Herrgott den Tag stehlen, *exp. (coll.)* to be lazy, *(lit.)* to steal the day from the dear Lord.

durchhängen, *v. (sl.)* unmotivated, *(lit.)* hang through.

eine ruhige Kugel schieben, *exp.* *(coll.)* to take it easy, *(lit.)* to push a calm ball.

einen Durchhänger haben, *exp.* *(sl.)* to have no motivation.

Faulpelz, *m.* lazy-bones, *(lit.)* lazy fur.

gammeln, *v.* bum around, *(lit.)* to rot.

Gammler, *m.* dropout.

Gesocks, *n.* lazy bum.

herumhängen, *v.* *(sl.)* hang out.

sich ins gemachte Nest legen, *exp.* to have it made, *(lit.)* to lie down in an already made nest.

sich kein Bein ausreißen, *exp.* not to exert oneself, *(lit.)* not to rip one's legs out.

keinen Drive haben, *exp.* *(sl.)* to have no motivation; *Note:* **Drive** is a term borrowed from English and pronounced as such.

(herum-) lungern, *v.* lazily hang about.

nicht mit dem Hintern hochkommen, *exp.* *(sl.)* to be lazy, *(lit.)* not to get up off one's butt.

Penner, *m.* *(sl.)* sleepyhead; *Note:* also used for tramp.

rumklamüsern, *v.* *(sl.)* bum around.

rumschnuddeln, *v.* *(coll.)* bum around.

Sandler, *m.* lazy-bones.

Schlafmütze, *f.* sleepyhead, *(lit.)* sleeping cap.

schlunzen, v. *(sl.)* hang out.

stinkend faul sein, *exp.* to be a lazy-bones, *(lit.)* to be stinkingly lazy.

Strawanzer, *m.* lazy-bones.

trödeln, *v.* waste one's time.

SMELL BAD, to *(stinken)*

drei Meilen gegen den Wind stinken, *exp.* to stink badly, *(lit.)* to stink three miles against the wind.

gotteserbärmlich stinken, *exp.* to stink to high heaven.

Mief, *m.* stench.

miefen, *v.* stink.

Muff, *m.* moldy smell.

muffig, *adj.* moldy.

wie die Pest stinken, *exp.* to stink to high heaven, *(lit.)* to stink like the plague.

wie ein Iltis stinken, *exp.* to stink badly, *(lit.)* to stink like a polecat.

zum Himmel stinken, *exp.* to stink to high heaven.

SPEAK, to *(sprechen)*

auf gut deutsch gesagt, *exp.* *(coll.)* to speak plainly, *(lit.)* to say it in good German.

blöken, *v.* *(sl.)* babble, *(lit.)* bleat.

blubbern, *v.* *(sl.)* babble.

das Maul aufreißen, *exp.* *(vulg.)* to speak, *(lit.)* to open one's snout wide.

jm. das Wort aus dem Mund nehmen, *exp.* to take the words out of sb.'s mouth.

jm. das Wort im Mund umdrehen, *exp.* to put words into sb.'s mouth, *(lit.)* to twist sb.'s words in their mouth.

den Mund aufmachen, *exp.* to speak up.

den Mund fusselig reden, *exp.* to talk until one is blue in the face, *(lit.)* to speak until one's mouth is fuzzy.

den Mund vollnehmen, *exp.* to speak big words, *(lit.)* to take a mouthful.

eine spitze Zunge haben, *exp.* to have a sharp tongue.

ein großes Mundwerk haben, *exp.* to be loudmouthed, *(lit.)* to have a big mouth-machinery.

einem ein Loch in den Bauch reden, *exp.* to pester sb. with chattering, *(lit.)* to talk a hole into sb.'s belly.

klönen, *v.* lengthy chatter.

labbern, *v.* *(sl.)* babble.

nicht auf den Mund gefallen sein, *exp.* never to be at a loss for words, *(lit.)* not to have fallen on one's mouth.

plaudern, *v.* babble.

posaunen, *v.* speak loudly.

sabbeln, *v.* chatter.

schnacken, *v.* blather.

schwazen, *v.* blather.

seibeln, *v.* *(sl.)* babble.

sülzen, *v.* *(sl.)* babble.

tröten, *v.* *(sl.)* speak loudly.

STORY *(Geschichte)*

alte Kamellen, *pl. exp.* old stories, *(lit.)* old camels.

Altweibergeschichten, *f.pl.* old wive's tales.

Altweibergeschwätz, *n.* old wive's tales

Altweibergewäsch, *n.* old wive's tales.

Aufgewärmtes, *n.* old stories, *(lit.)* reheated.

Geschichten erzählen, *exp.* to tell stories.

Seemannsgarn, *n.* seaman's yarn.

STROLL, to *(spazierengehen)*

sich die Beine vertreten, *exp.* to stretch one's legs.

bummeln, *v.* stroll.

dödeln, *v.* *(coll.)* stroll; *Note:* also to do sth. slowly.

flanieren, *v.* stroll.

schlendern, *v.* stroll.

Spritzfahrt, *f.* tour in a car.

Spritztour, *f.* tour in a car.

umherziehen, *v.* stroll from place to place.

STUBBORN PERSON *(eigensinnige Person)*

bockig, *adj.* bullheaded.

Dickkopf, *m.* stubborn person, *(lit.)* fathead.

dickköpfig, *adj.* stubborn *(lit.)* fatheaded; *Note:* **dickköpfig wie ein Esel sein/** to be as stubborn as a mule.

Dickschädel, *m.* stubborn person, *(lit.)* thick skull.

halsstarrig, *adj.* obstinate.

störrisch, *adj.* bullheaded.

stur, *adj.* bullheaded; *Note:* **sturr wie ein Ochse sein/**to be as stubborn as a bull.

zickig, *adj.* stubborn.

STUPEFIED, to be *(erstaunt sein)*
(See: **CRAZY, to go**)

ach du liebe Zeit! *Interj.* oh, heck, *(lit.)* oh, you dear time.

au Backe! *Interj. (coll.)* oh, heck.

aus allen Wolken fallen, *exp.* to be completely astounded, *(lit.)* to fall out of all the clouds.

aus den Latschen kippen, *exp. (coll.)* to be completely astounded, *(lit.)* to fall out of one's slippers.

baff, *adj.* flabbergasted.

da bleibt einem die Spucke weg! *exp. (coll.)* it took my breath away, *(lit.)* the spit stays away from one.

das ist allerhand! *exp.* that's quite something.

das ist ja ein starkes Stück! *exp. (coll.)* that's a bit much.

daß ich nicht lache! *exp.* don't make me laugh.

Donner und Hagel! *exp. (coll.)* I'll be darned, *(lit.)* thunder and hail.

Donnerwetter! *exp.* wow, *(lit.)* thunder weather.

dumm aus der Röhre gucken, *exp. (coll.)* to look stupefied, *(lit.)* to look out of the pipes stupidly.

du Schande! *exp.* what a shame.

echt Wahnsinn! *exp.* incredible.

echt Wahnsinnskiste! *exp. (sl.)* amazing, *(lit.)* real incredible box!

ein blaues Wunder erleben, *exp.* to get a nasty surprise, *(lit.)* to experience a blue wonder.

eine helle Freude haben, *exp.* to have fun, *(lit.)* to have bright fun.

Himmel, Arsch und Zwirn! *exp. (vulg.)* damn it, *(lit.)* heaven, ass, and thread!

ich denk, mich laust der Affe! *exp.* I'll be darned, *(lit.)* I think the monkey is delousing me.

ich glaub, ich spinne! *exp.* I'll be darned! *(lit.)* I think I must be crazy!

ich glaub, mein Hamster pfeift! *exp. (sl.)* I'll be darned! *(lit.)* I think my hamster is whistling.

ich glaub, mich knutscht ein Elch! *exp. (coll.)* I'll be darned, *(lit.)* I think a moose is kissing me.

ich glaub, mich streift ein Bus! *exp. (coll.)* I'll be darned, *(lit.)* I think a bus is scraping me.

ich glaub, mich tritt ein Pferd! *exp. (coll.)* I'll be darned! *(lit.)* I think a horse is kicking me.

Jessasmariaundjosef! *exp.* oh, my Lord; *Note:* Jesus-Mary-and-Joseph!

jetzt schlägts dreizehn! *exp.* I'll be darned, *(lit.)* now it's striking 13.

Kruxifix! *exp.* oh, my Lord.

mit den Ohren schlackern, *exp. (coll.)* to be stunned, *(lit.)* to flap one's ears about.

Pfeifendeckel! *exp.* no way, *(lit.)* whistle-lid.

platt, *adj.* flabbergasted.

Pustekuchen! *exp. (coll.)* nothing doing.

Schmarrn! *exp.* how stupid.

seinen Augen nicht trauen, *exp.* to be surprised, *(lit.)* not to trust one's own eyes.

jm. stehen die Haare zu Berge, *exp.* sb.'s hair is standing on end.

verblüfft, *adj.* astounded; *Note:* **verblüffend**/astounding.

verdattert, *adj.* astounded.

verdutzt aus der Wäsche gucken, *exp.* to look stupefied, *(lit.)* to look stupidly out of one's underwear.

verflixt und zugenäht! *exp.* damn it! *(lit.)* damned and sewn up!

vom Hocker fallen, *exp.* to be completely stunned, *(lit.)* to fall from one's stool; *Note:* **das reißt einen vom Hocker!**/that shocks one!

von den Socken sein, *adj.* to be flabbergasted, *(lit.)* to be out of one's socks.

was der Geier! *exp.* I'll be darned, *(lit.)* what the vulture!

jn. wie das siebte Weltwunder angucken, *exp.* stare at sb. as if he were the seventh wonder of the world.

wie der Ochs vom Berg dastehen, *exp.* be completely baffled, *(lit.)* to stand there like the ox from the mountain.

wie ein Auto gucken, *adj.* to be flabbergasted, *(lit.)* to stare like a car.

STUPID, to be *(dumm sein)*

---

angeknackst, *adj. (coll.)* stupid, *(lit.)* cracked.

ballaballa, *adj. (sl.)* nuts.

behämmert, *adj. (sl.)* nuts.

bekloppt, *adj. (sl.)* nuts.

beknackt, *adj. (coll.)* stupid. *Note:* **so was Beknacktes!**/what a load of rubbish.

belämmert, *adj. (coll.)* stupid.

bescheuert, *adj. (coll.)* stupid.

beschränkt, *adj. (coll.)* stupid.

blöd, *adj.* stupid; *Note:* sometimes also **blöde.**

brege, *adj.* stupid.

den Arsch offen haben, *exp. (vulg.)* to be cracked, *(lit.)* to have one's ass open: *Note:* **du hast wohl den Arsch offen, oder was?**/are you nuts or sth.?

den kann man in der Pfeife rauchen! *exp. (coll.)* what a stupid person, *(lit.)* one can smoke him in a pipe.

deppert, *adj.* stupid.

doof, *adj.* stupid; *Note:* **doof bleibt doof, da helfen keine Pillen**/once a fool, always a fool, *(lit.)* stupid stays stupid, no pills can help.

Dreck im Hirn haben, *exp. (vulg.)* to have dirt in one's brains.

drömelig, *adj.* stupid.

dumm wie die Nacht finster sein, *exp. (coll.)* to be extremely stupid, *(lit.)* to be as stupid as the night is dark.

dümmer sein als die Polizei erlaubt, *exp. (coll.)* to be extremely dumb, *(lit.)* to be dumber than the police allow.

dusselig, *adj.* stupid.

ein Brett vorm Kopf haben, *exp. (coll.)* to be stupid, *(lit.)* to have a board in front of one's head.

ein Loch im Kopf haben, *exp. (coll.)* to be off one's rocker, *(lit.)* to have a hole in one's head.

ein Rad ab haben, *exp. (coll.)* to be off one's rocker, *(lit.)* to have a loose wheel; *Note:* **du hast wohl 'n Rad ab!**/you must be off your rocker.

eine an der Waffel haben, *exp. (coll.)* to be off one's rocker, *(lit.)* to have one on the waffle.

eine lange Leitung haben, *exp. (coll.)* to be slow on the uptake, *(lit.)* to have a long connection.

eine Macke haben, *exp. (sl.)* to be off one's rocker, *(lit.)* to have a titmouse.

eine Mattscheibe haben, *exp. (sl.)* not to be with it.

eine Meise haben, *exp.* (*coll.*) to be nuts, *(lit.)* to have a titmouse.

eine Schraube locker haben, *exp. (coll.)* to have a screw loose.

einen an der Klatsche haben, *exp. (sl.)* to be off one's rocker, *(lit.)* to have one on the fly-swatter.

einen an der Waffel haben, *exp. (sl.)* to be stupid, *(lit.)* to have one on the waffle.

einen Dachschaden haben, *exp. (sl.)* to be stupid, *(lit.)* to have roof damage.

einen Detsch haben, *exp. (sl.)* to be cracked.

einen Fimmel haben, *exp. (sl.)*to be cracked.

einen Hammer haben, *exp.* to be crazy.

einen Klaps haben, *exp. (sl.)* to be stupid, *(lit.)* to have a smack (on the head).

einen kleinen Mann im Ohr haben, *exp. (sl.)* to be stupid, *(lit.)* to have a little man in one's ear.

einen Knacks weghaben, *exp. (sl.)* to be cracked, *(lit.)* to have gotten a crack.

einen Knall haben, *exp. (sl.)* to be off one's rocker.

einen Pieps haben, *exp. (coll.)* to be cracked.

einen Schuß haben, *exp. (sl.)* to be cracked.

einen Sprung in der Schüssel haben, *exp. (sl.)* to be off one's rocker, *(lit.)* to have a crack in one's bowl.

einen Triller unterm Pony haben, *exp. (sl.)* to be nuts, *(lit.)* to have a bird underneath one's bangs.

einen Vogel haben, *exp. (sl.)* to be off one's rocker, *(lit.)* to have a bird.

einen weichen Keks im Schuh haben, *exp. (sl.)* to be off one's rocker, *(lit.)* to have a soft cookie in one's shoe.

jm. einen Wink mit dem Zaunpfahl geben, *exp. (coll.)* to give a strong hint, *(lit.)* to wave to sb. with a fence-post.

Hirnie, *m. (sl.)* cracked person.

hirnrissig, *adj. (coll.)* cracked, *(lit.)* brain-ripped.

hirnverbrannt, *adj. (coll.)* cracked, *(lit.)* brain-burned.

langsam schalten, *exp.* to be slow on the uptake, *(lit.)* to switch slowly.

meschugge, *adj. (sl.)* nuts.

nicht alle Tassen im Schrank haben, *exp. (sl.)* to be slightly out of one's mind, *(lit.)* not to have all one's cups in the cupboard.

nicht bei klarem Verstand sein, *exp. (coll.)* to not be in one's right mind.

nicht ganz dicht sein, *exp. (sl.)* to have a screw loose, *(lit.)* to be not quite leakproof; *Note:* **du bist wohl nicht ganz dicht!**/you have a screw loose.

nicht ganz frisch sein, *exp. (sl.)* to be off one's rocker, *(lit.)* to not be quite fresh.

nicht ganz richtig sein, *exp. (sl.)* to not be in one's right mind.

nicht klar im Kopf sein, *exp. (sl.)* to not be quite right in one's head, *(lit.)* to not be clear in one's head.

nicht richtig im Oberstübchen sein, *exp. (sl.)* to not be right in one's mind, *(lit.)* to not be right in one's attic.

nicht richtig piepen, *exp. (sl.)*to have a screw loose, *(lit.)* to not chirp correctly; *Note:* **bei dir piept's wohl nicht richtig!**/you must be off your rocker.

plemplem, *adj. (sl.)* stupid.

saudumm, *adj. (sl.)* extremely stupid, *(lit.)* sow stupid.

schusselig, *adj.* scatter-brained.

schwachsinnig, *adj. (coll.)* feeble-minded.

so doof sein, daß es weh tut, *exp. (sl.)* to be so stupid that it hurts.

Spätzündung haben, *exp. (sl.)* to be slow on the uptake, *(lit.)* to have a late ignition.

spinnen, *v.* be crazy, stupid.

Tinte gesoffen haben, *exp. (sl.)* to be stupid, *(lit.)* to have drunk ink.

töffelig, *adj.* feeble-minded.

tölpelig, *adj.* feeble-minded.

trottelig, *adj.* twittish.

verblödet, *adj.* stupid.

verdummt, *adj.* stupid.

verkorkst, *adj. (sl.)* stupid.

vertrottelt, *adj.* stupid.

voll abgedreht, *adj.* dumb, *(lit.)* completely twisted.

von allen guten Geistern verlassen sein, *exp. (coll.)* to be out of one's mind, *(lit.)* to have been abandoned by all good spirits.

zu heiß gebadet haben, *exp. (coll.)* to have fallen on one's head, *(lit.)* to have bathed (in water that was) too hot.

T

TEASE, to *(necken)*

jn. auf den Arm nehmen, *exp.* to pull sb.'s leg, *(lit.)* to take sb. on one's arm.

jn. für doof verkaufen, *exp.* to pull sb.'s leg, *(lit.)* to sell sb. as being stupid.

jn. hops nehmen, *exp. (coll.)* to make fun of sb.

jn. veräppeln, *v.* pull sb.'s leg.

jn. verarschen, *v. (vulg.)* make an ass out of sb.

Verarschung, *f.* *(vulg.)* act of pulling sb.'s leg; *Note:* **das ist ja die reinste Verarschung/**that's outrageous.

jn. verhöksen, *v.* *(coll.)* pull sb.'s leg.

jn. verhonepipeln, *v.* pull sb.'s leg.

Verhonepiplung, *f.* the act of pulling sb.'s legs.

jn. verkackeiern, *v.* *(vulg.)* pull sb.'s leg.

jn. verkohlen, *v.* *(sl.)* pull sb.'s leg.

jn. verschaukeln, *v.* *(sl.)* pull sb.'s leg.

TELEPHONE *(Telefon)*

jn. an der Strippe haben, *exp.* *(coll.)* to have sb. on the phone, *(lit.)* to have sb. on the cable.

an der Strippe hängen, *exp.* *(coll.)* to be on the phone, *(lit.)* to hang on the cable.

jn. anklingeln, *v.* give sb. a ring.

bei jm. durchklingeln, *exp.* to give sb. a ring.

bei jm. durchrufen, *exp.* to give sb. a ring.

sich kurzschließen, *v.* give each other a ring.

TERMS OF ENDEARMENT *(Kosenamen)*

Most of the following terms apply to women as well as men.

Bärli, *n.* sweetheart, *(lit.)* little bear.

Herzblatt, *n.* sweetheart, *(lit.)* heart leaf.

Herzi, *n.* sweetheart.

Honigkuchen, *n.* honeycake.

Liebling, *m.* darling.

Mäuschen, *n.* little mouse.

Mausi, *n.* little mouse.

Schatz, *m.* darling, *(lit.)* treasure.

Schätzchen, *n.* darling, *(lit.)* treasure.

Schmatzipuffer, *m.* sweetheart.

Schnuckelchen, *n.* sweetheart.

Schnuckiputzi, *n.* sweetheart.

Spatzi, *m.* sweetheart.

Wonneproppen, *m.* sweetheart; *Note:* for a child.

Zuckerpuppe, *f.* sugar baby, *(lit.)* sugardoll; *Note:* for a woman.

THIN, to be *(dünn sein)*

aussehen wie der Tod persönlich, *exp.* to look like death, *(lit.)* to look like death in person.

aussehn wie Geist Leo, *exp.* to look like death, *(lit.)* to look like Leo the ghost.

bißchen dürftig sein, *exp.* *(coll.)* to be a little thin, *(lit.)* to be a little lean.

Bohnenstange, *m. (coll.)* beanpole.

dünn wie ein Besenstiel sein, *exp. (coll.)* to be as thin as a broomstick.

dünn wie ein Zwirnsfaden, *exp. (coll.)* to be as thin as a thread.

dürrer Hecht, *exp.* skinny pike.

dürr wie eine Bohnenstange sein, *exp. (coll.)* to be as thin as a beanpole.

Hobelspan, *m. (coll.)* wood shaving.

Klettergerüst, *n. (coll.)* beanpole, *(lit.)* climbing frame.

Knochengerüst, *n. (coll.)* bag of bones, *(lit.)* frame of bones.

Lulatsch, *m. (coll.)* beanpole.

mager, *adj.* lean.

nicht ein Gramm Fett haben, *exp.* to not have one gram of fat.

nichts als Haut und Knochen sein, *exp. (coll.)* to be nothing but skin and bones.

nichts auf den Knochen haben, *exp.* to have nothing on one's bones.

Splitter, *m. (coll.)* splinter.

verhungert aussehen, *exp. (coll.)* to look starved.

wie ein Sack Knochen sein, *exp. (coll.)* to be a bag of bones.

wie ein Strich in der Landschaft sein, *exp.* to be as thin as a rake, *(lit.)* to be only a line in the landscape.

THIRSTY, to be *(Durst haben)*

---

ausgetrocknet, *adj. (coll.)* very thirsty, *(lit.)* dried out.

einen trockenen Rachen haben, *exp. (coll.)* to have a dry throat.

THROAT *(Kehle)*

---

etw. (or jn.) am Hals haben, *exp.* to have to put up with sth. (or sb.).

Gurgel, *f.* throat.

gurgeln, *v.* gargle.

Hals über Kopf, *exp.* head over heels, *(lit.)* neck over head.

Hals- und Beinbruch! *exp.* break a leg! *(lit.)* neck and leg-break!

Kopf und Kragen riskieren, *exp.* to risk one's neck, *(lit.)* to risk head and collar.

Kragen, *m.* throat, *(lit.)* collar.

sich jn. vom Hals halten, *exp. (coll.)* to keep sb. away, *(lit.)* to keep sb. from one's neck.

UGLY, to be *(häßlich sein)*

---

erschreckend, *adj.* ugly, *(lit.)* scary.

Geschmacksverirrung, *f. (coll.)* lapse of taste, *(lit.)* taste aberration; *Note:* **unter Geschmacksverirrung leiden**/to suffer from a lapse of taste.

häßlich wie die Nacht sein, *exp.* *(coll.)* to be as ugly as the night.
häßlich wie die Sünde sein, *exp.* *(coll.)* to be as ugly as sin.
häßlich wie eine Schrulle sein, *exp.* *(sl.)* to be as ugly as a hag.
kotzhäßlich, *adj.* *(vulg.)* extremely ugly, *(lit.)* pukingly ugly.
potthäßlich, *adj.* *(coll.)* dead ugly.
Schreckschraube, *f.* *(sl.)* ugly woman, *(lit.)* scary screw.
total fertig aussehen, *exp.* *(coll.)* to look ugly, *(lit.)* to look completely done.
Vogelscheuche, *f.* *(sl.)* ugly person, *(lit.)* scarecrow.

UP TO DATE, to be *(auf dem Laufenden sein)*

am Ball sein, *exp.* *(coll.)* to be on the ball.
auf Draht sein, *exp.* *(coll.)* to be on the ball, *(lit.)* to be on the wire.
Flöhe husten hören, *exp.* *(coll.)* to know everything, *(lit.)* to hear the fleas cough.
im Bilde sein, *exp.* to be in the know.
schwer auf Zack sein, *exp.* *(coll.)* to be on the ball.
schwer drauf sein, *exp.* to be on the ball.
up to date sein, *exp.* *(coll.)* to be up to date; *Note:* a term borrowed from English.
wissen wo der Hase läuft, *exp.* *(coll.)* to know which way the wind blows, *(lit.)* to know where the rabbit is running.
wissen, woher der Wind weht, *exp.* *(coll.)* to know which way the wind blows.

W

WEAKLING *(Schwächling)*

fibselig, *adj.* undersized.
fipsig, *adj.* undersized.
Fliegengewicht, *n.* lightweight, *(lit.)* flyweight.
halbe Portion, *exp.* half-pint, *(lit.)* half a portion.
Halbstarker, *m.* half-pint, *Note:* also hooligan.
Kümmerling, *m.* *(sl.)* runt.
leere Hose, *exp.* *(sl.)* runt, *(lit.)* empty pants.
Leichtgewicht, *n.* lightweight.
Schwächling, *m.* weakling.
Spaddel, *m.* runt.
spaddelig, *adj.* runt-like.
Spargeltarzan, *m.* *(sl.)* runt, *(lit.)* asparagus Tarzan.
Unterirdischer, *m.* *(sl.)* little runt, *(lit.)* subterranean.
Waschlappen, *m.* *(sl.)* weakling, *(lit.)* washcloth.
Wicht, *m.* *(sl.)* weakling, *(lit.)* creature.
Zwerg, *m.* weakling, *(lit.)* dwarf.

WEEP, to *(weinen)*

auf die Tränendrüsen drücken, *exp. (coll.)* to cry, *(lit.)* to press one's tearducts.

sich die Augen aus dem Kopf weinen, *exp.* to cry one's eyes out.

flennen, *v. (coll.)* weep.

greinen, *v. (coll.)* weep.

heulen, *v. (coll.)* weep.

Krokodilstränen, *f.pl.* crocodile tears.

Kullertränen, *f.pl.* big tears.

nah am Wasser gebaut haben, *exp. (coll.)* to cry easily, *(lit.)* to have built close to the water.

plärren, *v. (coll.)* cry.

Rotz und Wasser heulen, *exp. (vulg.)* to cry hard, *(lit.)* to cry snot and water.

wie ein Schloßhund heulen, *exp. (coll.)* to cry hard, *(lit.)* to howl like a castle dog.

winseln, *v. (coll.)* whine.

WORK, to *(arbeiten)*

sich (eins) abrackern, *v. (coll.)* slave away.

Amtsschimmel, *m. (coll.)* office worker; *Note:* **Schimmel,** *m.* white horse; **der Amtsschimmel wiehert!**/that's bureaucracy for you.

auf Maloche sein, *exp. (coll.)* to be at work.

die Ärmel hochkrempeln, *exp.* to start working, *(lit.)* to roll up one's sleeves.

sich die Beine ausreißen, *exp. (coll.)* to work hard, *(lit.)* to rip one's legs out.

huddeln, *v. (coll.)* work sloppily.

malochen, *v.* work hard.

Rackerei, *f. (coll.)* slaving away.

ranklotzen, *v. (coll.)* graft.

schuften, *v.* slave way; *Note:* **sich eins abschuften**/to slave away.

Schufterei, *f.* slaving away.

sich den Hintern abarbeiten, *exp. (sl.)* to work one's butt off.

wühlen, *v.* slave away, *(lit.)* rummage; *Note:* **sich eins abwühlen**/to slave away.